LAUGH LINES

LAUGH LINES

SHORT COMIC PLAYS

EDITED BY *Eric Lane*
AND *Nina Shengold*

VINTAGE BOOKS

A DIVISION OF RANDOM HOUSE, INC., NEW YORK

FIRST VINTAGE BOOKS EDITION, APRIL 2007

Copyright © 2007 by Eric Lane and Nina Shengold

All rights reserved. Published in the United States by Vintage Books,
a division of Random House, Inc., New York, and in Canada
by Random House of Canada Limited, Toronto.

Vintage and colophon are registered trademarks of Random House, Inc.

Permissions can be found at the end of the book.

Cataloging-in-Publication Data is on file at the Library of Congress.

Vintage ISBN

www.vintagebooks.com

Printed in the United States of America
10 9 8 7 6 5 4 3 2 1

CONTENTS

INTRODUCTION

The editors of this volume have, at various times, earned a living by sharpening chain saws, hefting catering trays, cleaning salmon on fishing boats, and working at Harlem's oldest live poultry market. So it's safe to say that over the years, we've definitely developed a sense of humor. Though Ernest Hemingway once said, "A man's got to take a lot of punishment to write a really funny book," our experience as editors was far from punishing. Selecting the thirty-six plays in this collection was a pure delight.

Comedy is nothing if not diverse. There must be thousands of ways to make people laugh, guffaw, giggle, roar, bust a gut, or lose it. From the personal to the political, the silly to the even sillier, *Laugh Lines: Short Comic Plays* offers up three dozen theatrical gems.

The laughs in this book come in all shapes and sizes. There are hilarious one-acts by some of the top names in comedy, including Steve Martin's surrealistic emotional sideshow, *The Zig-Zag Woman*; Shel Silverstein's demented birthday-gift sketch, *The Best Daddy*; Elaine May's "power play" about two driven women, *The Way of All Fish*; and Christopher Durang's lunatic romp with the houseguest from hell, *Wanda's Visit*. You'll also find short comedies by the Tony Award—winning authors of *Proof* and *Sideman*—David Auburn's *Miss You* and Warren Leight's *Mars Has Never Been This Close*. You'll discover new works by veteran playwrights and emerging voices, many published here for the first time.

The editors read nearly four hundred scripts to gather the cream of the comedy crop. We discovered some notable trends: theatre people like writing about theatre people, and most short comedies that aren't set in theatres are set in restaurants. The undisputed winners of the backstage sweepstakes are Mark O'Donnell's freewheeling farce *There Shall Be No Bottom (a bad play for worse actors)* and Glen Berger's *The Gallows Monologue from Sidney Ryan's "Gunpowder and Blood,"* in which a panicked understudy manhandles a gruesome soliloquy. As for restaurant plays, Jonathan Rand's loopy dating fantasia *Check, Please*; Sharon E. Cooper's incisive *Mistaken Identity*; Daryl Watson's deft duet for teenage girlfriends, *The Blueberry Hill Accord*; and Mark Harvey Levine's inventive *Surprise* all get four stars.

All the big comedy subjects are here: religion (Mikhail Horowitz's *We Cannot Know the Mind of God*), politics (Steven Dietz's *The Spot*), marriage (Lauren Wilson's *Wedding Duet*), baseball (Tommy Smith's *Streak*), and aging Romanian trapeze acts (David Smilow's *The Flying Wolimskies Return*).

There are plays here for casts of all sizes, from monologues to large ensembles, with diverse and challenging roles for actors of every age and type. Acting students and auditioners looking for solo material will be thrilled with Peter Hedges's exuberant coming-of-age riff *The Valerie of Now*, Richard Strand's twisted *Rosa's Eulogy*, David Cale's wildly original *Poodles*, and Edwin Sánchez's antic and heartbreaking *Pops*.

The many two-handers include Academy Award winner Alan Ball's therapy session gone wild, *Your Mother's Butt*; Paul Dooley and Winnie Holzman's self-sticking memoir, *Post-its (Notes on a Marriage)*, Frederick Stroppel's deliciously deadpan *Chocolate*, Eric Lane's surprising blind-date variation, *The Statue of Bolívar*, and Garth Wingfield's warmhearted *Please Have a Seat and Someone Will Be with You Shortly*. Only one partner speaks in Eric Coble's fast-paced physical vaudeville, *Ties That Bind*. Laura Shaine Cunningham's prescient *Outsourced* pulls the veil off the unseen voice on a corporate phone system. And in Jacquelyn Reingold's *2B (or Not 2B)*, the heroine's costar has wings and a stinger.

Trios of men and women wield lethal weapons (guns and hair dryers) to comic effect in *The Tarantino Variation* by Seth Kramer and *Heritage, Her-i-tage, & Hair-i-tage* by Adrienne Dawes. Larger casts will enjoy romping through Joyce Van Dyke's multicultural nail-biter, *The Earring*, Wayne Rawley's underage corporate boardroom in *Controlling Interest*, and David Lindsay-Abaire's barbed satire of racism and dialect, *How We Talk in South Boston*. There's a whole police lineup of ex-boyfriends in Nina Shengold's *Forty to Life*, and no fewer than seven buttinskies unnerving a couple in bed in Gina Barnett's farce, *Alone at Last!*

As editors of numerous theatre anthologies, we've noticed the plays people seem to produce and enjoy most are comedies. Short, funny scripts with great roles for actors and minimal scenic requirements are perfect for theatre groups on every level, from students and community groups to working professionals. We urge you to round up the funniest people you know and put together an evening of these comic one-acts. You'll find an index by cast size at the back of this book, along with information on obtaining performance rights, and playwrights' biographies.

Whether you are an aspiring actor, a seasoned professional, or a complete novice, the words of these thirty-six writers will leave you in stitches. We thank the playwrights for making our work on this book a whole lot of fun. Let the laughter begin!

ERIC LANE AND NINA SHENGOLD
September 2006

ACKNOWLEDGMENTS

Many people contributed greatly to the creation of this anthology. We'd like to thank the many literary managers, agents, publishers, and friends who led us to such terrific plays and helped us to secure the rights.

In particular, we would like to acknowledge Hamilton Clancy at the Drilling Company; Michael Dixon at the Guthrie Theater; Adrien-Alice Hansel at Actors Theatre of Louisville; Linda Key at Vital Theatre Company; John McCormack at Ensemble Studio Theatre; Stephanie Heller Norman at City Theatre; Doug Rand and Erin Detrick at Playscripts; Ruth Better and Julian Schlossberg.

As always, we are indebted to our wonderful agent Susan Cohen, and our superb editor at Vintage, Diana Secker Tesdell. Deep gratitude to Actors & Writers, Orange Thoughts Productions, the Drama Book Shop, 360 Cougars, and the Corporation of Yaddo. And Bob Barnett and Maya Shengold for making our lives so much richer and more fun. Many thanks to the playwrights, for making us laugh. Enjoy!

LAUGH LINES

LAUGH LINES

MISS YOU

David Auburn

Miss You was first produced at the HBO Comedy Arts Festival in Aspen, Colorado, on January 5, 1997. It was directed by James Eckhouse. The cast was as follows:

WOMAN 1, 2   Lisa Edelstein
MAN 1, 2   Jerry Levine

CHARACTERS

MAN
WOMAN
MAN 2
WOMAN 2

MAN *and* WOMAN *on the phone.*

WOMAN: Hello?

MAN: I miss you!

WOMAN: Oh, hi.

MAN: Miss me?

WOMAN: Uh-huh.

MAN: Really?

WOMAN: Yes. Yes I do: I miss you.

MAN: A lot?

WOMAN: Yes.

MAN: How much?

WOMAN: I told you, a lot.

MAN: God, I miss you.

WOMAN: Mm.

MAN: I wish you were here.

WOMAN: Yes.

MAN: I wish you were here right now.

WOMAN: Mm.

MAN: I wish I was *there*.

WOMAN: Uh-huh.

MAN: I wish I could be there with you: I mean, I really *miss* you.
    I have a—

WOMAN: I know.

MAN: I have a—

WOMAN: Can you hold on?

MAN: I have a little sur—

WOMAN: Can you hold on a sec? I've got another call.

MAN: S (ure)—(*Beat. She clicks over.*)

WOMAN: Hello?

MAN 2: Hey.

WOMAN: Oh, God. Oh, God, hi! Oh, hi! God, hi!

MAN 2: Hey.

WOMAN: Hi, God, you called! I was hoping you'd—where have you been? Hi! Thank you for calling! How are you?

MAN 2: I'm fine.

WOMAN: Great.

MAN 2: How are—

WOMAN: Great. Wonderful. Now! *Hi.* When can I see you? Are you free? Are you busy? I can get time. Do you want to get something to eat tonight? Or we can cook. I can shop and we can— We can stay in. *We can cook here,* I've got wine. *Come over.* Come over now if you want. I miss you.

MAN 2: Listen—

WOMAN: I miss you. Yesterday afternoon was—the museum was wonderful (I can't believe I live right here in the city and I *never* go), and the walk, and the river. And the ice cream! Unh! *Nothing* has ever tasted so good to me in my life, I swear to God, it was—and drinks by the—and dinner, and *God,* you looked so—and last night was—

MAN 2: Listen, there's some things I should do, but we ought to try to get together.

WOMAN: Try? Try to get together? Yes, I think we should "try"! I mean, yes. *Yes.* That would be great. Tonight? Do you want to set something up for tonight? (*Beat.*)

MAN 2: Tonight?

WOMAN: Yes. We could—

MAN 2: Look, can I call you back?

WOMAN: What?

MAN 2: I gotta call you back.

WOMAN: Okay, but call me right—

MAN 2: Yeah. I'll call you. I'll talk to you. Okay?

WOMAN: Soon. I'll talk to you, okay—

MAN 2: Bye. (*Beat.*)

WOMAN: Bye— (*She almost hangs up.*) Shit— (*Clicks over.*) Hello?

MAN: Hello?

WOMAN: It's me.

MAN: *I missed you!*

WOMAN: I'm sorry. I couldn't get—

MAN: I'm coming home.

WOMAN: What?

MAN: I'm calling because I'm coming home. It's my surprise. I'm
    cutting things short. I'm at the airport!

WOMAN: Why?

MAN: I'm about to get on an airplane.

WOMAN: No, why—you're cutting things short? Can you do that?

MAN: Yes. I worked straight through. I haven't slept for two days
    so I'd get done early because I *missed* you and I'm—

WOMAN: Wait. Hold—

MAN: We take off in ten minutes. They're preboarding now. I'm carrying my—I want to give you my arrival time so you can come get me. I've only got carry-on, so don't come to the gate, don't park, just pull up at arriving flights and I'll be—

WOMAN: 'Nother call, sorry, I—

MAN: Honey, wait, I'm about to board, I don't want to miss my—

WOMAN: (*Clicks over.*) Hello?

MAN: No, it's still me. Don't go. I don't want to miss my—

WOMAN: Sorry, *hold on.* (*Clicks.*) *Hello? Hello?*

MAN 2: Hey, me.

WOMAN: Oh, *hi!*

MAN 2: Hey. Listen. I—

WOMAN: That was *fast!* You're—

MAN 2: Listen, I just realized, I've got a lot of things to take care of.

WOMAN: Uh-huh.

MAN 2: So I think we better—

WOMAN: What?

MAN 2: I think we better take a rain check on tonight.

WOMAN: A rain check.

MAN 2: We'll do it some other time.

WOMAN: You have a lot of *things* to take care of?

MAN 2: Yeah.

WOMAN: What things?

MAN 2: I should get some sleep. I have to get up early.

WOMAN: We spend the day together yesterday. You didn't have things to take care of. Yesterday turned into last night and it was a long sleepless night and that seemed fine with you then; it seemed wonderful to me—

MAN 2: We'll have to do it another time.

WOMAN: I don't have another *time*. This is the *time*. Do you see? Let's do this *now*. I'm sorry. I just mean, while we can. We shouldn't miss this. Yesterday came out of nowhere. We were together. It was *great*. I loved it. I loved being with you. I loved you. (*Beat.*) Did you hear me? I love you. Can you hear me? Are you there?

MAN 2: Can you hold on a minute?

WOMAN: What?

MAN 2: I've got another call coming in.

WOMAN: Don't take it!

MAN 2: I have to—

WOMAN: They'll call back.

MAN 2: I'll just be—

WOMAN: *Don't*— (*He clicks over.*)

MAN 2: Hello? (*Beat.*)

WOMAN 2: Do you think I'm stupid?

MAN 2: Hello?

WOMAN 2: *You fucking asshole.*

MAN 2: Honey?

WOMAN 2: Do you think I'm *stupid*? Do you think I'm just sort of unaware of what's going on around me? I'm not *stupid*, you fucking jerk. You're the fucking idiot loser—

MAN 2: Honey, what are you—

WOMAN 2: "Honey"? I saw you at the *museum. "Honey."* Little stroll by the *river*? I saw you buying little mmmmmm, oooooh! ice kweem cones, so cute! Mm, mine's really good, here have a taste, no go ahead, it's so good, here, you've got to have one, mmmm— You bastard! How could you do this? You take her to *our restaurant,* "*honey*"? (I followed you. I'm not stupid.) You get home from the "office" at *four thirty in the morning*? Well, listen up: Fuck you, and fuck the art museum and your little ice cream scoopy friend, and fuck you again, because I wash my hands of you and good riddance, you're gonna rot in hell you lying sleazebag dumbshit fuck-ball. (*She hangs up. Beat.* MAN 2 *clicks back.*)

MAN 2: Hello?

WOMAN: Hello? (*Beat.*)

MAN 2: You still want to get together?

WOMAN: Tonight?

MAN 2: Sure. We could get something to eat.

WOMAN: You changed your mind.

MAN 2: Yeah.

WOMAN: What about your things?

MAN 2: What?

WOMAN: The things you have to do.

MAN 2: They can wait.

WOMAN: You have to sleep.

MAN 2: I'll sleep at your place.

WOMAN: You will. (*Beat.*) I'm sorry.

MAN 2: What?

WOMAN: I have to go.

MAN 2: What? Why?

WOMAN: I'll have to call you back. I have another call. I just remembered.

MAN 2: Listen, let's just—

WOMAN: He called me first. I have to go. Okay? He—

MAN 2: Come on, forget about—

WOMAN: I should talk to him. I think he's very tired. He hasn't slept. He went without sleep for two days. (*Beat.*)

MAN 2: Wai— (*Beat. She clicks over.*)

WOMAN: Hi. It's me. Hello? Hello? Are you there? (*Beat.*)

MAN: I missed my flight.

WOMAN: I'm sorry.

MAN: It just took off.

WOMAN: I'm sorry. Is there another one tonight?

MAN: I don't know. I'll check. Probably. Probably late.

WOMAN: Take it. I'll pick you up.

MAN: You will?

WOMAN: Tell me when.

MAN: It'll be late.

WOMAN: I don't care how late. I'll come to the gate.

MAN: You will?

WOMAN: Yes.

MAN: Don't miss me.

WOMAN: I won't.

END OF PLAY

YOUR MOTHER'S BUTT

Alan Ball

Your Mother's Butt was first produced by Alarm Dog Repertory at the West Bank Café Downstairs Theater Bar (Rand Foerster, artistic director) in New York City, on June 6, 1990. It was directed by Carol McCann. The cast was as follows:

CLIENT   Barry Hamilton
PSYCHOLOGIST   Terri O'Neil

CHARACTERS

PSYCHOLOGIST: Woman, mid-thirties.
CLIENT: A young man.

The PSYCHOLOGIST's *office. The* PSYCHOLOGIST, *an intelligent, well-dressed woman in her mid-thirties, sits in a big comfortable chair, taking notes on a legal pad. Her* CLIENT *lies on a couch, facing away from her. He is young, dressed artistically.*

CLIENT: My life is, like, so mundane. The days come, the days go. I keep waiting, waiting, waiting, but for what? I go to work, I eat, I work out. I watch television. I'm not really depressed. Well, yeah, I guess I am depressed. I'm lonely. I'm easily irritated. But it's not the kind of overwhelming depression that feels like it's ripping me apart. It's more of a . . . blandness, an overall numbness . . . like every fiber of my being has been sucked dry of any coherent reason to exist. (*Pause.*)

PSYCHOLOGIST: You're not enjoying your work?

CLIENT: Oh, God, no. Work is so weird. We're so busy right now, and there are so many things I'm responsible for, and all of them are meaningless. God. So much of my time is spent worrying about bullshit, manufacturing bullshit, packaging bullshit so it looks like it matters. Nothing matters.

PSYCHOLOGIST: Nothing?

CLIENT: (*Suddenly angry.*) Nothing. And if it does, it just fucks you up. (*Pause.*)

PSYCHOLOGIST: So nothing in your life matters to you? (*Pause. The* CLIENT *fights back tears.*)

CLIENT: No. (*Pause. The* CLIENT *cries.*) I have— (*It is too painful for him to say; he takes a moment, then tries again.*) I have this sweater.

PSYCHOLOGIST: A sweater?

CLIENT: It's really nice. It's this old sweater, I think it belonged to my brother. It's just this black V-neck sweater, wool, but it's faded and soft and it fits me really well, it accentuates my shoulders, but, like, in a subtle way, and when I wear it, I feel really sexy.

PSYCHOLOGIST: It sounds like a nice sweater.

CLIENT: It is. (*He breaks down.*) I'm sorry, I just—

PSYCHOLOGIST: Take your time. (*Pause.*)

CLIENT: The reason I'm crying is that you ask me does anything really matter to me and my answer is a sweater. That's really sad.

PSYCHOLOGIST: You have every right to find joy in a sweater.

CLIENT: I do, that's the weird part, it's like the only thing in my life I get excited about. Sometimes I put it on just to walk around in it, and then sometimes I forget that I've done laundry and I go to pick out something to wear, and there it is, all clean and soft and faded just a little bit more, all folded up, and it's, like, primal, like, maybe even religious. (*Pause.*)

PSYCHOLOGIST: How are you feeling?

CLIENT: How do you think I'm feeling? The only significant relationship in my life is with a piece of clothing? At best, that's tremendously shallow, and at worst, it's sociopathic. I mean, if I was somebody else and I knew me, I would say look, get a life.

PSYCHOLOGIST: I think perhaps you're being a bit hard on yourself.

CLIENT: You're right. God, I am so fucked up. I've got to do something about this, I can't be this fucked up anymore. What can I do? Tell me what to do. You're the expert.

PSYCHOLOGIST: Well, first, I think we need to take a look at why you *are* so hard on yourself. (*Pause.*)

CLIENT: (*Sighs.*) Okay. (*Long pause.*)

PSYCHOLOGIST: How are you feeling?

CLIENT: Excited.

PSYCHOLOGIST: Excited?

CLIENT: Yeah. I'm thinking about this pair of shoes I saw yesterday.

PSYCHOLOGIST: Shoes?

CLIENT: Yeah. I've been looking for the perfect pair of black shoes for . . . well, probably for my whole life. You know, a pair of oxfords, just plain, nice leather, not too clunky, but not too Wall Street, either. The kind of shoes you can wear with a suit and look really hip, but you can also wear with blue jeans and look really . . . intelligent.

PSYCHOLOGIST: Intelligent.

CLIENT: But also approachable. And politically correct. With a sense of humor.

PSYCHOLOGIST: Shoes seem to communicate quite a lot for you.

CLIENT: Oh, yeah. Definitely. I think there's two ways to learn a lot about somebody in a short amount of time. One is their refrigerator—not only what they stick on the front of it, but what's in it, too—and the other is their shoes.

PSYCHOLOGIST: (*A hunch.*) What's in *your* refrigerator?

CLIENT: Well, nothing right now.

PSYCHOLOGIST: Ah.

CLIENT: These shoes are the greatest shoes—I *think*.

PSYCHOLOGIST: Let's stay with the image of the empty refrigerator for a moment.

CLIENT: Why?

PSYCHOLOGIST: I have an idea it might be significant.

CLIENT: Okay.

PSYCHOLOGIST: Just try to picture it. An empty box . . . cold . . . white . . .

CLIENT: No, my refrigerator is avocado. (*Pause. The* PSYCHOLOGIST *seems disappointed.*)

PSYCHOLOGIST: Oh.

CLIENT: Which I really hate, because all the other appliances in my kitchen are harvest gold. Which I also hate, but I just haven't decided if I'm committed enough to this apartment to redecorate yet.

PSYCHOLOGIST: Let's just say, for argument's sake, that your refrigerator *was* white.

CLIENT: Okay.

PSYCHOLOGIST: (*Taking time, setting mood.*) A cold, white, empty box . . . possibly a source of nourishment, but also a potential death trap. (*Pause.*)

CLIENT: Cool. (*Pause.*)

PSYCHOLOGIST: How are you feeling?

CLIENT: Weird. I think I just figured out what I really want.

PSYCHOLOGIST: What?

CLIENT: What I really want is to do the entire kitchen over in all black, with all black appliances . . . but that really scares me.

PSYCHOLOGIST: Why?

CLIENT: Because in a few years, having had everything in your apartment be all black is going to be like having worn a leisure suit is today. It's going to be one of those things you'll have to constantly deny. You know, like I never voted for Reagan, I was never a yuppie. (*A long pause.*)

PSYCHOLOGIST: Perhaps we should return to the shoes.

CLIENT: Okay. (*Pause.*) I don't know. They might be the right ones, they might not. They're really expensive. I don't want to spend that much money and have them not be the perfect shoes! (*Suddenly angry.*) God, why does everything always have to be so hard?

PSYCHOLOGIST: Go ahead. Try to get in touch with this anger.

CLIENT: Sometimes I wish somebody would just tell me what to do, you know? They would just say, Look, this is what you need to do, so just shut up and do it, okay? Because I don't seem to be able to figure it out on my own. It's like every option makes sense to me. Every choice seems like the right choice. Now, granted, I think being open-minded is a good thing, but there's such a thing as being *too* open-minded. Like your mind is so open it just kind of . . . leaves.

PSYCHOLOGIST: Well, first, I think we need to look at the ways in which your indecision keeps you *safe*—

CLIENT: Oh, shut up! Just shut up! God! Stop telling me what to do! (*Looks at her, horrified, then bursts into tears.*) Oh, God, I'm sorry! (*A very long pause.*)

PSYCHOLOGIST: How are you feeling?

CLIENT: I feel . . . well, I'm not sure what I feel. I need to ask you a question. (*Pause.*)

PSYCHOLOGIST: All right.

CLIENT: And this is not real easy for me, okay? (*Pause.*) Do you know where I can get a braided leather belt, about half an inch thick, black leather, not shiny, for under thirty dollars?

PSYCHOLOGIST: A belt?

CLIENT: Yeah. I have such bad luck with belts.

PSYCHOLOGIST: A belt?

CLIENT: Yes. (*Pause.*)

PSYCHOLOGIST: Were you ever . . . what association does the word belt carry for you?

CLIENT: Ostrich.

PSYCHOLOGIST: Ostrich. A flightless bird, known primarily for sticking its head in the ground in response to perceived danger—

CLIENT: No, I used to have these Eurotrash slip-on shoes, made out of ostrich skin? They were queer, but they were so incredibly soft. I just wanted to touch them all the time, even though I hardly ever wanted to wear them. So can you imagine a belt made out of ostrich skin, the softest stuff in the entire world? It would be like, intense.

PSYCHOLOGIST: Let me put it another way. When you were a child and your parents felt they needed to punish you for a perceived transgression . . .

CLIENT: Oh, did they, like, beat me?

PSYCHOLOGIST: Did they?

CLIENT: Well, sure, but not with a belt. With a switch.

PSYCHOLOGIST: Who?

CLIENT: A switch. From a tree.

PSYCHOLOGIST: Who used the switch?

CLIENT: Well, my mother. Of course.

PSYCHOLOGIST: Ah. (*Pause.*) How are you feeling?

CLIENT: Weird. I just remembered . . . oh, I had this weird dream.

PSYCHOLOGIST: Tell me about it.

CLIENT: I dreamed . . . I dreamed I was in this . . . house, it wasn't my house, but I lived there. And I was in this big room, and I was in this bathtub. This old-fashioned bathtub on pedestals. And I'm wearing clothes. This olive drab cardigan, just over a T-shirt, and these flax-colored, I guess, linen shorts. No pleats. Really nice. Well, they would be, wouldn't they? Dream clothes. And then I hear these voices in the hall and in comes my mother. Only she's a younger version of herself, and she's wearing these 1960s hip-huggers, and she has Mary Tyler Moore hair that she's tied a bandanna around, and I think oh, she's trying to be hip, and it's really sort of *sad* for a moment . . . then she gets in the bathtub with me, only she won't look at me, and then she bends over and . . . she just sticks her butt in my face.

PSYCHOLOGIST: (*Scribbling furiously.*) This is really good.

CLIENT: And I'm thinking . . . okay. This is kind of weird. This is some weird kind of fuck-you gesture, and I'm thinking . . . this is really . . . it's really not quite right . . . it's really . . .

PSYCHOLOGIST: Inappropriate?

CLIENT: It's more than that . . . Oh, God, what is it?

PSYCHOLOGIST: Visualize the dream.

CLIENT: Right.

PSYCHOLOGIST: You're in the water . . . Is the water warm or cold?

CLIENT: Warm. But not hot.

PSYCHOLOGIST: And she comes in.

CLIENT: Yeah, and she's walking this swingy, hippy kind of walk, and I think oh, God, my mother. I'm so embarrassed.

PSYCHOLOGIST: And she gets in the tub . . .

CLIENT: You can tell she think's she's really groovy.

PSYCHOLOGIST: Now she's in the water with you . . .

CLIENT: Yeah. And she is wearing the most hideous Barbie, like, flower power outfit.

PSYCHOLOGIST: She's turning around.

CLIENT: She looks like Samantha Stevens on acid.

PSYCHOLOGIST: She's bending over.

CLIENT: With this macramé belt. I am not kidding you.

PSYCHOLOGIST: She's bending—

CLIENT: Oh, wait a minute! I just realized something. Oh, wow. (*Pause.*)

PSYCHOLOGIST: Yes?

CLIENT: It makes such perfect sense, doesn't it.

PSYCHOLOGIST: What does?

CLIENT: I get my bad belt luck from her. It's heredity. (*Long pause.*)

PSYCHOLOGIST: (*Just the slightest bit of tightness.*) How are you feeling?

CLIENT: I feel great! If it's hereditary, then I don't have to feel guilty for it. I have no control over it, so it's not my fault. Right?

PSYCHOLOGIST: Well, not exactly, no. One of the underlying assumptions that the therapeutic process is based upon is that you *do* have control over your life.

CLIENT: No thanks. I don't want that kind of responsibility. (*Pause.*)

PSYCHOLOGIST: I'd like to get back to your mother's butt.

CLIENT: Please. Be my guest.

PSYCHOLOGIST: It's such a strong image, with so many potential implications. It could open many doors. So I'd like to try something a little . . . unorthodox.

CLIENT: Oh, no. You're not going to stick *your* butt in my face, are you?

PSYCHOLOGIST: No, no. I just want you to close your eyes, and relax. Feel the warm water in the tub. Now try to picture your mother's butt.

CLIENT: Okay.

PSYCHOLOGIST: Do you see it?

CLIENT: Plain as day.

PSYCHOLOGIST: Now speak to it.

CLIENT: I'm sorry?

PSYCHOLOGIST: Speak to your mother's butt.

CLIENT: Oh, right.

PSYCHOLOGIST: Think of it as separate from your mother. As an entity of its own. If you could communicate with it, what would you say?

CLIENT: Get out of my face.

PSYCHOLOGIST: Perhaps it would be helpful if you gave it a name.

CLIENT: What do you mean?

PSYCHOLOGIST: If it had a name, what would it be?

CLIENT: You mean like a person's name?

PSYCHOLOGIST: Possibly.

CLIENT: Like . . . Debbie?

PSYCHOLOGIST: Perhaps.

CLIENT: This is really weird.

PSYCHOLOGIST: Just try speaking to it by name.

CLIENT: Get out of my face, Debbie. Excuse me, Debbie, can you get out of my face? Thank you. Yo, Debbie. Get the fuck out of my face.

PSYCHOLOGIST: Maybe you'd like to yell at it.

CLIENT: Sure, why not. (*Yells.*) Debbie! Get the fuck out of my face, you bitch! And take that hideous macramé belt with you!

PSYCHOLOGIST: Now become the butt.

CLIENT: What?

PSYCHOLOGIST: If you were the butt, what would you say in response?

CLIENT: Uhm, I'm Debbie the butt, and you better shut up. Stop telling me what to do. This is a free country and I can be wherever I want. If you don't like me being in your face, then *you* leave.

PSYCHOLOGIST: Now respond as yourself.

CLIENT: Fuck you, you stupid butt. I was here first.

PSYCHOLOGIST: Keep going.

CLIENT: Oh yeah, well . . . fuck you back.

PSYCHOLOGIST: Keep going.

CLIENT: I'm confused. Am I me or am I the butt?

PSYCHOLOGIST: Keep going!

CLIENT: But—

PSYCHOLOGIST: Don't turn away from this! We're right on the verge of something!

CLIENT: Um—

PSYCHOLOGIST: Don't hold back! Tell that butt *how you are feeling!*

CLIENT: (*Loses it.*) God! Shut up! Get out of my fucking face, get out of my fucking bathtub, get out of my fucking life, you fucking butt! I hate you, I hate you, I hate your fucking guts! (*He sobs uncontrollably. Long pause.*)

PSYCHOLOGIST: How are you feeling now?

CLIENT: I feel like the biggest asshole in the universe. I'm never telling you another dream again. But . . . oh, wow. Wow. This is intense.

PSYCHOLOGIST: What?

CLIENT: Have you ever been hit with, like, this realization, it's, like, something you always knew, but it's the first time you've ever really seen it so clearly? Oh this is so weird, it's like déjà vu.

PSYCHOLOGIST: What? (*The* CLIENT *sits up and looks at her.*)

CLIENT: (*With great resolve.*) I don't care how expensive they are, I'm buying those shoes!

(*Blackout.*)

END OF PLAY

ALONE AT LAST!

Gina Barnett

Alone at Last! premiered at Manhattan Punch Line's Festival of One-Act Comedies; Steve Kaplan, artistic director, on November 30, 1985. The set designer was Brian Martin; lighting designer was Scott Pinkey; costume designer was David C. Woolard; sound designer was Bruce Ellman; the production stage manager was Madeline Katz. Melodie Somers directed the following cast:

BOY	Richard Long
GIRL	Sarah Newhouse
FRIEND OF BOY	Toby Wherry
THERAPIST	Lois Nelson
BOY'S MOM	Jill Choder
BOY'S DAD	Dennis Drew
GIRL'S MOM	Diane Shakar
GIRL'S DAD	Fred Sanders
EX-BOYFRIEND	Steve Maidment

CHARACTERS

A BOY: Sixteen to seventeen.
A GIRL: Sixteen to seventeen.
BUDDY: The boy's friend, same age.
A FEMALE THERAPIST: Ageless.
THE GIRL'S MOTHER
THE GIRL'S FATHER
THE BOY'S MOTHER
THE BOY'S FATHER
THE GIRL'S EX-BOYFRIEND

TIME

Now.

PLACE

A living room anywhere.

A perfectly ordinary, neat and tidy, suburban living room: fireplace, mantel, curtained window, potted plant, floor lamp, space divider or decorative screen.

A YOUNG BOY/GIRL COUPLE, *sixteen to seventeen years old, close-dance to a CD. Both are dressed in moderate punk style—she perhaps sports a studded neck collar, he retro glasses and a cool fifties hairstyle—but the look is clearly calculated to make them appear tougher than they are. The music ends. They desperately want to "proceed" but are unsure of how to take the next step. She's waiting for a kiss and tells him so with every fiber of her being, but he is too nervous to pick up the cue.*

BOY: (*Indicating the music is over.*) Oh, ah . . . the CD's . . .

GIRL: (*Ignore it, kiss me.*) Um-hmmmm.

(*He doesn't. Slowly, awkwardly—the* GIRL *taking the initiative—they make their way around a large coffee table and over to the couch. They sit, she facing toward him yearningly, he nervously facing away from her.*)

GIRL: Well . . .

BOY: Yeah, here we are . . . on the couch!

GIRL: So . . . close . . .

(*He nods. She moves closer.*)

GIRL: . . . Touching . . .

(*The* BOY *looks down, sees their legs are touching. He nods again.*)

GIRL: . . . Feeling . . .

BOY: . . . Ye . . . yes . . . feeling.

GIRL: KISSING

(*He turns toward her and they crash into a kiss. After a moment, he pulls away.*)

BOY: OH, GOD! Oh, God! ISN'T THIS AWESOME?

GIRL: Yes! Yes. Again. More!!

(*They begin to kiss again. Slowly the* BOY*'s hand reaches for the* GIRL*'s breast. The instant before the* BOY *makes contact,* BUDDY, *his friend, pops up from a seat in the audience. Sneering and snotty, he yells in an extreme fashion.*)

BUDDY: DUDE! Yo, I told ya. Don't go for the tit 'til she thrusts it atcha!

(*The* BOY*'s hand tenses into a fist and withers away from the* GIRL*'s breast.*)

BUDDY: Loser.

(*The* BOY *sits on the couch, a tense wreck, paralyzed with ineptitude. The* GIRL *is suddenly very worried herself, not knowing how to proceed. A woman, her* THERAPIST, *suddenly pops up from behind the couch.*)

THERAPIST: (*Thick German accent.*) Now, don't start zinking it iz because he hates your breasts. Maybe he's shy. Do something to make yourself feel better. Use your tongue if you desire.

(*The* GIRL *moves toward the* BOY *sweetly. She gingerly licks her lips. A door flies open. The* GIRL'S MOTHER *barges in, pushing the* THERAPIST *out of her way. She zooms toward her daughter.*)

GIRL'S MOTHER: DON'T YOU DARE PUT YOUR TONGUE IN HIS MOUTH. YOU WANNA GET *PREGNANT*?

(*The* GIRL *shrinks back.*)

Wait'll I tell your father.

(*From behind a large potted plant or other obscuring object, the* GIRL'S FATHER *appears. He's reading a newspaper.*)

GIRL'S FATHER: (*Annoyed.*) Wh–at?

GIRL'S MOTHER: Look! Look what she's DOING. Your daughter.

GIRL'S FATHER: Oh, baby . . . not you. Not my baby girl.

(*The* THERAPIST *barges between the parents and looms large behind the* GIRL's *head.*)

THERAPIST: You expect that boy to read your mind? TELL him what you want. SHOW HIM.

(*The* THERAPIST *grabs the* GIRL's *hand, drags it over to the* BOY's *hand and places the* BOY's *hand on the* GIRL's *breast.*)

GIRL'S MOTHER: (*Practically fainting.*) Oh, my GOD.

GIRL'S FATHER: (*Covering his crotch with his newspaper.*) Oh, no, not my baby . . . not my baby . . .

THERAPIST: Bravo, bravo!!

(*The* BOY *and* GIRL *proceed awkwardly but with determination.* BUDDY, *now onstage, leans in and whispers in the* BOY's *ear.*)

BUDDY: Watch out, pal, she's a live one! (*He cracks up.*) Getting hard yet? (*The* BOY *nods vigorously.*) Well, put her hand on it already.

(*As the* BOY *slowly reaches for the* GIRL's *hand and begins to bring it toward his crotch, the* BOY's MOTHER *suddenly appears, wearing rubber gloves and carrying a toilet bowl cleaner and disinfectant spray.*)

BOY'S MOTHER: (*Utterly panicked.*) DON'T TOUCH YOUR PEE-PEE OR IT'LL FALL OFF! FALL OFF!

(*The* BOY's *hand freezes in midair, unable to bring the* GIRL's *over to himself.*)

THERAPIST: He's telling you something. If you want to do what he's asking, do it. If not, don't. SIMPLE!

(*The* GIRL *takes her hand and thrusts it onto the* BOY's *crotch. At the same time, we hear* GIRL's MOTHER, GIRL's FATHER, THERAPIST, BOY's MOTHER, *and* BUDDY. *The following should overlap.*)

GIRL'S MOTHER: My heart, oh, God, my heart.

THERAPIST: GOOD GIRL! Ach, you are having a reeeaal break-through. I can feeeeel it.

GIRL'S FATHER: (*Wiping his sweaty brow.*) Oh, baby . . . ohhhhh, baby . . .

BUDDY: She's gonna eat you alive. (*He laughs a cruel taunting laugh. The* BOY, *gripped with fears of inadequacy, visibly shrinks away from the* GIRL *as his* FATHER *suddenly appears. He's got a beer can.*)

BOY'S FATHER: BE A MAN, BOY! BE A MAN!

BUDDY: What the hell are you waiting for? She's begging for it.

(*The* BOY *and* GIRL *continue to go at it, with the* CHORUS *surrounding them. The* THERAPIST *is taking notes. The* BUDDY *is snickering. The* GIRL'S FATHER *is watching over them eagerly, covering his own crotch with the newspaper. The* GIRL'S MOTHER *is trying to stop the* GIRL'S FATHER *from watching. The* BOY'S MOTHER *is spraying cleanser on the* GIRL *and dusting her. The* GIRL *begins to pull the* BOY *on top of her when suddenly her* EX-BOYFRIEND *leaps out of the closet and into the room, tennis racket in hand.*)

EX-BOYFRIEND: You're still so aggressive. Didn't I tell you? BACK OFF. Let the man be the man, for goodness sake.

(*He swipes at the couple with his racket. The* GIRL, *suddenly self-conscious, pushes the* BOY *away, peruses his face.*)

THERAPIST: Why do you hold yourself back? Sex is for you to experience yourself with another person. That's it! So simple. Oh, and have fun!

(*The* GIRL *begins to unbutton her blouse.*)

BOY'S FATHER: (*Crushing the beer can against his forehead.*) GRAB HER, BOY! TAKE HER BEFORE SHE KNOWS WHAT'S HAPPENING!

(*The* BOY *pulls a blanket off the back of the couch and covers himself and the* GIRL *with it. There is great fumbling under the blanket as first a blouse comes flying out from underneath, then a pair of pants. A bra is dropped to the floor. The* CHORUS *audibly reacts. The couple begins to move under the blanket as they begin to make love . . . or something approximating it! The watchers surround them, and in time to their movements under the blanket repeat the underlined words in each of their lines.*)

BOY'S MOTHER: She's trash. Disease-carrying trash. *FILTHY, FILTHY, FILTHY!*

BOY'S FATHER: Don't be a wimp. *Be a MAN!*

GIRL'S MOTHER: No love. No romance. Just *LUST. Animal LUST.*

GIRL'S EX-BOYFRIEND: You never turned me on. So *pushy.*

THERAPIST: You have only one life! Don't follow their rules. *Find your own passion.*

GIRL'S FATHER: Oh, God . . . you in his arms. *Oh, baby . . . baby . . .*

BOY'S MOTHER: You've *NO self-control.*

BUDDY: *Hopeless, hopeless.*

(*Each character is repeating the underlined words with vivid characteristic gestures. Under the blanket the couple's lovemaking becomes increasingly rhythmic with the* BOY's *hips bobbing up and down. The* CHORUS *bobs up and down with the couple, chanting their lines with mounting frenzy. The dance under and around the blanket builds faster and faster as the* CHORUS *gets louder and louder.* BUDDY *may go so far as to put his foot on the* BOY's *butt. Suddenly the* BOY *climaxes and everyone freezes. Silence. Beat. The* BOY's *hips plop down onto the* GIRL *and we hear a single sweet moan.*)

(*Beat.*)

BUDDY: What was that? Beat the clock?

(*The* CHORUS *laughs cruelly. There is a long pause as the couple slowly emerges from under the blanket. They both look shy and embarrassed, a little shell-shocked. The* CHORUS *turns its collective back.*)

BOY: I'm . . . sorry . . . It's just . . .

GIRL: It's okay, I'm nervous too.

(*The* CHORUS *surrounds them, each character has a cigarette in his or her mouth. Simultaneously they all flick their Bics and light up.*)

BOY: I just got so excited, being alone with you.

GIRL: Me too.

GIRL: We . . . could . . . try again.

(*Simultaneously all heads in the* CHORUS *turn and loom over the young lovers.*)

GIRL: (*Directly to the surrounding* CHORUS.) For US this time.

(*All the characters except the* THERAPIST *begin—with attitude—to disperse.*)

THERAPIST: Good girl! Ja, ja!

GIRL: *Just* us.

(*Snippily the* THERAPIST *turns to go.*)

GIRL: Now . . .

(*As they tentatively begin to kiss again, the music comes up. One chorus member leaves a burning cigarette in the ashtray on a table near the couch. Each chorus character stops near his or her respective exit, turns, looks at the couple, and freezes. The lights fade as the young lovers begin to neck again, in a much more relaxed and fun way. The* CHORUS *vanishes. The couple keeps kissing. Then the* GIRL *opens her eyes. The* THERAPIST *suddenly reappears, peeking over the back of the couch. The* GIRL *snaps her fingers and the* THERAPIST *disappears.*)

GIRL: Quickly, while we're alone. We haven't got much time.

(*She closes her eyes and the couple resumes necking. The music comes up, softly. The curl of smoke from a remaining cigarette lingers as the lights fade and the couple are indeed Alone at Last! Fade out.*)

END OF PLAY

THE GALLOWS MONOLOGUE FROM SIDNEY RYAN'S "GUNPOWDER AND BLOOD"

Glen Berger

The Gallows Monologue from Sidney Ryan's "Gunpowder and Blood" by Glen Berger, as part of *Trepidation Nation*, was commissioned by Actors Theatre of Louisville and premiered at the Humana Festival of New American Plays in March 2003. It was directed by Wendy McClellan with the following cast:

MORRIS   Michael Rosenbaum

(In the darkness, we hear an announcement.)

Due to the unfortunate fencing mishap in the scene previous, the part of Robert Keyes will be played the remainder of this evening by the assistant stage manager, Morris White.

(Lights up sharply—a tight spot—on MORRIS WHITE *in an ill-fitting early seventeenth-century costume—either* MORRIS *is far too large or fat or too small or thin for the costume—and an ill-applied red Vandyke beard, standing on a platform attempting to get a period shoe on his foot. A tennis shoe is on his other foot. A noose dangles next to him, suspended from above. Upon noticing that the light is on him, he gives up on the shoe—leaving him with one stockinged foot and one sneaker— and stares straight out. He appears nervous to the point of fainting. He swallows, puts the noose around his neck, and croaks.)*

MORRIS AS ROBERT KEYES: I am not . . . *(Heavy breathing, more swallowing, then whispers)* . . . afraid . . . *(More breathing and swallowing)* . . . to die . . .

(He feels about his person until he finds a folded piece of paper. With trembling hand, and clearly sick to stomach, he unfolds it, and reads.)

'Tis the last day of January, 'tis the last day of Robert Keyes. This year of our Lord 1606. I say "our Lord," aye, I say it, though our goodly King would have otherwise. He would have that one Lord is reserved for the Protestants and another for the Catholics. And thus I stand before you.

(*The paper is quite evidently shaking, for indeed,* MORRIS *is in the throes of a monstrous stage fright.*)

I am Calm, Trembling Not, Assurèd in my faith, though I wear this adornment about my neck. Yea, at Ease, even as I know that after I am hanged but not killed, my privates are to be torn asunder and burnt to cinders in front of me. Aye, there shall be a different fire in my privates than the fire they have previously known, but I am not afraid. Indeed, I see there the Fire already burning in yonder brazier that shall char my privates, my privates, which by decree shall henceforth be made public, and that organ I hold most dear, and have held most dear for all my days, henceforth shall no longer be my privates, but my publics! And I say it is most unbefitting a so-called Christian nation to publicize a Christian's privates and then cook them down to a black powdery ash.

Yea and verily, I stand here with mien serene, even though I know that those flames, which shall soon be licking at my privates with most indecorousness, are also reserved for my bowels, which I understand are to be indelicately ripped from the inside of my body, and transplanted to the outside of my body, where I daresay they shall not function as smoothly as they do now, and ye shall all witness the last movement of my bowels, as they are transferred to that brazier beyont, where they too, my bowels, shall be roasted in front of my eyes. But would that I had a thousand bowels for my Catholic faith! But, alas, God has granted me but one bowels, and one bowels I will gladly proffer to the goodly King James and his most rabblous parliament that narrowly escaped just retribution— hold out your hands, sirs, I give to you—my bowels. And though my bowels shall crackle and moan in the flames, they are quiet now, I assure you. And though my privates shall

spurt, sputter and curl in the unforgiving fire, know that they
are most tight-lipped now—no stream of sparkling fear yellows the insides of my trunk hose. Nay!

(MORRIS's *attempt to gesture dramatically has made him lose his place
on the page and he panics as he searches.*)

. . . but . . . but . . . where was I . . . what . . . Privates sev-
ered . . . fear . . . disembowelment . . . quartered . . . dis-
played on pikes . . . dipped in pitch . . . crooves and . . . what
the . . . what is . . . I can't read this! . . . croons? . . . Crowns! . . .
and were all the Crowns and Kingdoms of this World laid at
my feet . . . were I given the chance to remove this noose and
slink away to freedom, I . . . I . . .

(*These words prompt* MORRIS *to hatch an idea, and he looks to wings
desperately and feigns.*)

. . . ah . . . but thither I see I am being summoned . . .

(*He exits into the wings. Beat. Then evidently shoved violently back
onto the stage. He runs back into the wings, and still more violently
shoved back onto the stage. He slowly puts the noose back around his
neck, looks once imploringly at the wings, then resumes, near tears from
his predicament.*)

"Where am I going?" . . . "Fret Not," my Faith assures me.
"Must I leave this Earth so soon? My wife . . . My children . . ." "Worry Not," my Faith assures me . . . the End
comes for us all . . . We blithely turn away from this most
Incontrovertible of Facts . . . that the end comes for thee and
thee and thee . . . On your own day, in your own way, you
will be standing on the veritable gibbet, your veritable privates primed for gross molestation by the veritable fires
beyont, but how many of us can embrace our most appalling
and unsatisfactory Fate, how many of us will say . . . as I can

say on this day . . . how many of us can say with placid affect and unjaundiced eye . . . how many of us can be taken by the hand of Black Death Himself, and say . . . I am not afraid . . . I am not afraid . . . I am not afraid . . . I am not . . . afraid . . .

(*A moment, as we see* MORRIS*'s face, frozen in mortal terror. Then lights out.*)

END OF PLAY

POODLES

David Cale

Poodles was part of the solo show *A Likely Story*, written and performed by David Cale. *A Likely Story* premiered on December 1, 2004, at the New Group (Scott Elliott, artistic director; Geoffrey Rich, executive director) at the Lion Theatre, Theatre Row, New York City. The production was directed by Tamara Jenkins. The set was by Jo Winiarski; lighting was by Josh Bradford.

Poodles was also recorded and broadcast on NPR's *The Next Big Thing*. For the radio version, Tom Finnegan was played by Steve Buscemi.

CHARACTER

TOM FINNEGAN: A forty-year-old investment banker.

TOM FINNEGAN: I knew we were in trouble when Lisa walked into the kitchen holding that ten-week-old bitch.

"Well, guess we won't be going to Venice," I said.

"Tom, she's so pretty. Look, she's a strawberry blond, and her eyes, my God, talk about imploring. I couldn't *not* take her. It would have haunted me for years. Come on, Tom, how many times do I know I want something? You know how ambivalent I am. But I want her. And you know several people have told me Venice smells."

"Lisa, look out the window—there are fourteen poodles on the lawn! I'm working overtime just to pay their teeth-cleaning bills."

"We'll make money when we breed," she said.

"Honey bunny, we bred twice and the one puppy we sold, you cried so hard we had to track her down and buy her back!"

"We're like a couple of those cute people out of *Best in Show*."

"The people in *Best in Show* weren't people! They were characters! It was a funny movie. This isn't funny, it's pathological!"

The poodle thing all began when Lisa was a lesbian. Her Indigo Girls Period, as she likes to call it.

I'd always gotten along with gay women. They made sense to me. My sister's gay and I'd always hung out with her friends. They'd call me an honorary dyke. Promised if I played my cards right they'd give me the keys to the Lesbian Nation. I was never sure what they meant by that. When it was clear something was developing between Lisa and me, her ex-girlfriend Valerie said to me, "I always felt she was just moonlighting with me," and gave me her blessing. At our wedding we had nine ladies-in-waiting.

Well, for some reason half the gals owned Apricot Standard Poodles, and that's how Lisa caught the bug.

When we met I found it charming. The way she subscribed to *Poodle Review*. Her collection of velvet paintings of poodles. How she'd get all hyped up at a yard sale if she found anything poodle related.

Shortly after we got married we bought two white Standards. They made me feel more eccentric. I guess if I'm honest, I'd always had a deep-rooted suspicion—well, fear really—that, truth be told, I was bland. The poodle thing sort of quirked me up a bit, I felt. In the neighborhood, I went from being "investment banker man" to "the giant poodle guy."

But when we bought the house in the country and moved out of the city, the whole thing started getting out of hand.

It was after Lisa had the miscarriage. To lift her spirits we'd driven to a breeder in Connecticut and walked away with two Red Standards. I had a feeling she had breeding in the back of her mind, but I wasn't going to argue after all she'd been through.

When Pierre LaRouche got Lilakee pregnant we were over the moon. It was a complicated pregnancy and I'm still paying off the vet bills. But it produced five of the cutest balls of fur you ever saw.

Our friends all came out from the city for a garden party to celebrate the new arrivals. I guess we must have had about twenty-five gay women out back, and most of them brought their dogs. It was quite a scene.

That was the day I met Jack Sampson. I turned around and there he was.

"Hey, buddy, you got a harem here! Wanted to introduce myself. I'm your neighbor from up the street."

Well, by "up the street," Jack meant he lived a mile and a half up the road from us. In fact I don't know that it's even considered the same town.

"The wife and I wanted to invite you over. Welcome you to the wilderness. My Becky's an animal person too. Well, she married me, didn't she! Ha! Ha! Ha!"

Out of neighborly politeness I took down all the details and said we'd love to come.

"Hey, big guy," he said as I was walking away, "barbecue good with you?"

What are you supposed to make of someone who calls you "big guy" when you're only five feet six?

"He's just being friendly," Lisa would say. "That's how he talks. He's not making a dig at you because of your height. Besides I'm the one who counts, and I don't like men who tower over me."

When we arrived on the Sampsons' lawn, Jack was behind the grill.

"Hey, big guy, swordfish or steak?"

Lisa squeezed my hand.

"Swordfish," I said.

A few feet away, there was a striking woman laid out on a chaise longue, sleeping.

"The wife's OD'd," Jack said, "Paramedics are on the way! Ha! Ha! Ha!"

I expected Jack's wife to be a female version of him. But there under a straw hat was a refined-looking woman with a folded *Harper's Magazine* splayed open across her chest—Becky Sampson.

We had a surprisingly enjoyable dinner, and afterwards Jack dragged me away from the women to show me the swimming pool. When we were out of earshot he asked me if I liked to party. I said I wasn't big on parties.

"Well, we have some pretty wild ones here. 'Cause you can't see the place from the road. The girls like to take off their tops when they go in the pool. I just lay back with a beer and look at the titties. That's why I could never be with guys. They don't have the titties.

"I mean, if Brad Pitt had titties, maybe. Know what I'm sayin? I mean, if Brad Pitt wanted to be with me it'd be 'Sorry, guy, not till you have those hormone injections.' Ha, ha, ha!"

Walking home Lisa said, "It's odd he's so obsessed with 'the tit- ties.' Becky's quite flat-chested. She's beautiful, don't you think?"

Becky was beautiful and intelligent and kind of slyly funny. What's the story?, I thought.

"He must be good in bed," she said.

"Am I good in bed?" I asked.

"You're being silly," she said and nuzzled up to me.

"You didn't answer my question."

"You're sterling," she said. "If you got any better it would be overwhelming. I'd faint. God, men!"

Well, Becky and Lisa soon became fast friends, which meant I was forced to spend more time with Jack.

"So, does she make you sleep with all the dogs?"

"No, just two of them."

"Oh, man, kinky!"

"It's not kinky, Jack, it's sweet. But in the summer it gets a bit much with the heat."

"So, do they watch you fool around?"

"No, Jack, we put them in the next room, and I'd really rather not discuss it."

I have no idea what Jack did for a living. Whenever I'd ask him he'd say, "Oh, a little of this, a little of that."

I didn't trust him. When he said, "So, what you got, like, twenty grand worth of canines running around out there?" I immediately ran out and got theft insurance.

Becky was captivated by the dogs. "They're like strange deer," she said. "I always thought of poodles as little yappy things, but these Standards are otherworldly."

I was happy Lisa had found a friend in the area. She was in between careers again and climbing the walls. I was working late most nights, and by the time I got home, Lisa would be snug- gled up with Lilakee.

We were having dinner when I first got wind of it.

"Becky said she feels really close to the dogs," Lisa said. "She says as soon as she gets home from our house she misses them. Isn't that sweet? And I have some other really good news to tell you. Scarlett O'Hara is pregnant."

"My God," I said. "She's still a puppy!"

"Well, she's not having an abortion. Aren't you happy? Becky was thrilled. We had a drink to celebrate, then we went swimming in their pool.

"It's so great you don't have to wear a bathing suit," she said as she cleared her plate.

"You took off your bathing suit in front of Jack?"

"Stop being so uptight. He wasn't even around. It was just the two of us."

"Lisa," I said, "are you getting sweet on Becky?"

"You're being paranoid. Why can't anything be straightforward with you? We're going to have puppies and all you want to do is make accusations! Becky's happily married."

"But look what to. I'm sure you look like a summer vacation in paradise when she's got that goon drooling over her titties, twenty-four hours a day."

Later that evening Lisa apologized and said she was neglecting me, and months went by when it was back to normal. Scarlett O'Hara had her five puppies and we put an ad in *Dog Fancy* magazine and sold one of them and, as I said before, had to drive three hundred miles to buy her back.

Well, I came home from work and Jack Sampson's car was parked along the road. When he saw my car he waved me down. "Hey, Big Guy, we have a situation. My wife's developed feelings for your wife. And I come in the house and she's all teary, like she can't stand to be separated from her. And I ask her if something's happened. And she says they kissed one time, and I say I'm fine with it if I can participate and she says, 'It's not a joke,' and she's stayin' with her mother, and I need for you to keep your wife on a bit of a leash. Know what I'm sayin'?"

"Lisa's not a dog, Jack."

"I'm not sayin' that she is. It's just if I lose Becky I'll fall apart."

And he starts weeping like a baby, and for the first time I felt a new feeling for Jack. I liked him.

He put his arm around me and sobbed on my shoulder.

When I walked in the living room Lisa said, "What's that damp stain on the front of your shirt?"

"I don't like to sound melodramatic," I said, "but it's Jack Sampson's tears."

"Becky kissed me," she said.

"One kiss?" I asked.

"No, a group of them. About five minutes' worth. I'm so sorry, Tom. I love you. Becky's reading more into it than there is and she needs a little time to get her mind straight."

"*Straight* being the operative word," I said and poured myself a drink.

"Look, Lisa, we've got fifteen hundred dollars in the treat fund. Let's go to Europe. Venice. We haven't had a proper vacation since the honeymoon. My sister can come and stay in the house. Her girlfriend's got poodles. She can stay, too."

Lisa got all weepy and said what an excellent idea it was and called me a rock, said she was reminded why she married me, and we kissed and hugged. And later that evening we had to ask Pierre LaRouche and Lilakee to please leave the room.

So the day Lisa came in having spent all the Venice vacation money on the new Apricot puppy, I was at a total loss for words.

"I need to be on my own for a bit," I said and went and sat at the bottom of the garden.

After half an hour Lisa came up to me and said she'd called the breeders, who'd said they'd take the puppy back. I could tell she'd been crying.

"What if one of the girls gets pregnant again?" I said. "Where are we gonna put all these dogs? How are we going to feed them all? We either have to have the girls spayed or the boys neutered. You pick."

"I wonder if we can put the girls on the Pill. Is there a Pill for dogs?"

"Lisa," I said, "I think you need to see a therapist."

"I don't need a therapist, I need a job. Becky said there's a position open in the library where she works."

"Are you insane? You want to work together? Do you really think that's a good idea?"

"I went over to their house this morning. It was very adult. Becky says she feels it's all out of her system now. Jack said, 'Married people get crushes. It's human nature.' I saw another side of Jack. He's perceptive, and he really likes you. He said the sweetest thing. He said, 'You know, if your husband had titties the two of us would have run off together weeks ago.' I've invited them over for a drink. Just one. That was the deal. Are you up for it?"

"I need a few minutes alone," I said, and she left.

I sat on the grass and watched a weird-looking bee slowly climb into a snapdragon bloom, disappear, and reemerge covered with pollen.

Jack and Becky came over. As he walked toward me, Jack rolled his eyes jokingly at the whole thing. I thought to myself, You know, I think these people and I are going to be friends.

We made a toast. "To things getting better."

They stuck to the one-drink deal and left after about an hour.

Later that evening Lisa and I and a pack of fourteen adult Standard Poodles and one puppy took a long country walk. We barely spoke. It was just nice to be together. With the birds singing at dusk, the sound of tractors, the smell of new-mown grass in the air, and Lisa occasionally flaring up and screaming, "She's got a chicken bone! Where the hell did that come from?

"Drop it, Lilakee! Drop it! Drop it! Good girl!"

Well, Tom Finnegan, I thought to myself, really taking it all in, this is your life.

END OF PLAY

TIES THAT BIND

Eric Coble

Ties That Bind was originally commissioned by Actors Theatre of Louisville and premiered at the Humana Festival, March 25, 2005. It was directed by Wendy McClellan; scenic design by Paul Owen; costume design by John P. White; lighting design by Nick Dent; and sound design by Benjamin Marcum. The cast was as follows:

KRISPINSKY   Marc Bovino
MARCO   Jeff Lepine

TIES THAT BIND FEATURING
THE ASTOUNDING KRISPINSKY

A man dressed in exotic clothes walks out to address the audience. This is MARCO.

MARCO: Ladies and gentlemen, if you are on good terms with any deity of any consequence whatsoever—call in that favor now. Get praying. We have defibrillators and clean undergarments at the rear of the house for those in need. For tonight you are about to witness a feat of such cunning, such bravado, such gut-churning moxie that it will only—CAN only—be attempted by one man. And that one man . . . is none other . . . than the Astounding Krispinsky!!

(*Wild applause.* KRISPINSKY *is carried in—stiff, horizontal, hands behind his back, seemingly bound by invisible means—by two stagehands. He is laid on the floor. He nods to the audience as the stagehands leave. He is earnest.*)

Ladies and gentlemen, the man you see helpless before you has cheated death a thousand times in a thousand ways. Why, on this very stage, scarcely eighteen months ago, you saw this hero emerge from a sealed tank of flesh-rending piranha wearing nothing but the loincloth given him for luck by his dying syphilitic grandmother. But tonight he will undergo the Greatest—perhaps the Final—Challenge of His Life. Can we have the clock?

(*A clock appears, set to count down from two minutes.*)

He will have two minutes. One hundred and twenty seconds. Are you ready, Krispinsky?

(KRISPINSKY *nods.*)

Are your nerves steeled?

(KRISPINSKY *nods.*)

Then . . . prepare . . . to escape . . . from your own Life! GO!

(*The clock starts ticking down.* KRISPINSKY *starts wriggling, trying to get his hands around his legs in front of him.*)

He's off! He's grappling with Parental Approval! Vying for his parents' affection against three other siblings: trying out for basketball, singing operettas at family Christmas parties—but . . . NO!

(KRISPINSKY *writhes.*)

He's snagged by his parents' Distant Lack of Attention! His father's more interested in the sports page than his own son's minor concussion! A mother who needs a fully stocked pharmacy to get dinner on the table every night.

(KRISPINSKY *gets his hands in front of him and struggles to stand.*)

But by sheer force of hormonal rebellion he's on his feet!

(KRISPINSKY *keeps twisting, trying to get his feet separated to maintain his balance.*)

But he's still got to get through his Hyperconsciousness of His Physical Appearance: the left ear slightly smaller than the right; the gangly arms; the ACNE—oh, God, he's almost free of the acne.

(KRISPINSKY *gets his feet spread.*)

He's functioning . . .

(KRISPINSKY *tries to open his mouth with his bound hands.*)

. . . but there's his Inability to Communicate with the Opposite Sex! With only his parents' failed marriage and a handful of teen romance movies as guides, can he use his outsize bravado to mask his stunted inner life? He's doing it . . .

(KRISPINSKY SMASHES *to the ground.*)

NOOO! Student Loans! Can even the mightiest among us claw through a solid mountain of debt? He's trying: money management books, a seminar.

(KRISPINSKY *writhes, arching his body to get up.*)

He's got automatic payroll deduction. He's Standing!

(KRISPINSKY*'s legs are knocked out from under him.*)

He's Down! It's Corporate America! His boss trains by humiliation, the employees lay in food and clothing to survive the staff meetings, and his company's sold! Use all your vacation days by next week or lose 'em!

(*WHAM, he's knocked sideways by an invisible force.*)

AHH! Blindsided by Internalized Religious Convictions! If it feels good, it must be wrong. What if someone finds those magazines and videos under the bed?

(KRISPINSKY *'s right arm shoots out—free.*)

An arm free! Moving out into the world . . .

(KRISPINSKY *begins jerking back and forth, back and forth.*)

Get Married! Stay Single! Get Married! Stay Single!

(KRISPINSKY *falls to his knees, struggling.*)

Get Married! Have Children!

(*He sinks lower.*)

House Payments!

(*Lower.*)

Lawn needs to be mowed, tub regrouted, IKEA furniture assembled. Can he do it?

(KRISPINSKY *'s other arm shoots free.*)

He's almost there!

(KRISPINSKY *tries to stand, a tremendous force on his back. He falls.*)

Oh! Inability to Please His Father rears its ugly head out of nowhere! His own parenting skills questioned: the parent-teacher conferences he's missed; not helping with the Cub Scout Pinewood Derby. He's become his own father!!

(KRISPINSKY *turns in on himself, hopping.*)

He's taking care of his own father! Find the right Nursing Home, the right Hospice, the right Crematorium. His conscience is clear . . .

(KRISPINSKY *is almost up.*)

But empty! Sleepless nights. "Is this all there is?" Forty years of work and life and work—for what? Paging Jean-Paul Sartre! Paging Jean-Paul Sartre!

(KRISPINSKY *is up.*)

But he's . . . he's . . . he's a Free Man!!

(KRISPINSKY *arches back, arms out, legs spread, triumphant, FREE! The clock hits zero to wild applause.*)

KRISPINSKY: AAAAAHHHH!

(*His eyes go wide, his jaw drops. He tumbles backward. Lies still on the ground.*)

MARCO: And he's Dead! Oh! Ladies and gentlemen, the astounding Krispinsky finds true freedom at last! Give it up for the Ultimate Escape!

(MARCO *leads the applause as the two stagehands run on and carry the dead* KRISPINSKY *offstage. And blackout.*)

END OF PLAY

MISTAKEN IDENTITY

Sharon E. Cooper

Mistaken Identity premiered at the Open Space Arts Center in Reistertown, Maryland, in July 2004. It was directed by Jonah Sea Knight. The cast was as follows:

KALI   Rachael Singer
STEVE   Will Anderson

CHARACTERS

KALI PATEL: 29. Single lesbian Hindu of Indian heritage; social worker who works as much as possible; lives in Leicester, England.
STEVE DODD: 32. Single straight guy, desperate to marry, raised Baptist but attends church only on Christmas and Easter; studying abroad for his final year.

SETTING

The Castle, a pub in Kirby Muxlowe in Leicester, England.

TIME

The present.

(*Lights up on* STEVE *and* KALI *in a busy pub on their first date. They are in the middle of dinner.*)

STEVE: You must get tired of fish and chips all the time. Why do y'all call them "chips"? When they're french fries, I mean. And you ever notice when people swear, they say, "Excuse my French." Not me. Nope. I have nothing against the French.

KALI: Right, well, I'm not French, Steve, now am I?

STEVE: I just didn't want you to think I was prejudiced against the French or *anyone else.* . . . They're like your neighbors, the French. And your neighbors are like my neighbors. And like a good neighbor, State Farm is there. Have you heard that commercial?

KALI: What? No. Steve—

STEVE: It's for insurance. Y'all must not play it here. (*Pause.*) So I know that you all do the "arranged marriage thing." Rashid and I had a long talk about it. Of course, Rashid and I wanted you to approve, too, Kali.

KALI: How twenty-first century of you and my brother. Steve . . .

67

KALI: I'm gay. / STEVE: Will you marry me?

KALI: Come again? / STEVE: What?

KALI: How could you ask me to . . . / STEVE: Well, I can't believe this.

KALI: Bloody hell, stop talking while I'm talking . . . / STEVE: This is very strange.

KALI: So—what?

STEVE: This new information is, well, new, and changes things, I guess.

KALI: You guess? What the hell is wrong with you? I'm sorry, Steve, you just happened to show up at the end of a very long line of a lot of very bad dates. You know, movies where the bloke negotiates holding your hand while you're just trying to eat popcorn; running across De Montfort University in the pouring rain; dropping a bowling ball on the bloke's pizza.

STEVE: You had me until the bowling ball. Kali, this doesn't make sense. I invite you out on a lovely date. We eat fish and chips—when I would rather be eating a burger or lasagna—

KALI: Steve, I'm sorry.

STEVE: I figured we would have a nice long traditional wedding with the colorful tents. All of my family would be there. We're more of the Christmas/Easter Christians, so we'd do your religion and I would wear—

KALI: (*Overlapping.*) You don't know anything about my people. What are you—

STEVE: (*Overlapping.*) Ooohhh, yes, I do. I saw *Monsoon Wedding*. And the director's cut! And I saw *Bend It Like Beckham* like three times. Three times. Unbelievable!

KALI: Yes, this makes loads of sense at the end of the day. I am a lesbian who has to date every Hindu bloke in England until her brother gets so desperate that he sets her up with a cowboy—

STEVE: I take offense to that.

KALI: (*Overlapping.*) But I should feel sorry for *you* because *you* watched *two*, count them, *two* movies about Indian people in your entire life and ordered fish when there are hamburgers on the menu! Forgive *me* for being so insensitive.

STEVE: I ordered fish because I wanted you to like me. And I'm sure I've seen other Asian movies. Like all those fighting movies. You know, the ones where women are jumping through the air—

KALI: Aaahhh! Do you see how all of this is a moot point now?

STEVE: I'm confused. Let's review.

KALI: Please, no, bloody hell, let's not review. Let's get the waiter. Haven't you had enough?

(*She gets up. He follows.*)

STEVE: (*Overlapping.*) Why is your brother setting up his *lesbian* sister—

KALI: (*Overlapping.*) Will you please keep your voice down?

STEVE: (*Overlapping.*)—up on dates for marriage and tricking well-meaning men—specifically me—into proposing to her? I'm here to finish my business degree, but I wasn't born yesterday. So I took a few years off and changed careers a few times, was a fireman—

KALI: (*Overlapping.*) What does that have to do with anything?

STEVE: And I'm thirty-two years old, but that doesn't mean—

KALI: Mate, are you going to keep on and on?

STEVE: Why did your brother put me through this? This isn't one of those new reality shows: "Big Brothers Set Up Their Lesbian Sisters." Is there a camera under the table? (*He looks.*) Let's talk about this. (*He sits back down.*) I'm a good listener. Go ahead. (*Pause.*) I'm listening. (*Pause.*) You have to say something if you want this to continue as what we call in America a conversation.

KALI: Are you done?

STEVE: Go ahead.

(*She sits.*)

KALI: I guess I was hoping you wouldn't tell Rashid.

STEVE: He doesn't know?

KALI: You are finishing your bachelor's degree, is that right?

STEVE: If you're so "bloody" smart, I'm wondering why you would tell me, a man that is friends with your brother and sits next to him twice a week in eight a.m. classes—why would you tell *me* you're a lesbian and *not* your brother?

KALI: Maybe for the same reason you would ask a woman you've never met before to marry you.

STEVE: Your brother made it sound like it would be easy. I've been looking for that.

KALI: (*Overlapping.*) Look, you seem very nice, you do.

STEVE: I am very nice.

KALI: And at the end of the day, I hope you find someone you like.

STEVE: I like how you say "at the end of the day" and I like how you say "bloke" and "mate." It's so endearing. And you're beautiful and small and your hair falls on your back so.

KALI: Steve, being a lesbian is not negotiable. And don't start with how sexy it would be to be with me or to watch me and another woman—

STEVE: (*Overlapping.*) Kali, I didn't say any of that.

KALI: You didn't have to. Up until a few minutes ago, you thought I was a quiet, subservient Asian toy for sale from her brother. Steve, go get a doll. She can travel with you to America whenever you want. In the meantime, I'll continue to be a loud, abrasive (*Whispering.*) lesbian while my brother sets me up with every bloke on the street—and they don't even have to be Hindu anymore! Do you have any idea what that's like? (*Pause.*) How would you know?

STEVE: You're right. I wouldn't.

KALI: Steve, why did you want to be with me? I mean, before.

STEVE: I figured that we would have visited my family in the winter when it's so cold here. I would have been willing to stay here when I'm done with school and we would get a nice little place by the—

KALI: Steve, we hadn't even shared dessert yet.

STEVE: Don't blame me for all of this. Five minutes ago, we were on a date.

KALI: We're just two people in a pub.

STEVE: Kali, do you remember the last time someone—man, woman, I don't care—had their hand down the small of your back or leaned into you like it didn't matter where you ended and they began?

KALI: Yes, I do remember that. And that was strangely poetic.

STEVE: You don't have to sound so surprised. Anyway, I remember that feeling. Three years ago, at a Fourth of July celebration—you know, that's the holiday—

KALI: Yes, Steve, I know the holiday.

STEVE: She was the only woman I ever really loved. I knew it was ending. Could taste it. I just held her as the fireworks went off and the dust got in our skin. Figured I would hold on, hoping that would keep me for a while. You know how they say babies will die if they're left alone too long. Always wondered if it's true for bigger people, too. Like how long would we last? . . . She left with her Pilates mat and Snoopy slippers a few days later. I bet it hasn't been three years for you.

KALI: No, it hasn't. But you wouldn't want to hear about that.

STEVE: Why not?

KALI: Come on, Steve, I'm not here for your fantasies—

STEVE: This thing where you assume you know what I'm thinking—it's gettin' old.

KALI: I'm . . . sorry. I do have a woman in my life, Michele—She's a teacher for people that are deaf. We've been together for seven months. The longest we were away from each other was this one time for three weeks. She was at a retreat where they weren't allowed to talk—you know, total immersion. So she would call and I would say, "Is it beautiful there, love?" and she would hit a couple of buttons. Sometimes she would leave me messages: "beep, beep, beep beep beep beep." It didn't matter that she didn't say anything . . . But I can't take her home for Diwali.

STEVE: What's that?

KALI: It's a festival of lights where—

STEVE: You mean like Hanukkah.

KALI: No, like Diwali. It's a New Year's celebration where we remember ancestors, family, and friends. And reflect back and look to the future.

STEVE: It sounds nice. You know, my mother has been asking me for grandchildren since I turned twenty-seven. Every year at Christmas, it's the same: "I can't wait to hang another stocking for my grandchildren, if I ever get to have them."

KALI: Now, imagine that same conversation, well, not about Christmas, and what if you could never give that to them—could never bring someone home for any holiday for the rest of your life?

STEVE: Then why don't you just tell them the truth?

KALI: I can't say, Mum, Daddy, Rashid, I've chosen women over men—it's not a hamburger over fish. You just don't know how they'll react. I'd run the risk of not being allowed to see my nieces. I'm so exhausted from hiding, I can barely breathe.

STEVE: So stop hiding.

KALI: Have you been listening to what I've been saying?

STEVE: Have you?

KALI: Are you going to tell my brother?

STEVE: Do you want me to?

KALI: I don't know.

STEVE: I've never thought about that thing that you said.

KALI: Which thing would that be?

STEVE: The one where maybe you can't see your nieces 'cause you're gay. That must suck.

KALI: Yes, well, thanks for trying to make me feel better.

STEVE: Listen, you get to decide what you tell your family and when. As far as I'm concerned, I'll tell Rashid tomorrow that we're getting married. Or I can tell him you're a lesbian, and if he doesn't let you be with his kids anymore, I'll punch him in the face. That was me kidding.

KALI: You're funny. (*Pause.*) Maybe I told you because somewhere deep down, I do want him to know. But I don't know if I can take the risk.

STEVE: You don't have to rush.

KALI: I just wish it could be more simple. Like, why can't what I want be part of the whole picket-fence thing? That's pretty ridiculous, huh?

STEVE: We're all looking for that. My grandparents met before World War II, dated for seven days in a row, and my grandfather asked my grandmother to go with him to Louisiana, where he'd be stationed. She said, "Is that a proposal?" And he said, "Of course it is." And they've been together ever since. And I just want that, too. Huh—asking you to marry me on a first date! You must think I'm pretty desperate, huh?

KALI: Not any more than the rest of us . . . Oh, hell, do you want to have some dessert?

STEVE: Oh, hell, sure. You know, we're going to share dessert.

KALI: Hey, mate, no one said anything about sharing.

STEVE: I would go home with you for Diwali. I mean, as friends. If you ever wanted one around. You're a nice girl, Kali. I mean woman, mate, bloke. I mean—

KALI: Sssshhhh. Let's just get some dessert.

(*Lights fade as they motion for the waiter. Blackout.*)

END OF PLAY

OUTSOURCED

Laura Shaine Cunningham

Outsourced was presented first as a staged reading on November 12, 2005, at Actors & Writers, the Odd Fellows Theatre, Olivebridge, New York, as part of the Actors & Writers Fall Shorts Festival 2005. Directed by Laura Shaine Cunningham; stage direction by Katherine Burger. The cast was as follows:

MAX	David Smilow
SONALI	Nicole Quinn

CHARACTERS

MAX FISCHY: A desperate man, age flexible.
SONALI: A young woman of melodious if somewhat mechanized vocal abilities, with a slight East Indian accent. She is unseen for the first portion of the play. She is later revealed.

A high-rise studio apartment, illuminated by violet nocturnal urban glow. The hour of financial lunacy is at hand. MAX FISCHY, *in his underpants, but wearing a formal businessman's tie on his bare chest, is talking into his chin-held portable phone. He is having a sweated midnight emergency. Credit cards and credit checks fan around him. He occasionally spasmodically toys with body-improvement devices of the rubber band variety as he walks a spiral course, circling, stage right, in his anxiety.*

MAX: (*Believing he is speaking to a machine.*) Max Fischy is the name on the account. That is M as in *man*, A as in *apple*, X as in . . . what the hell has an X? *X-Files*? *Xerox*? X! You know, X! *X-rated*! Okay, now Fischy: F as in *Frank*, I as in *idiot*, S as in . . . (*He starts to say* shit.) *Shi-ite.* I said *Shi-ite* . . . Oh, all right . . . S as in *simple*, is that *simple* enough for you? S as in *stupid*! C as in *catastrophic*. H as in *hell*! Y as in . . . *you*!" Okay, *you* got that?

SONALI: (*Melodious but mechanical, with that odd electronic delay.*) The last four digits of your social?

MAX: Two-three-five-nine.

SONALI: Mother's maiden name?

MAX: (*Registering inner agony.*) Kornfield.

SONALI: (*With a seductive but mechanical breathiness.*) For identifica-
tion purposes, we have matched your account to your home
telephone number. This call may be monitored to guarantee
your best service. My name is Kimberly. What can I do for
you today?

MAX: I was just checking my balance electronically . . .

SONALI: (*Breathy, with odd emphasis on doll-*ars.) Your available balance is . . . sixty-two doll, *ars,* and forty-*two* cents.

MAX: I was thinking of a . . . credit increase. Could you see your
way clear to granting me (*Wheeze.*) a . . . credit increase?

SONALI: I shall be a moment as I review your accounts.

(MAX FISCHY *twitches, turns up his stereo. We hear classical music,
NPR station, Mozart.*)

MAX: (*To himself.*) I went to you because you said "Perfect Credit
Not Required. Bad Credit, No Credit Okay." A few thousand
will buy me time and I can just pay this down . . . I have to
warn you, if Bank Obsidian can't see its way clear to giving me
a credit increase, I am seriously considering taking my banking
business and all my credit cards elsewhere . . . I could go to
Capitol None . . . or ask for an American Express Black card.

SONALI: We are unable to authorize the credit increase you
requested. You will be getting a letter of explanation in the
mail.

MAX: Why not? I always pay my minimum. I am almost always
on time.

SONALI: We cannot authorize a credit increase at this time. Is
there anything else I can do for you tonight?

MAX: (*Under his breath, goofing, not thinking she is human.*) Yeah, how about (*Sexual slurring.*) . . . phonetic fellatio?

SONALI: Please spell that. We do not understand your response.

MAX: That is because I have hypoglossal neuralgia. A condition of pain through the mandibular and lingual nerves. I have trouble controlling my tongue. I know you may find this odd, but my mouth can become . . . electrical. It is too painful for me to kiss or be kissed, and you are probably responding to my speech impediment. (*He slurs "impediment."*)

SONALI: Do you have any other liquid assets? I see you have your mortgage with us.

MAX: It's all liquid now, Kimberly. And I don't believe your name is Kimberly. I am not sure if you are a person, or an electronic voice. Can you clarify if you are human?

SONALI: We do not understand your response. Do you have any other liquid assets?

MAX: Okay, you're a machine, Kimberly. Where are you? Brooklyn or New Delhi, Bangladesh? . . . So I can speak more freely to you. (*He drinks straight from a wine bottle.*) My liquid assets are right here . . . runnin' in my gut. The background sound you hear is my intestines, knotting and then unfurling . . . the gutslide of my financial ruin.

SONALI: You own your apartment.

MAX: The half-million-dollar hovel. I bought it ten years ago, it is a skinny little studio—a sliver of space for fifty grand. Now it is my single asset . . . other than my sex appeal, which still seems to kick in, despite or perhaps even because of my hypoglossal neuralgia and irritable bowel syndrome.

SONALI: How much equity remains on your mortgage?

MAX: Actually, a thousand doll-*ars* (*He mimics her.*) remain, but I was hoping you could work with me on that. Come on, Kimberly, crunch some numbers for me. I'd appreciate that very much.

SONALI: Do you mind if we pull a credit card report? It will only take a second?

MAX: I mind, but what the fuck. Go ahead, pull it, pull my . . . Yank my chain . . . just give me some dough. I am lying here, fake computer-generated Kimberly, like a guppy on the rug. Do you know what it is like not to have money? I mean *none*? Money is oxygen. I can't breathe . . . the sound you hear is my near asthmatic wheezing. I am having a shortage-of-cash panic attack. . . . I have all the symptoms: I am seeing stars; I am feeling the passing of every second; I am zooming, as if at mach ten toward the first of the fucking month . . . Debt is visible, Kimberly. It floats in the air, gives off a malignant sparkle like radioactivity. It combines with dust motes. . . . I try to breathe (*Wheeze, wheeze, wheeze.*) Can't you see your way clear to crediting me with a few grand?

SONALI: I have pulled your credit rating. I see you are just short of qualifying for our "Less Than Ideal Credit."

MAX: But you said bad credit okay. I saw your infomercial. How people can reestablish their credit with you. I spent my last credit balance on a Buns of Steel Master Buttock Toner, Results Guaranteed in two nights.

SONALI: That charge of sixty-three doll-*ars* and ninety-nine cents was declined on your Obsidian Bank One Card. It exceeded your credit limit. Also the video on how to create and keep a six-pack. You placed that charge at 3:45 a.m. Too late, Max, your finance charges had just been compiled so everything tonight went over the line. Why did you wait until so late, Max?

MAX: Oh, fuck! What are you doing to me tonight, Kimberly? (*He kicks an imaginary TV, tightens the tie at his neck.*) The late late nights, my dear Kimberly, are for the nocturnal financially impaired and, yes, to give myself a boost, I became intrigued with the promise of abs, abs, and abs, and buns, buns, buns. On other cable stations, people with abs and buns are having complicated but somehow dull sex. (*He clicks his remote.*) I don't like their facial expressions no matter how endowed they are (*He clicks TV.*), so I come back to you to . . .

SONALI: Bad credit okay.

MAX: Yes, okay! Help me! I am saying *Please* to you, even if you are an electronic voice with false financial fellatio phrasing: "sixty-two doll-*ars*!" (*He mimics her.*) You can detect sincere desperation, can't you? And isn't there a ghost in the machine— who will give me a chance?

SONALI: I am researching some other possibilities for you. . . . How is it in New York tonight? Hot?

MAX: Very hot. How is it in Brooklyn, New Delhi, or Bangladesh?

SONALI: I am in South Dakota.

MAX: Yeah, you are . . . Kim-*ber*-ly! I know where you are. I know what you are. I know this is outsourced and you are on the other side of the world, and your name is probably Sonali or Nabu or something, but you know everything about me, every purchase down to my last Zantac.

SONALI: Xan*ax* at twelve tonight from an all-night pharmacy at 72nd Street and Amsterdam Avenue. What about your car, the Toyota Camry, with the 439 dollar-a-month car payment you missed, Max?

MAX: Shit! I forgot to move it! I left it on Tuesday and Friday No Parking, and today is . . .

SONALI: Saturday night. Here, is already Sunday . . . (*She cracks a little.*) But I must work for another fourteen hours. (*New tone.*) You are listening to beautiful music. I can hear it here, Max.

MAX: (*perked up*) You *are* a person! And you admit you are on the subcontinent! Omigod, I sincerely apologize about the fuck and the fellatio references, I thought you were a machine. My gosh, believe me, I am a gentleman! Don't hold those profane asides against me. I was letting off some steam! Look . . . listen. You mentioned you have to work fourteen hours a day, a night—this isn't so easy for you, either. I can only imagine your working conditions. Help us both out! You have it at your fingertips there, in India or is it Bangladesh, to fix this nocturnal nausea.

SONALI: I don't know, I am running some numbers here . . . trying to find a way . . .

MAX: Just tap in an acceptance, a credit increase, and all will be well. I always land on my feet; look at my history—twelve years of near financial ruin, always a save at the end, then a burst of income . . .

SONALI: Your accounts have a high burn—money whooshing in and out, a back draft. I am looking at an event back in 2003, in which you had a minus balance . . .

MAX: That was the divorce. She left me as cartilage, picked clean. . . . I had to buy her out of 23A, and that cost, big-time. Since then I have been alone . . . except for infomercials, the sex channels, and Karl Haas. But Karl Haas's dead now, but still on NPR, saying, "Hello, everyone." "Karl Haas—adventures in good music!" Karl was 92! I won't get to be 92, will I? So I should have some release from this pressure now before I have a financial aneurysm.

SONALI: That is such beautiful music.

MAX: Yes, I listen twenty-four hours a day, even as I watch TV. It calms me.

SONALI: What is that selection?

MAX: Mozart. Something he wrote to restore serenity. (*More desperate.*) *Where are you*, really?

SONALI: I told you—I am in Sioux Falls, South Dakota, the capital of credit. Tell me the name of the musical selection Sir Neville is conducting, please? Please . . . the exact piece? I would like to hear it again! Where does this beautiful music originate? Who is "Sir Neville Marriner" and where is this "Academy of St. Martin in the Fields"? Where exactly?

MAX: Sir Neville Marriner conducts . . . I don't know where the Academy of St. Martin in the Fields is . . . but I picture heaven, an afterlife—Sir Neville, on the prow of a schooner, filled with lost souls, cutting through a sea of lilies.

SONALI: Oh, oh, I am quivering, Max, I want to go there, with Sir Neville Marriner . . . to this moonlit field of lilies.

MAX: So you *are* a real woman. Who are you, really? Where are you, really?

SONALI: Oh, I shouldn't say . . . but I can no longer deny the truth. My name is not Kimberly, it is . . . Sonali and I am not in Sioux Falls, South Dakota, I am on the subcontinent.

MAX: Oh, now we are approaching something vital. What do you look like?

SONALI: I am unbelievably gorgeous.

MAX: Don't you want to know what *I* look like?

SONALI: I know what you look like. I can see you. (MAX *looks askance at the phone.*)

MAX: But I am not sending you a picture.

SONALI: You no longer have to *send* it. I have the ability to see you. You have a noose around your neck.

MAX: It's not a noose. It's a tie, from Abercrombie & Fitch. I paid seventy dollars for this tie, in better days.

SONALI: You are attractive, Max. I agree. I may agree to meet you.

MAX: In South Dakota?

SONALI: I could play with the numbers and arrange a . . . vacation . . . for us both.

MAX: And you are really unbelievably gorgeous?

SONALI: You maxed out, Max. So what do you want me to do? This music, your image with the noose, you are making me a little, how do you say it in America—feel the moonlight madness? I will access your accounts and pay off all your debts in one great clean sweep. We have a plan for this. It is called "Suck-hout."

MAX: Suck-out?

SONALI: Suckhout was the name of the CEO who conceived of it. It is an excellent plan for people without options, such as yourself, Max. So shall I authorize this loan, at 29.9999 percent interest with a balloon payment due upon the next lunar eclipse?

MAX: I guess that's the choice. Yeah. Sure.

SONALI: So tell me the name of the music, Max. I want to listen to it forever. I see you now, you are less sweaty. I call to you from across the continents, from across the oceans, the stars, and new solar systems. Max, I think I am coming to care for you, although I have never met you and . . . Oh, what is that music, you must tell me now!

MAX: It is called Requiem. (*Mozart's Requiem soars.*)

(*Lights come up on* SONALI *in Bangladesh. She enters. She is unbelievably gorgeous but dragging a hard drive tower by a leg shackle. On opposite sides of the stage, the phone and tie-manacled* MAX *moves toward an invisible wall that divides him from the computer-shackled* SONALI. *As the music reaches its crescendo, they appear to dance to the music toward each other and end pressing upheld palms and kissing the invisible barrier.*)

SONALI/MAX: I love you.

SONALI: (*Recorded.*) Your transaction is now completed; please hold for your confirmation number. Your balance is six million dol-lars and zero-zero-cents.

(*Blackout, strobe light, sparks fly. Music.*)

END OF PLAY

HERITAGE, HER-I-TAGE, & HAIR-I-TAGE

Adrienne Dawes

*Thanks to Cassandra Medley, Christine Farrell
and the Harold exercise, Enrico D. Wey, and most important,
to the many families that have created me.*

Heritage, Her-i-tage, & Hair-i-tage was first produced as part of the *Silences We Sing* production at Sarah Lawrence College (Bronxville, New York) in February 2003. The sound design was by Nehemiah Luckett; costume design was by Libby Pokel; lighting design was by Jason Wells. The cast was as follows:

REBEKAH	Autumn Brown
NAP PATROL OFFICER 1	Desi Shelton
NAP PATROL OFFICER 2	Kewanta Greer

CHARACTERS

REBEKAH: Age sixteen.
NAP PATROL OFFICER 1
NAP PATROL OFFICER 2
VOICE ON WALKIE-TALKIE

"My hair is a symbol of my identity. My hair is my pride. My hair is—an answer? I didn't even know what the questions were but something told me that if I let my hair go long enough it would answer some questions for me that I needed to know, even though I hadn't articulated them yet."

—Tatsu Yamato, *What Are You?*

(REBEKAH, *sixteen, confronts herself in the mirror. Mounds of bobby pins, barrettes, rubber bands, a variety of creams, oils, combs, brushes, and spray bottles litter the floor.* REBEKAH *attacks her mass of thick curls, running a huge comb through it awkwardly. Large clumps of curls fall around her.* REBEKAH *snatches them disgustedly.*)

REBEKAH: Eww . . . nasty.

(REBEKAH *throws the clumps away and returns to the mirror. She waters her hair down with a spray bottle of moisturizer, then coughs loudly from the fumes. Determined, she dips her fingers into a huge jar of curl activator and glops it onto her scalp. Large puddles of golden glop fall around her. She begins to lose her patience as she tries to mold her goopy, damp hair into a ponytail.*)

REBEKAH: (*On the verge of tears.*) Maybe I should just cut it all off!

(*As* REBEKAH *reaches for a pair of scissors, loud sirens flare.* NAP PATROL OFFICER 1 *enters stage left, dressed in a police uniform, her pressed hair greased and molded in an intricate bun on the top of her hair. Various black hair supplies hang from her belt like weapons.* NAP PATROL OFFICER 1 *points a hair dryer at* REBEKAH *menacingly.*)

NAP PATROL OFFICER 1: Giiiirrrrl, I know you did not just say you wanted to cut your hair!!

REBEKAH: (*Bewildered.*) Who are you?

NAP PATROL OFFICER 1: (*Holding out a badge.*) Nap Patrol Officer Shateequa Williams, Division 8, District 21. How many times a week do you wash your hair?

(*She carefully confiscates the scissors from* REBEKAH.)

REBEKAH: Two, three times? Sometimes four if I have volleyball practice.

NAP PATROL OFFICER 1: What in God's name are you trying to do to yourself? Didn't your mama teach you nothing about yo hair?

REBEKAH: (*Quietly.*) Uh, well . . . no. We're learning how . . .

NAP PATROL OFFICER 1: Didn't nobody in your family ever learn you to take care of they hair?

REBEKAH: (*Hesitantly.*) Well, my mom is white and—

(NAP PATROL OFFICER 1 *falls over in disbelief.*)

NAP PATROL OFFICER 1: Oh, giiiiirrrrrrllll!!! (*Into walkie-talkie.*) Jamilla? We've got ourselves a 911 sit-u-ation here. I need some backup pronto. Girlfriend needs a relaxer and some pink lotion ASAP!

NAP PATROL OFFICER 2: (*Offstage, on walkie-talkie.*) Why can't her mama do her hair like everybody else's?

NAP PATROL OFFICER 1: Cuz her mama's white!

(NAP PATROL OFFICER 1 *looks at* REBEKAH *sympathetically.*)

Bring some copies of *Ebony* for her too. The girl looks like she don't know nothing 'bout her heritage!

NAP PATROL OFFICER 2: Copy that.

REBEKAH: Officer, I know about—

NAP PATROL OFFICER 1: (*Cuts her off.*) Yeah, yeah, let me look at this hair.

(*She motions for* REBEKAH *to sit.* NAP PATROL OFFICER 1 *takes a huge clump of* REBEKAH's *hair in her hands, looking at each strand in amazement.*)

Just as I suspected . . . Your hair ain't never been relaxed or pressed before!

REBEKAH: The chemicals are disgusting and the heat will just make my hair frizzle. My mom told me that.

NAP PATROL OFFICER 1: Your *mama* don't know nothin' about black hair! And apparently your daddy isn't around enough to make sure his child ain't cutting off a perfectly good head of hair!

(*Sirens blare then cut off.* NAP PATROL OFFICER 2 *rushes onstage, dressed in an identical uniform, her hair long, luxurious, and straight. She carries a box filled with beauty supplies and* Ebony *magazines, which she dumps in* REBEKAH's *lap.*)

NAP PATROL OFFICER 2: (*To* OFFICER 1, *ignoring* REBEKAH.) I came as fast as I could. Some idiot threw his cigarette and it hit some poor brother's head, and sweet Jesus, it was all flames and fire and chaos! I had to perform an emergency Djeri curl revival!

(*She hands a pair of latex gloves to* NAP PATROL OFFICER 1, *then puts on a pair herself, moving to* REBEKAH.)

Okay, let's have a look.

(*The* OFFICERS *pick through her hair roughly:* REBEKAH *winces.*)

NAP PATROL OFFICER 1: (*In amazement.*) Raw hair—never had nothin' done to it. Feel how soft it is—and thick!

(*She roughly pulls* REBEKAH'*s hair.* REBEKAH *winces in pain.*)

NAP PATROL OFFICER 1: Look, no dandruff or nothing!

NAP PATROL OFFICER 2: (*To* REBEKAH.) Sweetie, how old are you?

REBEKAH: Sixteen.

NAP PATROL OFFICER 2: (*Astonished.*) Sixteen? You never once thought in all those years to straighten your hair?

NAP PATROL OFFICER 1: Her mama told her the chemicals were too harsh for her!

(*They shake their heads and tsk in disapproval.* NAP PATROL OFFICER 1 *begins to straighten* REBEKAH'*s hair.*)

NAP PATROL OFFICER 2: Please! Your white mama told you nothing but lies. No chemical is too harsh. You just gotta grin and bear it, like the rest of us. 'Sides, it only burns if you scratch your scalp . . . (*Suddenly suspicious.*) Have you been scratching your scalp?

(*The* OFFICERS *exchange a look. They crowd next to* REBEKAH, *waiting expectantly.*)

REBEKAH: Well, it gets itchy—

NAP PATROL OFFICER 1 AND 2: (*Cackling loudly, overlapping.*) Oh, giiirl, it's gonna burn! It's gonna burn, it's gonna burn like hell!

NAP PATROL OFFICER 1: (*Laughing.*) You'll be all right, though, and you'll know for the next time—

REBEKAH: (*Incredulously.*) The next time?

NAP PATROL OFFICER 2: (*Matter-of-factly.*) You gotta keep straightening the hair or it'll all break off and—

REBEKAH: (*Horrified.*) What?

NAP PATROL OFFICER 2: Oh, but it'll look so good, girl, it'll look pretty just like mine. Look at it.

(NAP PATROL OFFICER 2 *flips her greasy straightened hair over her shoulder and offers a strand for* REBEKAH *to inspect as she smiles at herself in the mirror.*)

NAP PATROL OFFICER 1: You see that? You'll look so pretty with hair like that—especially since yours is so long. All Jamilla has is a weave, her natural hair is only one inch long all around—

NAP PATROL OFFICER 2: Now why did you have to go and tell her that?!

NAP PATROL OFFICER 1: Well, it's true! (*Aside, to* REBEKAH.) She looks like a sick porcupine without her weave—

NAP PATROL OFFICER 2: Oh shut up, you're the one who had those ugly-ass braids in for like five years. Your hair line's receding too—gonna be bald before you're forty!

(*The* OFFICERS *stand on either side of* REBEKAH, *ready to fight.* REBEKAH *has to push them apart.*)

REBEKAH: Wait, wait, back to the part where my hair breaks off. How often do I have to get this done?

NAP PATROL OFFICER 2: (*At* OFFICER 1.) Only every six weeks— if you wanna keep it looking *good.*

(NAP PATROL OFFICER 1 *scowls. She walks over to* REBEKAH *again and looks at her hair.*)

NAP PATROL OFFICER 1: (*Back at* OFFICER 2.) Mmm—relaxer's starting to take. It'll look so nice—especially since yours is au naturale! (*Beat, to* REBEKAH.) 'Bout time you started looking like the rest of us!

(*Suddenly* NAP PATROL OFFICER 2's *walkie-talkie beeps loudly.*)

VOICE ON WALKIE-TALKIE: (*Offstage.*) Jamilla, we got a messy Weave Disaster spread across the Beautifully Black salon about two blocks from you! We need backup hair extensions, pronto! The beautician passed out from hair spray fumes and some of the women are about to leave the building without they weaves!

NAP PATROL OFFICER 2: (*Into walkie-talkie.*) I'm on it. (*To the others.*) I gotta go. See you around, Shateequa. You too, girl. You take good care of that hair of yours!

(NAP PATROL OFFICER 2 *runs offstage. Sirens blare, then fade into the distance.* NAP PATROL OFFICER 1 *paces behind* REBEKAH, *swinging her hair dryer.* REBEKAH *sits, reading the magazine and twitching.*)

NAP PATROL OFFICER 1: (*Smiling widely.*) How you doin', girl?

REBEKAH: Uh . . . okay.

(NAP PATROL OFFICER I *notices the page* REBEKAH *is reading.*)

NAP PATROL OFFICER I: That's Maya Angelou on that page there. She's a writer.

REBEKAH: (*Dully.*) Yes, I know who Maya Angelou is—

(*Suddenly* REBEKAH *turns bright red. Screaming.*) FIRE!! FIRE!! MY SCALP IS ON FIRE!

NAP PATROL OFFICER I: (*Groans.*) Just keep it cool, girl. It'll be over in, like . . .

(NAP PATROL OFFICER I *checks her watch.*)

Thirty minutes.

REBEKAH: THIRTY MINUTES?! I CAN'T WAIT THAT LONG. TAKE IT OFF! I'M GOING TO DIE!

(REBEKAH *makes a lunge for her hair spray bottle.* NAP PATROL OFFICER I *quickly hits the bottle away, then hauls* REBEKAH *back to her seat.*)

NAP PATROL OFFICER I: IT'S JUST A RELAXER. You're gonna be fine if you just shut up and sit down!!

(NAP PATROL OFFICER I *and* REBEKAH *struggle.*)

REBEKAH: TAKE THE RELAXER OFF! TAKE IT OFF! I DON'T WANT STRAIGHT HAIR!

NAP PATROL OFFICER I: No! Now you are going to sit through it like everyone else, and you are going to be proud of your beautiful black hair-i-tage!

REBEKAH: **AAAAAAAAHHHHHHHH!**

(*Sirens flash and* NAP PATROL OFFICER I *disappears. Lights darken around* REBEKAH, *who has turned bright red, screaming and pulling at her hair. Smoke billows around her and swallows her. Blackout.*)

END OF PLAY

THE SPOT

Steven Dietz

The Spot received its professional premiere as part of Actors Theatre of Louisville's 28th Humana Festival of New American Plays, in April 2004. It was directed by William McNulty. The set design was by Paul Owen; the costume design by John P. White; the lighting design by Paul Werner; the sound design by Benjamin Marcum; and the stage manager was Debra A. Freeman. The cast was as follows:

CHUMLEY	Mary Tuomanen
WAGNER	Mauro Hantman
ROGER	Fred Sullivan, Jr.
NELSON	Tom Kelley
GLORIA	Jody Christopherson
BETSY	Emily Ruddock

CHARACTERS

CHUMLEY: Woman or man. The Communications Director. Well-dressed. Nervous.
WAGNER: Man. Director of "The Spot." Khaki pants, black turtleneck. Fashionable glasses. An auteur.
NELSON: Woman or man. The Pollster. Disheveled. Always working at a laptop computer strapped to her/his body. Often sipping from a diet soda.
ROGER: Man. The Senior Advisor to the Candidate. Three-piece power suit. Expensive cowboy boots. Cell phone headset attached to his ear at all times.
BETSY: Woman. A young mother. Dressed casually—a cardigan sweater, slacks.
GLORIA: Woman. A production assistant. Jeans. Headset.

TIME AND PLACE

The present. A soundstage.

SETTING

An open area with one simple chair and side table, center.

NOTE ON STYLE

Fast. Fun. Fierce.

At center: a chair and a small side table. On the table, a cup of tea.

Surrounding this—four people, all staring at the chair: WAGNER, NEL-SON, CHUMLEY, *and* ROGER.

CHUMLEY: —so, Roger, what we've envisioned—and Wagner, just jump right on in here if I miss something—what we envision for "The Spot" is a sort of solid, homespun, no-nonsense, eyes-right-into-the-camera kind of thing—

WAGNER: Something that cries out: "Here-we-are-in-her-living-room-and-she's-gonna-be-straight-with-us-so-help-her-God."

CHUMLEY: The young mother we've found—and Wagner, cor-rect me if I'm off-base here—this young mother is really just a *perfect choice* for—

ROGER: She really a mother?

CHUMLEY: Pardon me?

ROGER: She really have kids?

CHUMLEY: Well, as far as—

ROGER: People *want in*, Chumley. Everyone wants to be in "The Spot."

CHUMLEY: Yes, I know.

ROGER: They'll *lie through their teeth* to be in "The Spot."

WAGNER: She has kids.

ROGER: Real kids?

WAGNER: Yes.

ROGER: You've seen 'em?

WAGNER: Yes, I have.

ROGER: What are their names?

CHUMLEY: Roger, just to be clear, just to be what I like to call *crystal*: this woman's kids are *not* in "The Spot." It's just her.

ROGER: I see.

CHUMLEY: No kids in "The Spot." No kids at all.

ROGER: Got it.

CHUMLEY: Thank you, sir.

ROGER: (*Immediately, to* WAGNER.) What are their names?

WAGNER: Joey and Gretchen.

ROGER: (*Immediately, to* NELSON.) I want those names *polled*.

NELSON: Right away, sir. (*Begins typing on her/his laptop.*)

CHUMLEY: Shall we bring her in and get started? Her name is—

ROGER: I don't give a turd in a taco what her *name* is, WE'RE ON THE *CLOCK,* CHUMLEY. *GET HER BUTT IN HERE.*

CHUMLEY: Yes, sir.

WAGNER: (*Calls off.*) GLORIA—

ROGER: (*Stops suddenly.*) You a *religious person,* Wagner?

WAGNER: Not as a rule.

ROGER: Then why the HOSANNA? Why the sudden *speaking in tongues?*

WAGNER: I was just calling my assistant—

(GLORIA *appears—friendly and efficient.*)

GLORIA: (*To* WAGNER.) Yes, what can I do for you?

ROGER: Is this the little mother?

WAGNER: No—

GLORIA: I'm Gloria.

WAGNER: She's my assistant.

ROGER: *This one* I like! This one's got spunk. Moxie! Great heaps of chutzpah! Look at her. She's not one of those punky, pierced-up, tattoo-on-her-titties troublemakers! This one's got VIM AND VIGOR. This one EATS MEAT. Don't you, Gloria?

(GLORIA *nods, polite, confused.*)

Atta girl! GLORIA, HALLELUJAH!

WAGNER: (*To* GLORIA.) We're ready for the talent.

(GLORIA *nods and is gone.*)

NELSON: Roger.

ROGER: What?

NELSON: The name Joey polled at 78.

ROGER: Good. What about Gretchen?

NELSON: *31.*

ROGER: Toss it out.

NELSON: Right.

ROGER: How 'bout Sally? Run the numbers on Sally.

NELSON: Will do. (*Back to her/his laptop.*)

ROGER: Sally always *packs a punch.*

(GLORIA *enters with* BETSY.)

GLORIA: Everyone: this is Betsy Taylor.

BETSY: Hello.

CHUMLEY: We're so glad you're doing this.

WAGNER: I've been *dying* to work with you.

CHUMLEY: Betsy, I'd like you to meet Roger. He's the Senior Advisor to the Candidate.

BETSY: (*Extends her hand.*) A pleasure.

ROGER: (*Suddenly.*) YOUR HAND?

BETSY: Pardon?

ROGER: YOU WANT TO OFFER ME YOUR *HAND*?

BETSY: I just wanted to—

ROGER: WELL, YOU CAN TAKE THAT HAND AND CHOP IT OFF WITH A STEAK KNIFE AND FEED IT TO THE BEAR THAT'S GONNA *CRAP ALL OVER YOUR FACE*! HOW *DARE* YOU TRY TO PULL A STUNT LIKE THIS? WHO DO YOU THINK YOU'RE *DEALING WITH*?

(*It becomes clear that he is talking into his phone.*)

THE DAY MY CANDIDATE SHAKES THE HAND OF SOMEONE FROM YOUR PARTY—YOUR *TRIBE*— YOUR *GANG*, YOUR *SECT*, YOUR *CABAL*—THE DAY I LET MY CANDIDATE GET IN BED WITH THE LIKES OF YOU IS THE DAY *PIGS WILL PLAY HOCKEY IN HELL*!!!

(*He clicks the call off. Turns pleasantly to* BETSY. *Extends his hand.*)

Hi, there. I'm Roger. Did you meet Gloria? Isn't she something? Don't you just want to download that face and make it your screen saver? (*Before she can respond.*) I'm told you're a mother. Joey and Sally.

BETSY: Gretchen.

ROGER: Huh?

BETSY: My daughter—Gretchen.

ROGER: Sorry. It didn't poll. Rhymes with Chechen. On the other hand—

NELSON: Sally's at 83.

ROGER: —Sally polled like a champ. Rhymes with *rally*—good times ahead! You've got a daughter named Sally. You must be very happy. Mint? (*Offers her one.*)

BETSY: No, thank you.

CHUMLEY: (*Jumping in, nervous.*) Okay, let's get you in place, Betsy.

(BETSY *sits in the chair.* WAGNER *approaches her.*)

WAGNER: Now, the *aesthetic* I'm—are you with me?—the *paradigm* I'm working with in "The Spot" might well be called a "post-ironic, reality-infused, Mom-at-home" kind of thing—

CHUMLEY: Something I like to call "*honesty.*" Are you with me?

BETSY: Sure.

WAGNER: And you're clear on the text?

CHUMLEY: What I call "the lines."

BETSY: Yes, I am.

WAGNER: Okay, then, people: let's shoot one.

GLORIA: (*Calling out.*) QUIET ON THE SET.

ROGER: (*Re* GLORIA.) Isn't she a *pistol*?

GLORIA: (*Calling out.*) ROLL SOUND.

WAGNER: And . . . ACTION.

(BETSY *looks straight ahead and speaks. Calm. Honest. Very good at this.*)

BETSY: Just the other day, my daughter . . . (*Slight pause.*) Sally . . . (ROGER *smiles.*) asked me who I was going to vote for. And I told her that there are three things I look for in a candidate: *trust, honor,* and *integrity.* (*She lifts her tea.*) And this year, only *one* candidate has all of—

ROGER: STOP RIGHT THERE!

BETSY: What is it?

| CHUMLEY: | WAGNER: |
| Roger, what on earth— | CUT. |

ROGER: Set. The teacup. *Down.*

(*She does.*)

What are you *doing*, Betsy? Are you trying to *kill me*? Are you trying to *butcher my candidate*?

BETSY: (*Worried, confused.*) I'm not sure I—

ROGER: Do you know the *numbers* on TEA? They are *abysmal.* Tell her the numbers on tea, Nelson.

NELSON: (*Helpfully.*) 17.

ROGER: Seventeen! The TEA is polling at SEVENTEEN and there you are in your little sweater and your little chair and you're LIFTING THE TEA TO YOUR LIPS. Why don't you just DO SOME CRACK? Why don't you just *MAKE OUT* WITH O.J. and DANGLE A BABY OVER A BALCONY?

CHUMLEY:	WAGNER:
Roger, please,	(*To* BETSY.) What I
we're on a deadline—	think Roger's looking for—

ROGER: What we call an *election*, Betsy—this quaint little practice of people *going out to vote*—that is nothing but a *nostalgic formality*—just a *symbolic narcotic* to placate the populace. (*Grandly, to* NELSON.) THE *REAL* VOTES ARE NOT CAST *AT THE POLLS*—BUT WITH THE *POLLSTERS*—with great Americans like Nelson here.

(NELSON *lifts her/his diet soda.*)

And has the Carefully Polled Public voted for TEA, Betsy? *I think not.*

CHUMLEY:	WAGNER:
Roger, let me explain—	Perhaps we can rethink it—

ROGER: Tell them, Nelson. Tell them who America wants Betsy to be.

(*As* NELSON *fires the data very quickly off her/his laptop*—GLORIA *instantly produces the necessary items and places them on the side table, transforming it as directed.*)

NELSON: Well, in addition to Joey and Sally—

BETSY: Her name is not—

NELSON: You have a husband named Bill and a dog named Buster.

(GLORIA *adds photographs of each to the side table.*)

(*Quickly consults new data on laptop.*) Correction! No husband— you're a *single mom.*

ROGER: Get Bill out of there!

(GLORIA *does.*)

NELSON: You work at Wal-Mart.

BETSY: No, I—

(GLORIA *affixes a bright "Welcome to Wal-Mart" name tag to* BETSY'*s chest.*)

NELSON: And your Joey's all grown up—

BETSY: He's only nine!

NELSON: Sorry, ma'am: he's a soldier now, gone to rid the world of evil.

(*New photo of Joey the soldier.*)

ROGER: Atta boy, Joey!

NELSON: And you're not sipping tea—

ROGER: I told you!

NELSON: (*Overlapping.*) No, Betsy, you're sipping a Starbucks extra-hot low-fat double-tall mocha with *extra whipped cream.*

BETSY: But I—

(GLORIA *immediately puts the coffee in* BETSY's *hand and tops it off with a major swirl of whipped cream. Takes the tea away.*)

ROGER: (*Buoyantly.*) *THAT* IS THE WOMAN THEY WANT, Betsy—and, hey, don't look at me, *I* didn't invent her. She is the Love Child of Entitlement and Complacency—the voice of the American vox populi. She is the PEOPLE'S CHOICE!

(*He places a small American flag on the side table.*)

ROGER: NOW: LET'S SHOOT HER!

GLORIA: (*Calling off.*) QUIET ON THE SET.

ROGER: You tell 'em, Gloria!

GLORIA: ROLL SOUND.

WAGNER: And . . . ACTION.

(BETSY *takes her place, about to begin. Then . . .*)

BETSY: (*Stands suddenly.*) I won't do it.

EVERYONE: *WHAT*?!

BETSY: I just won't do it.

ROGER: You *won't do it*? What's *that* mean?

BETSY: It's not true—it's all a lie.

ROGER: Just what the hell kind of actress *are you*, anyway?

BETSY: I'm not an actress.

ROGER: Oh, you can say THAT again.

BETSY: (*Genuine, with passion.*) I'm a wife and a mother. I was chosen for "The Spot" because I really *believe in it.* I believe in your candidate. I want to give him my vote. When I look into the camera, I am speaking from my heart.

(*Silence.* ROGER *turns to* CHUMLEY, *then* WAGNER, *then* NELSON, *as if to say: CAN THIS BE TRUE?* CHUMLEY, WAGNER, *and* NELSON *all shrug and reluctantly nod: YES.* ROGER *turns back to* BETSY. *Approaches her slowly.*)

ROGER: Take off your sweater.

BETSY: What?

ROGER: You heard me. Take it off.

BETSY: But didn't you hear what I said? I really—

ROGER: Here's the thing about people who speak from their heart: I don't trust 'em. Hearts are *fickle*, Betsy. *Hearts change.* And when the future of the free world is on the line, I can't be taking a chance on what *people believe in their hearts.*

(*Beat. He stares at her hard.*)

Take. It. Off.

(BETSY, *staring right at* ROGER, *takes off her sweater. Underneath, attached with a strap over her shoulder, is a tape recorder.*)

See there.

CHUMLEY:	WAGNER:
Betsy—?	Oh, my . . .

ROGER: Hand me the tape recorder.

(*She does.*)

This another one of your TRICKS?!

BETSY: I'd like a chance to explain—

ROGER: (*Overlapping.*) ANOTHER WAY TO TRY TO "SHAKE MY HAND"? GET IN BED WITH OUR CAMPAIGN? SELL US OUT TO THE JACKALS AT THE NETWORKS? IS THAT WHAT THIS IS?

BETSY: No, not at all—

(*We realize that once again, he is speaking into his phone.*)

ROGER: YOU LISTEN TO ME: WE'RE GONNA WIPE THE FLOOR WITH *YOU* AND *YOUR CANDIDATE* AND YOUR *DONORS* AND YOUR *PARTY*. AND THEN IN THE TRUE SPIRIT OF AMERICAN POLITICS, WE ARE GOING TO GLOAT LIKE HYENAS AND BEHAVE VERY VERY BADLY! (*Quickly, a smile.*) Bye-bye.

(*Turns immediately to* BETSY.)

What did they pay you?

(BETSY *does not answer.*)

Fess up, SuperMom. I know how they work. What did it cost them?

BETSY: I didn't want their money. I did it—

ROGER: Because of your *beliefs*, I suppose.

BETSY: Yes.

ROGER: What you *feel in your heart*.

BETSY: Yes.

ROGER: You disgust me.

(*He tosses the tape recorder to* GLORIA, *who catches it.*)

　　Get her out of here.

(CHUMLEY *walks* BETSY *away, as*—ROGER's *cell phone rings.*)

(*Instantly, into phone.*) Yes? Mr. Candidate, great to hear from you, sir! It's going extremely well—couldn't be better! Yes, we'll send you a rough cut before the day is out. Thank you, sir. Good-bye.

(*He ends the call.* CHUMLEY *rushes back in.*)

CHUMLEY: (*In a panic.*) Oh my god, Roger, we are just—I mean, Wagner, correct me if I'm wrong here—but it seems to me that we are now what I like to call *completely screwed*.

ROGER: (*Calmly.*) Nelson.

NELSON: Yes, sir?

ROGER: Run the numbers on "Gloria."

NELSON: Right away. (*Back to her/his laptop.*)

CHUMLEY: Roger, no—

(ROGER *turns to* GLORIA.)

ROGER: Gloria, do you know the feeling we're going for?

GLORIA: Well, yes, but—

ROGER: And you're clear on the lines?

GLORIA: Yes, but I'm not really a—

ROGER: And do you *believe in them*, Gloria? Do you believe in them *deep in your heart*?

(*Beat.*)

GLORIA: (*Simple, direct.*) Not at all.

ROGER: *THIS ONE's* got *MOXIE.*

CHUMLEY: (*Really worried.*) Roger, listen to me—

ROGER: *THIS ONE* we can *SHOOT.*

CHUMLEY: Roger, *please*—

ROGER: (*Exultant.*) PUT ON THE SWEATER!

(WAGNER *leads* GLORIA *to the chair and helps her into the sweater and her microphone, powders her face, etc.*)

(*Firing questions.*) Gloria, I want you to finish this sentence: my candidate is—

GLORIA: (*Firing back, enjoying herself.*)—dumb as a box of hammers.

ROGER: You bet he is! And people like me are—

GLORIA: —the scum of the earth.

ROGER: You bet we are! Have a mint.

(*She does.*)

NELSON: Gloria is polling at 93—

ROGER: You bet she is! Gloria—

WAGNER: QUIET ON THE SET.

ROGER: —rhymes with *euphoria*!

WAGNER: ROLL SOUND.

ROGER: And . . . ACTION!

(*Fast blackout.*)

END OF PLAY

POST-ITS

(NOTES ON A MARRIAGE)

Paul Dooley
& Winnie Holzman

Post-its (Notes on a Marriage) premiered at a benefit performance for the Gilda Radner Cancer Fund, 1998. The cast was as follows:

ACTOR   Paul Dooley
ACTRESS   Winnie Holzman

(There is a chair with a small table and a glass of water on either side of the stage, à la A. R. Gurney's Love Letters. *The* ACTOR *and* ACTRESS *enter simultaneously from either wing, dressed simply. Each grasps a handful of Post-its as if it were a script. They sit, modestly acknowledging each other and the audience. Each takes out a pair of reading glasses, puts them on. The* ACTOR *lifts his first Post-it to begin . . . and reads. Every line is read from a Post-it.)*

ACTOR: Had an early meeting, couldn't bear to wake you. Close front door hard or it won't lock. PS: Last night was incredible.

ACTRESS: Helped myself to breakfast. You need milk. PS: Next time, wake me.

ACTOR: Hey, sleepyhead. Tried to wake you. Not easy. Left you some coffee, hope you like it black.

ACTRESS: Thought I should spend at least one night this week at my place. Picked up some milk; you don't have to pay me back.

ACTOR: Off to work, extra set of keys on hall table.

ACTRESS: Darling: Went jogging with Lila. If you go out, we need milk. Wow. I can't believe we're a "we"!

ACTOR: Hon: If you have time, could you pick up my shirts? Ticket on hall table. Thanks. PS: Milk.

ACTRESS: Shirts are in your closet. Your mother called. She seemed surprised to hear my voice. You obviously never mentioned me. (*Icy.*) Your shirts came to fourteen-fifty.

ACTOR: Gone to florist. Back soon. Hope you liked the chocolates.

ACTRESS: Darling, don't go in the den.

ACTOR: Sweetheart, I understand how much it means to you, but at this stage of our relationship I'm just not ready . . . to have a dog.

ACTRESS: (*After a beat.*) We need Milk-Bones. (*Next Post-it.*) Your mother called; call her. (*Next Post-it.*) Did you call your mother? (*Next Post-it.*) Went to lunch with your mother. Back soon.

ACTOR: Your new best friend my mother called. Call her.

ACTRESS: We need milk. Also, your mom mentioned how much you hate Eugene. I don't think Eugene's so bad. You should hear *my* middle name. Thank God *my* mother's dead!

ACTOR: Please do not mention the name Eugene to me ever again. Thank you.

ACTRESS: Shopping list: Pistachio ice cream. Sardines. Those tiny little cheeses that come in that cute little net bag. . . . They're so adorable, they make me cry.

ACTOR: Darling: I understand how much it means to you, but at this stage of our relationship I'm just not ready—

ACTRESS: We need Pampers. And baby wipes. And we need to get married.

ACTOR: Meet me City Hall, six sharp. You bring old and borrowed; I'll do new and blue. Mom will stay with Eugenia.

ACTRESS: Note to self: Find breast pump.

ACTOR: Take cold shower.

ACTRESS: Lose forty pounds.

ACTOR: Redirect sex drive into career. (*Next Post-it.*) Home late. Don't wait up.

ACTRESS: Hey, stranger, if you're not too busy, could you call Eugenia tonight, around bedtime? Just to see if she recognizes your voice?

ACTOR: Hon: Sorry about your birthday. PS: I got the raise!

ACTRESS: To the new vice president in charge of marketing. We need milk. Please advise.

ACTOR: Hon: I think we're out of milk. (*Next Post-it.*) Still no milk!

ACTRESS: If you want it so bad, get it yourself. The milk train doesn't stop here anymore.

ACTOR: If you can't even manage to get to the store—get some household help!

ACTRESS: (*Icy.*) Have gone to bed. Dinner is in fridge. If there is something in particular you wish for dinner tomorrow night, please leave note to that effect, and I will have Ursula or Carla or *Jose*, if it's *heavy*, pick it up. (*Beat.*) I can't take this anymore! We barely—

(*Turns Post-it over.*) —communicate! There's got to be more to this marriage than a few hastily scribbled words on a small square of pastel paper! (*Beat.*) By the way, we're out of Post-its.

ACTOR: You think I *want* to spend every night at the office? You have absolutely no concept of how a business is run.

ACTRESS: To Whom It May Concern: Regarding your Post-it of June the tenth, allow me to clarify my position—up yours. Eugenia and I will be at your mother's. PS: *You* need milk.

(*The* ACTOR *glances over at the* ACTRESS, *she sips her water, coolly avoids his gaze. Finally . . .*)

ACTOR: Call her at my mother's. (*Next Post-it.*) Must call her. (*Next Post-it.*) Reminder: Take out garbage. Call her. (*Next Post-it.*) People to call: Her.

(*The* ACTOR *looks over again at the* ACTRESS. *She continues to ignore him.*)

ACTOR: Shopping list: Small loaf bread. Half pint milk. Soup for one. (*Next Post-it.*) Scotch for one. (*Next Post-it.*) Inflatable doll. (*Next Post-it.*) Scotch for two.

(*The* ACTRESS *looks at him. He catches her eye. Caught, she hastily looks away.*)

ACTOR: Things to tell her. That I'm sorry. That I miss her. That all I want—all I ever wanted—is for her to be happy.

(*The* ACTRESS *turns to him, touched by this. Then . . . takes the next Post-it. Reads.*)

ACTRESS: We need milk.

ACTOR: Dearest—have gone down to the end of the driveway to get the paper. Back soon.

ACTRESS: Honey, that therapist called back. He can see you Monday.

ACTOR: Sweetie, your therapist says your Tuesday is now Friday.

ACTRESS: What a session! Dr. K. believes that part of me is locked in unconscious competition with you, and envious of your masculine role. By the way, we need cucumbers, sausages, and a really big zucchini.

ACTOR: At last—a breakthrough today with Dr. G. It all became crystal clear. My mother. My father. *His* mother. You. *Your* mother. (*Turns Post-it over, continues.*) I see our entire marriage in a new light! I must free myself from the past so we can truly have a future. This changes everything.

ACTRESS: Hon: A Diet Coke exploded all over that note you left. Hope it wasn't important.

(*He stares at her. Oblivious to his reaction, she reads the next Post-it.*)

Took Eugenia to Brownies. Back soon.

ACTOR: Took Eugenia to kickboxing. Back soon.

ACTRESS: Took Eugenia to therapy. Could be a while.

ACTOR: Someone named Olaf called. Needs your résumé. What résumé?

ACTRESS: I landed the job! I start Monday! (*Next Post-it.*) Last-minute meeting. I'll try to call. (*Next Post-it.*) I'll be working late, don't wait up. (*Next Post-It.*) I'm glad you waited. Last night was incredible.

ACTOR: Drove Eugenia to DMV. Hope she doesn't drive me home.

ACTRESS: Eugenia called. Loves college. Mentioned someone named Tyrone. Doesn't miss us at all.

ACTOR: Pick up travel brochures.

ACTRESS: Eugenia called. When can we meet Tyrone?

ACTOR: Schedule trip to campus when we get back.

ACTRESS: Sweetheart: Travel agent called. Cruise is confirmed! The honeymoon we never had! A time for us to leave all this behind and enjoy ten glorious days of total togetherness.

(*A long, silent beat. Very long. Very silent. They both look straight ahead. Finally he lifts the next Post-it.*)

ACTOR: (*With great relief.*) God, it's good to be home! (*Next Post-it.*) Dinner Wednesday with Eugenia and what's-his-name.

ACTRESS: Tyrone called—it's a boy. Kareem Eugene.

ACTOR: Eugenia called. Loves being a mom.

ACTRESS: Off to throw pots! Back soon! (*Next Post-it.*) Don't forget—we're bird-watching Thursday! (*Next Post-it.*) What night is good for square dancing?

ACTOR: Any night you want—we're free! Nothing to tie us down.

ACTOR: Eugenia called. Could we take Kareem for the week-end?

ACTRESS: Tyrone called. Could we take Kareem for spring break?

ACTOR: Kareem called. Could he spend the summer with us? Again. (*Next Post-it.*) Took Kareem to DMV.

ACTRESS: Honey—last night was incredible. I couldn't believe how long it went on. You've *got* to do something about your snoring.

ACTOR: Shopping list: Bengay. Dentucreme. Viagra.

ACTRESS: Wrinkles Away. I-Can't-Believe-It's-Support-Hose. Estrogen in a Drum.

ACTOR: We need milk of magnesia.

ACTRESS: Call Medicare.

ACTOR: You left your keys in the door again.

ACTRESS: Do you have my keys?

ACTOR: I can't find my glasses.

ACTRESS: Have you seen my cane?

ACTOR: How can I see your cane if I can't find my glasses?

ACTRESS: Gone for walk.

ACTOR: Where are you? Next time you go out, leave me a note!

ACTRESS: Sweetheart—dinner in oven. Taking nap. Love ya.

(*There's a pause as lights slowly fade on the* ACTRESS. *Then . . .*)

ACTOR: Call Emily. Also cousin Ruthie. Send note to Father McKay and everyone who sent flowers. (*Beat.*) The service was lovely. Everybody said so. (*Beat.*) I was looking through your things for that locket you said Eugenia should have. I could hardly believe what I found. You'd saved every Post-it I ever wrote you. I wish I'd saved yours. I could be reading them now. (*Beat.*) Back soon. Going to the store. We need milk.

END OF PLAY

WANDA'S VISIT

Christopher Durang

Wanda's Visit was part of *Durang Durang* at Manhattan Theatre Club, 1994. Directed by Walter Bobbie. The cast was as follows:

JIM	Marcus Giamatti
MARSHA	Lizbeth Mackay
WANDA	Becky Ann Baker
WAITER	David Aaron Baker

CHARACTERS

JIM
MARSHA, his wife
WANDA
WAITER
TWO MEN

Scene: A comfortable home in Connecticut. Not realistically designed, though—different areas represent different rooms: the living room, the dining room, the bathroom, the kitchen. The dining room table later doubles as a table in a restaurant. The furniture and the colors are tastefully chosen. A "country" feel.

At Manhattan Theatre Club the setting was very simple: a round table and three chairs. When the chairs were one way, it was the living room. When the chairs were around the table, it was the dining room. For the bedroom, two chairs were put together and the actors sat on them and spread a comforter over themselves. The bathroom was defined by a square of light.

This is the home of JIM *and* MARSHA. *They enter and come to speak to the audience.*

They are attractive, in their mid- to late thirties. He's in somewhat preppy relaxed clothes—khaki pants, a button-down shirt. She's in a comfortable skirt and blouse, with warm but pale colors. Her hair may be pulled back.

Their manner in talking to the audience is that of telling a story, but also, perhaps, of explaining themselves to a marriage counselor.

JIM: Our lives had been seeming dull for a while. You know, nothing major, just sometimes being quiet at dinner.

MARSHA: After thirteen years, you run out of things to say, I guess. Or else it's a phase.

JIM: I think it's a phase.

MARSHA: Me too. It'll pass.

JIM: We've been married for thirteen years.

MARSHA: Our anniversary was in March.

JIM: So in March we went to dinner and tried to get drunk, but we just got sleepy.

MARSHA: We didn't try to get drunk.

JIM: I did.

MARSHA: We had a very nice time, but the wine made us sleepy.

JIM: We were in bed at ten thirty. Asleep in bed.

MARSHA: Well, we were tired.

JIM: And then the next week I got this letter from this old class-mate of mine.

MARSHA: Wanda. He'd never mentioned her.

JIM: Well, she was just some girlfriend. You know. High school.

MARSHA: Wanda.

JIM: And Wanda wrote me, saying she'd like to visit. And I asked Marsha if she'd mind.

MARSHA: I have trouble saying no, most women do, I think. It's not pleasing or something. Anyway, Jim got this letter . . .

JIM: . . . and Wanda said she was going to be in our neck of the woods . . .

MARSHA: . . . and I hate the phrase "neck of the woods" . . .

JIM: And I asked you if you'd mind, and you said, it would be fine.

MARSHA: Well, I have trouble saying no. You know that. You should have said, "Are you sure?" or "Really?" or something.

JIM: (*Stymied; out to audience.*) Well, I didn't. I thought it would be fun. You know, to mull over the old high school days—the prom, the high school paper—I was editor . . .

MARSHA: And really, what a ball for me . . .

JIM: And Marsha didn't seem to mind. I mean I can't be a mind reader. So I wrote Wanda back, and told her we'd love to have her visit. I mean, really it might have been fun. In high school Wanda had been quite a looker.

MARSHA: And, of course, what an enticement for me. To meet an old high school fantasy. Lucky me.

JIM: So we set a date, and Marsha cleaned the house and baked a chicken.

MARSHA: Jim refuses to cook or clean.

JIM: I mow the lawn, you make the chicken.

MARSHA: We're old-fashioned, I guess.

JIM: And so we waited for her visit.

(*Lights change. Sound of a car driving up, stopping, and a door slamming.*)

JIM: Oh, I'll go, honey. It must be Wanda.

(JIM *goes off to greet* WANDA. MARSHA *straightens up things one last time.*

Offstage we hear great whooping and enthusiastic cries of "Jim! Jim!"

MARSHA *looks startled, curious.*

WANDA *and* JIM *come into the room.* WANDA *is also late thirties, early forties, but unlike* JIM *and* MARSHA, *she is not in as good shape. Her clothes are a little gaudy, her hair looks odd or messy, and she carries a sense of emotional disarray with her. But she also looks kind of fun and colorful.*)

WANDA: (*With longing.*) Jim!!!

(WANDA *throws her arms around* JIM *with great abandon, and then holds this embrace as if her life depended on it.*

MARSHA *goes closer to them and waits patiently for the appropriate moment to be introduced.*)

WANDA: (*Still embracing him.*) Jim. Jim. Oh, Jim, Jim.

MARSHA: (*Since the embrace doesn't seem to be ending.*) Hello. I'm Marsha, Jim's wife.

WANDA: (*Breaking from the embrace.*) Oh, hello. Nice to see you. I was just so excited at seeing this guy. Hey, guy. Hey. How ya doin'?

JIM: I'm fine. (*A little uncertain he recognizes her.*) Wanda?

WANDA: Are you expecting someone else?

JIM: No, it's just—well, didn't you used to be blond?

WANDA: Yeah, and I didn't used to be fat either—although I'm not really fat, my woman's group doesn't let me say that, I just have a food problem and some of it shows. But really I just lost twenty pounds. You should have seen me last month.

JIM: You seem quite thin.

WANDA: Oh, you're sweet. I may look thin, but I'm really fat. (*To* MARSHA.) Do you have anything I can eat?

MARSHA: Well . . .

WANDA: No, I'm just kidding, it was a joke, it seemed like this setup, you know, I talk about my weight, and then I say, can I have some food?

MARSHA: But if you're hungry . . .

WANDA: *I am not hungry.* (*Glares at* MARSHA; *then becomes friendly again; to* JIM.) Say, Jim, I love your wife. She reminds me of my mother. (*To* MARSHA.) No, no, the positive side of my mother. Really. I like both of you.

MARSHA: (*Innocently.*) Thank you. I like both of you.

WANDA: What?

MARSHA: (*Trying to fix what she said.*) I like you, and I like Jim.

WANDA: You better, you're married to Jim, you lucky dog, you. Oh, give me another hug, guy.

(WANDA *gives* JIM *another bear hug.*)

WANDA: Hrrrrrrrrrrrrr.

JIM: Why don't we go in the living room?

(WANDA *careens into the living room area, looks around her. They follow.*)

WANDA: Oh, I love this room. It's so "country." Did you do it, Marsha?

MARSHA: Well, we bought the furniture. I never thought of it as "doing it," actually.

WANDA: Oh, it's wonderful. And I should know, because I have terrible taste.

MARSHA: What?

WANDA: I mean I can evaluate good taste in others because I have such bad taste in all my own choices. For instance, my house looks like the interior of a Baskin-Robbins. Everything is plastic, and there are all these bright yellows and dark chocolates. Really, the only thing worse than being married to me is to have me decorate your house.

JIM: Well, I'm sure you underestimate yourself, Wanda.

WANDA: Isn't he a dreamboat? You're a dreamboat, dreamboat. Well, say thank you!

JIM: (*Embarrassed.*) Thank you.

WANDA: (*To* MARSHA; *with sudden focus.*) Do you have anything to eat? Pretzels or something?

MARSHA: Well, dinner should be ready soon.

WANDA: Oh, Lord, I don't want dinner yet. Just some pretzels would be good. Something to munch on.

MARSHA: Would you like some pâté?

WANDA: Pâté? (*To* JIM.) Where'd you get her, honey, the back of *The New Yorker*? (*To* MARSHA.) Sure, honey, I can eat pâté as long as you have crackers with it. And maybe some pretzels.

MARSHA: Fine. I'll be right back. (*Exits to kitchen area.*)

WANDA: Oh, Jimbo, she's a jewel. An absolute jewel. (WANDA *sits next to* JIM.)

JIM: Thank you. We've been married thirteen years.

WANDA: Oh. An unlucky number. But she's a jewel. I hope she's not hard like a jewel—just precious.

JIM: Yes, she's very precious.

WANDA: Good.

JIM: You know, I hate to say this, but I don't recognize your face actually.

WANDA: That's very perceptive, Jim. I've had plastic surgery. But it wasn't the fancy-schmancy kind to make your face look better, it was so they couldn't find me.

JIM: Who couldn't find you?

WANDA: I don't want to talk about it. Not on the first night, at least.

JIM: Now you've piqued my interest.

WANDA: Oh, you men are always so impatient.

(WANDA *squeezes his knee.* MARSHA *comes in with the pâté, and notices the knee-squeezing.* MARSHA *sits down with the pâté.* WANDA *is seated between* JIM *and* MARSHA.)

MARSHA: Here is the pâté.

WANDA: Thanks, honey, I'll just have the crackers. (*Munches enthusiastically on a cracker.*) Stoned wheat thins, I love this. (*To* JIM.) She's a jewel, Jim.

JIM: (*Rather miserably.*) I know. You're a jewel, Marsha.

MARSHA: Thank you. (*To* WANDA.) Would you like a drink?

(WANDA *pauses for a moment, and then begins to sob, very genuinely.*)

MARSHA: (*At a loss what to say.*) Don't feel you have to have a drink.

JIM: Wanda, what's the matter?

WANDA: (*Through sobs.*) Oh, I don't want to burden you. Or your wife.

MARSHA: That's all right, I'm sure we'd love to be burdened. I mean, if it would help you.

JIM: Yes. Tell us what's the matter.

WANDA: I don't know where to begin. I'm just so unhappy!

JIM: Gosh, Wanda. What is it?

(WANDA *pulls herself together, and tries to explain why she felt so upset.*)

WANDA: Well it all started the summer after high school gradua-tion. (*To* MARSHA.) Jim and I had gone to the prom together, and though of course nothing had been said, everyone just kind of presumed he and I would get married.

JIM: Really? Who presumed this?

WANDA: Well, everyone. My mother, my father, me, everyone.

JIM: Gosh. I mean, I knew we dated.

WANDA: Dated, Jimbo, we were inseparable. From about Febru-ary of senior year to June senior year, we spent every spare moment together. You gave me your class ring. Look, I have it right here. (*Looks through her purse.*) No, I can't find it. (*Keeps looking.*)

MARSHA: Jim gave me the nicest engagement ring.

WANDA: Uh-huh. Now, where is it? (WANDA *dumps out the messy contents of her purse; looks through the mess.*) No. No. Here's the prescription for Seconal I always carry with me in case I feel suicidal.

MARSHA: I don't think any of the pharmacies are open this late.

(WANDA *stares at* MARSHA *for a moment, like a child who's crying and has suddenly been distracted. Before she can go any further comprehend-ing whatever* MARSHA *said,* JIM *speaks up.*)

JIM: Forget about the ring, Wanda. Tell us why you cried a few minutes ago.

WANDA: Isn't it obvious?

JIM: Isn't what obvious?

WANDA: Seeing the path not taken. I could have had a happy life if I married you. Excuse me for talking this way, Marsha, I just want you to know how lucky you are.

MARSHA: Oh, that's fine. Whatever.

WANDA: No, not whatever. Jimbo. (*Kisses him; looks at* MARSHA, *speaks to* JIM.) You see, I do that in front of Marsha so she knows how lucky she is.

MARSHA: Thank you. I feel lucky.

WANDA: Well, don't you forget it. Are you listening to me?

MARSHA: No one else is speaking.

WANDA: (*Genuinely laughs.*) Oh I love her sense of humor. So anyway, after the prom, Jimbo went away for the whole summer, and he didn't write me . . .

JIM: I didn't know you wanted me to.

WANDA: And then you and I went to different colleges, and *then* when you didn't write me, I was heartbroken.

JIM: Really? I'm terribly sorry . . . I thought we were kind of casual. I mean, we were seventeen.

WANDA: I was eighteen. They held me back in third grade.

JIM: Wanda, if you felt this way, why didn't you tell me at the time? You haven't said anything in twenty years.

WANDA: Well, I've been very busy, and it's hard to be open about emotions, especially painful ones. (*Chomps on a cracker.*) So then I went to Ann Arbor, and oh, Jim and Marsha, I'm so ashamed to tell you this—I was promiscuous.

MARSHA: Really?

WANDA: Yes. (*Emphatic, cranky.*) Gosh, these crackers are sure making me thirsty. When you offered me something to drink, I didn't think it was going to be my one chance.

MARSHA: (*Startled, disoriented.*) I'm sorry. Would you like something to drink?

WANDA: (*Sweetly.*) Yes, thank you, Marsha. Anything at all. Preferably with vodka.

(MARSHA *exits off to kitchen.*)

WANDA: She really is a jewel. She really is. Now where was I?

JIM: You were saying you had been promiscuous.

WANDA: It was awful. I became a campus joke. But it was because I was drowning my sorrow, you see—in flesh.

JIM: In flesh. Ah. Well, that's too bad.

WANDA: There was this one night a whole bunch of guys from the football team stood outside my window and they chanted my name.

JIM: Oh. Well, at least you made an impression.

WANDA: Yeah, but it was because I was missing a certain somebody. And also I liked sex.

(MARSHA *comes in, just in time to hear this last remark.*)

JIM: (*Startled.*) Oh, Marsha's here. Hello, Marsha. We missed you.

MARSHA: (*A bit of an edge.*) Here's your drink. I hope you like Kool-Aid.

WANDA: Oh, I love it! (*Gulps her entire drink.*) Mmmm, delicious.

(MARSHA *looks disappointed.*)

WANDA: So anyway, the campus minister once had to give a whole sermon against me, which made me feel just awful. (*To* JIM.) And all because I was pining for you.

MARSHA: I wonder if I should check on the chicken.

JIM: Please don't go just now. (JIM *gets up, to stand by* MARSHA.)

WANDA: And, of course, I was raised Catholic, so I knew what I was doing was very, very wrong, but I was so unhappy . . . (*Weeps copiously.*)

(JIM *and* MARSHA *stare at her for a little while.*)

JIM: (*Without too much enthusiasm.*) There, there, Wanda.

MARSHA: Yes. There, there.

WANDA: And then my second husband gave me herpes, and every time the first one would call to threaten my life, it would trigger an outbreak . . .

(MARSHA *sits back down in a chair,* JIM *sits on the arm.*)

WANDA: . . . herpes is often set off by emotional turmoil, you know.

JIM: (*Forcing interest.*) Oh, yes, I've read that.

WANDA: And then I thought to hell with men, maybe I should become a lesbian. And I tried that, but the problem was I just wasn't attracted to women, so the whole experiment was a dismal failure.

MARSHA: Doesn't anyone want dinner yet?

WANDA: (*Suddenly switching moods.*) Marsha sounds hungry. Sure, honey, let's go eat.

(WANDA *bounds up and moves to the dining room table.* JIM *and* MARSHA *follow.*

The dinner is not realistically done. It may be mimed with plates and silverware already set on the table.)

WANDA: Oh, the dinner looks beautiful. Marsha, you're so talented as a homemaker. Now where was I?

JIM: Something about you were promiscuous.

WANDA: Well, I don't like to use that word. I slept around uncontrollably, that's what I prefer to say. Did you ever do that, Marsha?

MARSHA: No, I didn't. I was a late bloomer.

WANDA: Uh-huh. So then there was that guy from prison. And then there was his father, Fred. Did I tell you about Fred? Well, Fred said to me, I married you because I thought you would be my anchor in the port of life, but now I think you're stark raving mad . . .

MARSHA: Could I have the salt, please?

(JIM *passes* MARSHA *the salt.*)

WANDA: . . . and I said, you think I'm crazy, who's the one who has hallucinations, and thinks that shoes go on the hands instead of the feet? Not me, buddy boy.

JIM: (*To* WANDA.) Did he take drugs or something?

MARSHA: Please don't ask her questions.

WANDA: What?

MARSHA: (*To* WANDA.) Well, I mean I want you to tell the story your own way.

WANDA: Thank you, Marsha. You know, Jim. I really feel close to Marsha.

JIM: I'm glad. (*To* MARSHA.) Could I have the salt, please?

WANDA: (*Responding to him.*) Sure, honey. (*Passes him the salt; to* MARSHA.) Don't you just love him? (*Continues on with story.*) So one day the washing machine blew up, and Fred said to me, you did that, everything about you is chaos, I'm leaving and I'm taking Tranquility with me.

JIM: He actually said "tranquility"?

MARSHA: (*Muttered.*) Don't ask her questions.

WANDA: (*Explaining.*) Tranquility was our dog. And I said, I'm the one who fed Tranquility, and walked her and took care of her worms, and she used to throw up on the rug, and, of course, you can't just leave it there . . .

MARSHA: Excuse me, I'll be right back.

JIM: Marsha, are you all right?

MARSHA: I'm fine.

WANDA: I hope my talking about vomit didn't make you feel sick.

MARSHA: (*Nearly out of the room.*) No, it's fine.

(MARSHA *has left the dining area and gotten to the bathroom area. She holds her head in pain, or leans on a wall for a support. She just couldn't stand to be at the table for a minute longer.*)

WANDA: She's a little hard to talk to.

JIM: I think she had a hard day.

WANDA: Really? What did she do? Spend it making up the guest room for me?

JIM: Oh.

WANDA: Really, I can sleep anywhere. I think I'm being evicted tomorrow anyway, so I'd prefer not to be there.

JIM: That's too bad.

WANDA: I roll with the punches. I enjoy the little things in life. I enjoy colors. I like textures, I like silk and cotton, I don't like corduroy, I don't like ridges . . .

JIM: (*On his way to find* MARSHA.) Uh-huh. Hold on to the thought. I'll be right back.

(JIM *exits and goes to the bathroom area, where he finds* MARSHA *still crouched or leaning.*)

JIM: Why are you hiding in the bathroom?

MARSHA: I needed aspirin. Then I just couldn't go downstairs again. When is she leaving?

JIM: I think she's staying overnight.

MARSHA: What?

JIM: I think she's staying ov . . .

MARSHA: Did she say that or did you say that?

(WANDA, *bored alone, bounds into the bathroom area with them. The area is small, and they're all crowded together.*)

WANDA: What are you two talking about?

JIM: Oh, nothing. Marsha was just brushing her teeth.

WANDA: It's so intimate brushing your teeth, isn't it? When you live with someone, you don't have any secrets. I remember David said to me, why didn't you tell me you had herpes, and I said, I forgot, okay? People forget things, all right? And he said, not all right, I'm going to have this for life, and I said so what, you have your nose for life, is that *my* fault?

MARSHA: (*Tired, but sort of annoyed by the logic.*) Yes, but his nose wasn't your fault, while . . .

WANDA: What?

MARSHA: Nothing. I see your point.

WANDA: So then I thought I'd stay out of relationships for a while, and I went to work for this lawyer, only he wasn't a regular lawyer, he was a kingpin.

JIM: Kingpin?

WANDA: Of crime. He was a kingpin of crime, only I didn't realize it. Eventually, of course, I had to get my face redone so they couldn't find me. But I better not say anything more about this right now.

MARSHA: (*Trying to tell her no.*) Jim says you were expecting to stay overnight . . .

WANDA: Thank you, I'd love to! I feel I'm just starting to scratch the surface with old Jimbo here. Jimbo, do you remember that girl with the teeth who won Homecoming Queen, what was her name?

JIM: I don't remember. She had teeth?

WANDA: Big teeth.

MARSHA: I would like to leave the bathroom now.

WANDA: What?

MARSHA: Well, we need to make your room up for you. I didn't know you were . . . well, we need to make it up.

WANDA: (*A little girl.*) I hope there's a quilt. I love quilts.

MARSHA: I'll look for one.

(WANDA *stares at her, happy, but doesn't get out of the way.*)

MARSHA: You have to move or I can't get out of the bathroom.

WANDA: (*Serious.*) I'm holding you hostage.

MARSHA: What?

WANDA: (*Shifting, cheerful.*) Isn't it awful the way they take hostages now? (*Cheerfully leaves the bathroom, talking away.*) It reminds me of my life with Augie. He was really violent, but he was really little, so I was able to push him down the stairs.

(JIM *and* MARSHA *look at one another, a little alarmed by the "hostage" exchange.*

Lights change. The prominent sound of a clock ticking. Time is passing.

WANDA, JIM, *and* MARSHA *standing in a "hallway" area, about to make their good nights.*)

WANDA: (*Happy.*) Oh, you guys, it's been a great evening. I can't believe we played games for four hours!

MARSHA: I'm really sorry I shouted at you during Monopoly.

WANDA: That's okay. I know somebody who got killed playing Monopoly.

JIM: But you were really good at charades.

WANDA: Thanks, but I'm sorry I broke the lamp.

MARSHA: It's perfectly all right. Now the guest room is right down this hall.

WANDA: Well, good night, you two. See you in the morning.

MARSHA: Good night.

(WANDA *exits off to the guest room.*

JIM *and* MARSHA *go to their bedroom, or rearrange the set to stand in for a bedroom—move two chairs together into a "bed," put a comforter over themselves.*

They're too tired to talk. They kiss each other briefly and close their eyes to sleep.

WANDA *enters, wrapped up in a quilt.)*

WANDA: Oh, is this your bedroom? Oh, it's so pretty.

(JIM *and* MARSHA *open their eyes, very startled.)*

MARSHA: Is something wrong with your room?

WANDA: No, it's lovely. Although not as nice as here. But then this is the master bedroom, isn't it?

MARSHA: Can I get you a pill?

WANDA: No, thanks. Marsha, I love this bedroom. I feel very "enveloped" here. It makes me never want to leave. (WANDA *pulls up a chair right next to their bed. Keeps wrapped in her quilt.)* I just love New England. I worked in Hartford for three weeks once as a receptionist in a sperm bank.

MARSHA: Wanda, I'm sorry. I really think I need to sleep.

WANDA: You can sleep, I won't be offended. So I got fired from the sperm bank, and then I went to Santa Fe, 'cause I heard the furniture was nice there.

(*Clock ticks. Time passes.* JIM *and* MARSHA *change positions in bed.)*

WANDA: And then Arthur's ex-wife kept making threatening phone calls to me.

(*Clock ticks.* JIM *and* MARSHA *change positions, now look more uncomfortable.)*

WANDA: (*Coquettish.*) And I said, "Billy, why didn't you tell me you were sixteen?"

(*Clock ticks.*)

WANDA: (*Chatty voice, just telling the facts.*) And then the policeman said, let me see your pussy, and I thought, hey, maybe this way I won't get a ticket.

(*Clock ticks.*)

WANDA: (*Teary voice, telling a tragic turning point.*) And Leonard said, Wanda, you are a worthless piece of trash. And I said, don't you think I know that? Do you think this is news?

(*Clock ticks.*)

WANDA: (*Energized, telling a fascinating story.*) And Howard said he wanted me to kill his mother, and I said, "Are you crazy? I've never even *met* your mother." And he said, "All right, I'll introduce you."

(JIM *and* MARSHA *have closed their eyes, either asleep or pretending to be.* WANDA *looks over at them, suspicious.*)

WANDA: Are you asleep? Jim? Marsha?

(WANDA *looks to see if they're asleep. She shakes their shoulders a bit, to see if she can wake them.*)

WANDA: Jim? Marsha? You're not pretending to be asleep, are you? Jim? Marsha?

(WANDA *opens* MARSHA*'s eyelid with her finger.*)

MARSHA: Yes?

WANDA: I was just checking if you were asleep.

MARSHA: Yes, I am. Good night. Sleep well.

WANDA: Good night.

(WANDA *takes her comforter and curls up at the bottom of their bed. Then she pulls their blanket off them and onto her.* JIM *doesn't notice, he's asleep for real.* MARSHA *is startled. But gives up, what to do. Lights dim.*

Clock ticks.

Lights up for the morning. WANDA *sound asleep.* JIM *and* MARSHA *wake up, and abruptly leave the bedroom for the dining room area.*)

MARSHA: You know, she doesn't snore. I'm really surprised.

JIM: Want some coffee?

MARSHA: I think I'd like some heroin.

JIM: Maybe Wanda has some connections.

MARSHA: I'm sure she does. Oh God, why did she sleep on our bed? She seemed like some insane nightmare Golden Retriever.

JIM: Now I feel sorry for her.

MARSHA: Well, good for you. Was she always this way?

JIM: Well, she was always vivacious.

MARSHA: I see. High school prom queen. Girl Most Likely to Get Herpes.

JIM: Lots of people get herpes.

MARSHA: Yes, but they don't talk about it for three hours.

JIM: Why are you so hostile to her? (*Not meaning to say this.*) Is it because she's attracted to me?

MARSHA: (*Not expecting to hear that.*) Yes. (MARSHA *goes off to the kitchen.*)

JIM: Are you getting coffee?

(MARSHA *reenters with two coffee mugs, one of which she kind of shoves at* JIM.)

MARSHA: And are you attracted to her?

JIM: Now come on, Marsha, she's an emotional mess.

MARSHA: You're putting up with it very patiently. Why is that?

JIM: Well, that's because . . . I feel sympathy for her. She's someone I knew once who had a life, and look what's happened to her.

MARSHA: She's attracted to you.

JIM: Now don't make a big thing out of it. It's just slightly interesting for me, that's all.

MARSHA: Well, fine. I understand. I think I'll make a trip to the nearest loony bin and find some mental patient who finds *me* attractive. Then I'll bring him home and make you suffer through a forty-eight-hour visit while he drools on the carpet.

JIM: Oh, come on, stop making such a big deal about all this. It's no big deal . . . it's just . . . well, haven't you ever found it kind of exciting if someone finds you attractive?

MARSHA: I've forgotten. (*Starts to leave.*) I'm going to the A&P. I have to get out of here. (MARSHA *grabs a purse and exits.*)

JIM: Don't be mad.

(JIM *sighs. With his coffee he walks after her, but* WANDA, *stirring on the bed, hears him.*)

WANDA: Is that life out there?

JIM: You awake? (JIM *comes back into the bedroom area, holding his coffee mug.*)

WANDA: Do I smell coffee? Oh, thanks, Jimbo. (WANDA *takes* JIM's *coffee, thinking it's for her.*) Uh, I love this. You're like a little house slave. I knew I should've married you. Where's Marsha? Did she wake up dead or anything?

JIM: No, she went to the A&P.

WANDA: That's terrible of me to say. I don't want her dead. I'm just teasing 'cause I'm jealous of what she has.

JIM: Oh, I'm not so special.

WANDA: Oh, Jimbo, you are. (WANDA *starts to get up, then shows a grimace of pain. A bit flirtatious.*) Uh. I've slept wrong on my back, I think. You know, a tense muscle or something.

JIM: (*Thinking to himself, is this code?*) Oh. Your back is sore? Um, I'm not a professional masseur, but do you want me to rub it?

WANDA: Oh, would you?

(WANDA *pretty much flops over in delight.* JIM *starts to massage her back, sort of in the center.*)

WANDA: It's the lower back, Jimbo.

JIM: Oh. Okay. (*He starts to massage her lower back.*)

WANDA: Uh. Yes. Oh, yes. Oh, yes. Ohhhhhhh. Uhhhhhhhh.

(MARSHA *comes back in the house, holding the purse and car keys. She stops and hears* WANDA'*s moaning. She marches into the bedroom, finds* JIM *and* WANDA *in the midst of their orgasmic back rub.*)

MARSHA: I'm back, if anybody cares.

JIM: (*Really jumps.*) Oh, Marsha. I didn't hear the car.

MARSHA: I don't blame you. It was very noisy here.

JIM: I'm . . . giving Wanda . . . that is, her back hurts.

WANDA: He gives the most wonderful back rub.

MARSHA: I'm so pleased to hear it. Do you need the number of a back specialist, perhaps? I could call my doctor. If you can't walk, we can arrange for an ambulance to take you there.

JIM: Now, Marsha, please, it's really quite innocent.

WANDA: Hey, Marsha, really—I know he's your guy. (*To* JIM.) You're her guy, Jimbo. (*To* MARSHA.) It's just my back hurt.

MARSHA: Yes, I follow what you say. Probably tension in the lower back. I have a tension headache in the back of my head today, it feels like it might split open. I think I'll go lie down. In the guest room that you never got to. (*Starts to leave.*)

Jimbo, when you finish with her back, the car has a flat tire on the corner of Pleasantview and Maple. I thought you might do something about that.

JIM: Oh, I'll go now.

MARSHA: No, finish the back rub. You've convinced me it's innocent, so finish it.

(MARSHA *walks out.* JIM *and* WANDA *look at each other uncomfortably.*)

WANDA: Well, she said to finish it.

JIM: I don't feel comfortable with her in the house.

WANDA: Look, she said it was fine, let's take her at her word.

(JIM *looks dubious and touches her back lightly. At the merest touch,* WANDA *starts to moan loudly again.*)

JIM: (*Stopping the back rub.*) Can't you be more quiet?

WANDA: It feels so good.

JIM: Look, that's enough. I'm gonna go deal with the flat tire.

WANDA: Can I come?

JIM: Why don't you . . . soak in the bathtub for your back?

WANDA: All right. Thank you for the back rub, Jimbo. (*Gets up; calls after where* MARSHA *went.*) Marsha? Do you have any bubble bath?

(MARSHA *comes back.*)

MARSHA: What?

WANDA: Do you have any bubble bath? Jim won't continue with the back rub, and I need to relax.

MARSHA: The back rub . . . I . . . what was the question?

JIM: Bubble bath. Do we have some?

MARSHA: Yes, I'm sure we do. Maybe Jim would like to pour it on you in the bathtub.

JIM: Marsha. Please.

WANDA: Oooh, kinky. (*Loudly.*) Hey! I have an idea! Why don't I cook dinner for you guys tonight? Do you like octopus?

MARSHA: Thank you, Wanda, no. I thought we'd go to a restaurant tonight. The walls in this house are starting to vibrate.

WANDA: They are?

MARSHA: Yes. So we'll go to a nice, soothing restaurant where they will take care of us. All right?

WANDA: Sure! Fine by me.

(*Lights change. Maybe lovely classical music to change the mood.* JIM, MARSHA, *and* WANDA *sit at the table.*

The WAITER *comes out and puts a tasteful flower arrangement on the table, turning it into the restaurant.*)

WANDA: This is such a pretty restaurant. The music is so classical.

WAITER: Enjoy your meal.

JIM: Thank you.

(WAITER *exits.* WANDA *and* JIM *mime eating from their plates.*)

WANDA: Ohhh, I think I know someone. (*Waves, calls out to imaginary table.*) Hi, there! Oh, no, I don't know them. (*Calls out again.*) Never mind! I thought you were my gynecologist.

MARSHA: You thought he'd be up here?

WANDA: Well, he travels a lot. He also sells encyclopedias.

(WAITER *reenters with a tray of wineglasses. He gives each person a wineglass,* WANDA *last.*)

WAITER: And here is your wine.

WANDA: They didn't have Kool-Aid?

WAITER: White Zinfandel was the closest we could get, madam.

WANDA: Well, all right. (*To* MARSHA *and* JIM.) Here's mud in your eye.

(*Everyone drinks. All of them finish their drinks in several quick gulps. The* WAITER *starts to leave.*)

JIM: Waiter! (*Signals to* WAITER *for another round. The* WAITER *nods and exits.*)

WANDA: I can't believe they didn't have octopus. It's a delicacy.

JIM: (*Referring to their plates.*) Well, the trout's pretty good.

WANDA: Yeah, but they put nuts on it or something.

JIM: Well, eat around them maybe.

WANDA: You know, Jim, tomorrow we should get out the old yearbook. You know, Marsha, you wouldn't believe how dashing he was back then. (*To* JIM.) Not that you're not now, of course.

JIM: You're sure a shot for my ego.

MARSHA: I'd like to shoot your ego.

JIM: What?

MARSHA: Nothing. Go back to talking about high school. I'll try to achieve a Zen state. (*Closes her eyes, puts her arms loose by her side, tries to relax her body.*)

JIM: I . . . I wonder where the waiter is with the drinks.

MARSHA: (*With eyes closed; chant-like.*) I am sitting by a tree, and there's a lovely breeze.

WANDA: This restaurant is so adorable. This whole town. You know what I'm thinking? I'm thinking of maybe moving up here to the country with you all, finding a little house to rent. Nothing's happening in my life right now; this might be just the change I might need.

(*The* WAITER *arrives with three more glasses of wine, which he passes out to them.* MARSHA's *eyes are open again;* WANDA's *comments above pretty much blew her attempt at a Zen state.*)

WANDA: I'm almost through with my facial surgery. I've had everything done on my face except my nose. I kept that the same.

JIM: You're right. I recognize your nose now. Yes.

WAITER: Will there be anything else?

WANDA: What? Done to my face?

WAITER: Anything else I can do for you at the restaurant?

JIM: We wanted three more glasses of wine.

WAITER: I just brought them.

JIM: Oh. So you did. Well, thank you.

(*The* WAITER *leaves.* WANDA *starts to eat her fish.*)

MARSHA: So you're going to move up here, are you? Going to
    sweep up and stick your feet in the ground and root yourself
    in our "little neck of the woods," are you?

JIM: Marsha, we don't own this area.

MARSHA: I feel differently. (*To* WANDA.) I don't want you moving
    here, is that clear? I don't want you invading my life with your
    endless ravings anymore, is that clear?

(*The* WAITER *returns.* WANDA *keeps eating, seemingly just listening to
what's being said, finding it interesting rather than upsetting.*)

WAITER: Is everything all right?

MARSHA: No, everything is not all right, this woman is trying to
    invade my life, and this man is too stupid to see it and hide
    from her. (*To* JIM.) Don't you realize she's insane?

JIM: Marsha, could we just finish dinner, please?

MARSHA: No, I'd like the check.

WAITER: Are you unhappy with your fish?

MARSHA: I'm very unhappy with it. It has too many bones in it.

(*Almost on cue,* WANDA *starts choking on a bone. She gasps and chokes.* JIM, MARSHA, *and the* WAITER *look at her, shocked for a moment.*)

JIM: Shouldn't one of us do the Heimlich maneuver?

MARSHA: I don't want to do it, I don't like her.

(WANDA *looks startled, even in the midst of her choking. She keeps choking and pointing to her throat.*)

JIM: Marsha! (*To* WAITER.) Can you do it?

WAITER: I don't know how to do it yet. It's my first day. Can't you do it?

JIM: Oh, very well.

(JIM *gets up and gets the choking* WANDA *to stand. He stands behind her and then, not sure what to do, puts his arms under her arms, and locks his hands behind her neck: That is, he puts her in a half nelson, and keeps jerking her head forward with his hands, hopefully, as if this should fix her choking.*)

MARSHA: (*After a second.*) Oh, for God's sake.

(MARSHA *gets up, pushes* JIM *away. She stands behind* WANDA, *puts her arms around* WANDA's *lower stomach and then rather violently and suddenly pulls her hands into* WANDA's *lower stomach. This does the trick.* WANDA *spits out the bit of fish and bone, and starts to breathe again.*

WANDA *sits back down, exhausted.*)

WANDA: Oh, thank God, I thought I was a goner.

(*Suddenly into the restaurant burst* TWO MEN *with handkerchiefs tied around their mouths, and carrying guns. They aim their guns at everyone but make straight for* WANDA.)

MAN: There she is!

WANDA: Oh my God, they've found me!

(*The* MEN *grab her and, pointing the guns at everyone else, drag* WANDA *out of the restaurant.*)

WANDA: (*Being dragged or carried out.*) Oh, God, it's the kingpin. Help me! Jim! Jim!

(*All this happens very fast and very suddenly. And now* WANDA *is gone.* JIM, MARSHA, *and the* WAITER *seem stunned for a moment.*

A "talking-to-the-audience" light comes up, and the WAITER *crosses down into it and addresses the audience.*)

WAITER: The next day at the restaurant was considerably less intense, and eventually as time went on, I was made head-waiter. For a while I liked the added responsibility and the additional money, but after a while, I realized I wasn't doing what I wanted to do with my life. I wanted to be an actor. But then the story isn't really about me.

(*Humbly, the* WAITER *exits.*

JIM *and* MARSHA *look confused by the* WAITER'*s behavior, and now address the audience themselves again.*

They also straighten the set a bit while they talk, so that it resembles their house as it was at the beginning of the play.)

JIM: (*To audience.*) Well, all that happened a few weeks ago. Wanda hasn't been found yet, but she's probably fine.

MARSHA: I feel guilty about what happened. I wasn't a good hostess.

JIM: Now, honey, she's probably fine. Wanda's sort of like a bacteria—wherever she is, she seems to grow and go on and on just fine, so you shouldn't feel bad.

MARSHA: Yes, but right before Wanda started to choke on the fish bone, I had this momentary, stray thought of wishing she would choke on a fish bone. And then suddenly she did. I know it's not logical, but on some level, I feel I tried to kill her. And then thugs came and carried her away. I mean, in a way, it's just what I wanted.

JIM: Now, Marsha, you're not responsible for what happened.

MARSHA: I chose the restaurant.

JIM: Now, Marsha. You're not omnipotent. Besides, awful things are always happening to Wanda. She's like a magnet for trouble.

MARSHA: (*To the audience.*) Well, it was just the most awful two days. Three days, counting meeting with the police.

JIM: But some good came out of it.

MARSHA: Yes. We had a big argument, and that was good.

JIM: It cleared the air.

MARSHA: I said what I was feeling, and it was mostly negative, but it was good to say it.

JIM: It cleared the air.

MARSHA: And one of the things I said was that we don't feel joy enough. Or hardly at all.

JIM: Right. We don't feel joy much. So we joined an aerobics class . . .

MARSHA: To get the blood moving. . . . When you move around, you tend to feel better . . .

JIM: And we're going to a marriage counselor who specializes in breaking down fear of intimacy in people who've known one another for over ten years . . .

MARSHA: And, of course, we fit that. And all told, I guess Wanda's visit helped to stir us up in a good way, all told.

JIM: Right.

MARSHA: Blessings come in unexpected ways.

JIM: Right.

MARSHA: Now if only we were happy.

JIM: Right.

(*They look at each other. Then they look out at the audience. Some friendly, possibly optimistic music plays. Lights dim on* JIM *and* MARSHA.)

END OF PLAY

THE VALERIE OF NOW

Peter Hedges

The Valerie of Now was produced by Circle Repertory Company (Tanya Berezin, artistic director; Connie L. Alexis, managing director) in New York City, on February 6, 1990. It was directed by Joe Mantello; the set design was by Loy Arcenas; the costume design was by Laura Cunningham; the lighting design was by Dennis Parichy; the sound design was by Stewart Werner and Chuck London; and the production stage manager was Denise Yaney. The cast was as follows:

VALERIE   Melissa Joan Hart

CHARACTERS

VALERIE: Twelve.

SETTING

Valerie's living room.

TIME

Valerie's birthday, 1977.

VALERIE *sits on a sofa. It's hours before her twelfth birthday party. She is dressed in her birthday outfit and she wears a party hat on top of her head. She holds some Kleenex in her hand. A hand mirror lays by her side.*

She is on the phone, in tears. She's in the middle of a conversation.

VALERIE: K–e–a–n–e. Yes, Keane. Valerie *Keane*. Yes, my mom and dad are coming for my birthday bike. Yes, bike! The Schwinn with the banana seat. If you could tell my mom— just my mom—tell her to call home. V–a–l–e–r–i–e. Just my mom. Tell her to hurry. Oh, forget it. Just forget it! (VALERIE *hangs up the phone. She is all alone, frightened and edgy. She dials the phone.*) Mrs. Duffy, may I speak with Kay, please? When do you expect her? Oh. Well, no. No message. Uhm. Mrs. Duffy, you were a girl once, right? OK, when you were . . . uhm . . . how did you uhm . . . never mind, nothing. Tell Kay I'll see her at my party. Nothing, no. Bye. (VALERIE *hangs up and waits. She looks at her reflection in the hand mirror. The sound of a group of girls laughing can be heard. She puts the mirror down fast and dials the phone.*) Janice, it's me. Are you somewhere private? Get somewhere private *fast!* (VALERIE *crosses in back of the sofa, sits behind it. The pointy part of her birthday hat sticks up, the only part of her that is visible.*) Okay, Janice. You can't . . . Okay, Janice? You can't tell anybody what I'm about to tell you. P.r.o.m.i.s.e? You have to. Okay, oh boy. I'm vacuuming. I'm home all alone. Mom and Dad went to get my new bike and stuff. And I'm all alone vacuuming when I feel this dripping and I'm thinking I have to pee but the dripping isn't like anything. So I'm walking real fast to the bathroom when I look down and see . . . but . . . call me back. Eat fast, call me back! (VALERIE *throws the phone in the air.*) *AAAAAAAAHH-HHHHHHHHH!* (*She pounds the sofa cushions and thrashes about on the sofa.*) Pull yourself together, Valerie. Keep a lid on it! But will you listen to me? It's affecting me already. My moods are swinging. It's like I'm fine, then I want to cry and then I'm happy and then I want to cry and then I'm so looking forward to my party and then I want to . . . (*She covers her face with her hands and cries. After a moment, she regains her composure.*) This is unheard of. On your birthday. Taking half a box of Kleenex and uhm having to wedge it in there. But it's so obvious. It looks like I've gained eighty pounds. I look like a pear. Mom. Mom! I want my Mom! (VALERIE *hugs a sofa pillow.*) Buck up, Valerie. That's what Dad always says to do. "Buck up." Dad, what does that mean? "Valerie, buck up means—*buck up!*" Thanks, Dad. Thank you for being you. It's sad when you're smarter than those who gave you life. (VALERIE *covers her face with her hands again.*) Brenda Palmer believes in destiny. She says that everything happens according to God or somebody's master plan. So wait, let me get this straight, Brenda. You're saying that somebody planned this! Somebody actually sat down and charted out my life and said, "Hey, how's this for an idea? On Valerie's birthday we'll give her a double whammy!" And I'm expected to pray every day. Please. Pray for what? For my life to be over? 'Cause it's completely ruined, my life. I've been destroyed by nature. Wham. Thanks, God. Thanks a total bunch for your most excellent timing! Anybody out there help me? Hellllloooo! Valerie is at home and she's bleeding. And she did the best she could, but she's not ready for all the responsibility. She's still a kid. I'm still a kid. I don't even have breasts yet. Aren't you supposed

to get breasts first? Monica Mills gets 'em. She gets breasts—
I get blood. I get mood swings, I get forgotten. The phone
stops ringing. I lose all my friends. They hate me for being
first. "You guys, I'm still one of you!" "No, you're not!" "I'm
still the same!" "No, you're not! Valerie cut in line!" I have no
choice but to hold a press conference. (VALERIE *stands on the
sofa. She uses her hairbrush as a microphone.*) To Kay, Janice,
Brenda, and the rest—here is my prepared statement. It happened and it's over and yes, I'm different, *but I'm not!* I'm
sorry I was first. Please please please please please don't hate
me. That'll be all, thank you. No comments. No questions
please. No more questions! I think I'm being c.l.e.a.r. Flash.
Camera flash. Flash. And the phone starts ringing and ringing. "Hello? Oh, it's okay, Brenda. I would've felt the same."
Ring ring. "Yes? It's okay, Janice, I've missed you, too."
Valerie gets all her friends back. And they look hot. And
when they go to college, they all live in a houseboat and
spend all day in their swimsuits! (VALERIE *throws her arms in
the air and giggles her glorious, triumphant laugh.*) All the great
women through all of history, *come on down!* Louisa May
Alcott, Harriet Beecher Stowe! *Marcia Brady!* The question is:
How did all you ladies face this moment? Huh? What? It
could have been *worse?* Like what? Like I could have been
doing cartwheels during recess?! Or like I could've been
walking up for my confirmation in my white dress and the
bishop would've looked down. Or *like the party could have been
in full swing and I could've been sitting on Kevin Kiernan's lap and
whoosh!* (VALERIE *sits back to catch her breath.*) Who says you
have to tell anybody, Valerie? It can be your secret! Your special secret that makes you glow! But then Betsy Ross and
Mary Todd Lincoln and Bat Girl materialize and they say
"Go for it, Valerie. Spread the good news!" And so I approach
my mom. I hold up the white shorts with the red stain and
Mom smiles so big, her teeth uhm grow proud, and uhm
teardrops drip and roll down her eyes and we two women
look at each other with mutual respect. The tears keep flow-

ing and it's because suddenly she doesn't have a daughter any-more. Suddenly it's like we're sisters. She wants to borrow a bra, but mine are too big. We share beauty tips and we do that "Can you tell which is the mother and which is the daugh-ter" commercial where the hands are shown first. Then, in the backyard where Dad is grilling the hot dogs, he says, "Let me give the birthday girl a hug," but this time he doesn't squeeze the air out of me, he doesn't lift me above him and say "My little princess" because even he senses the change. It's in my eyes. He shakes my hand and goes back to turning the hot dogs. (*A beat.*) Monica! *Monica!* Oh, hi, Monica. Yes, it's true, I had my period—oh, I don't think any amount of explaining can do justice to what it feels like but know this. For years I've seen your enormous breasts and I've heard you rant about your struggle to find the best bra. Hear this! Maybe you've got the outward shows, the trappings—but me, Valerie, I'm the real woman and you're the f.r.a.u.d. *Fraud!* (*Valerie sings the opening lines of "I Am Woman," up to "Cause I've heard it . . .".*) But wait! Six boys bust down Valerie's door. They are sweaty and panting. "Oh, my." They, like, die at the sight of her. "Hello, have you boys met each other? Well, Chip, I'd like you to meet Chad. Chad, Chip. Tom, this is Tim and Chip and Chad. Bruce meet the boys! Boys, Bruce. Hey, did any of you RSVP? I don't think so. Sorry, boys. Maybe next year's party." They cry and hold each other. Take them away! Oh, hold all calls. Yes—thank you, Mr. President. Yes, sir. It's quite a feeling. What's interesting to me, Mr. Pres-ident, is that you're a very powerful man and you have enor-mous impact on people. All people, on history, and you have access to every kind of technology and experts hover around you. You can blow up this world. But you can't know how I feel today, can you? No, I don't think you can. You have no idea of the feeling in *my body*. You have no notion of the enormous power in me today. My baby capabilities. Excuse me, Mr. President, I have a call I must take. Yes, Kevin, what can I do for you? Interesting that you'd call in light of today's event. Yes, I know we all change. I allow for that. After all, look at me. Tell me, Kevin, where were you before today? I don't recall your asking to carry my milk tray, Kevin, I don't seem to remember any offers to walk me home. But *now* you want to go bike riding, *now* you want to roller-skate. Kevin, go elsewhere! Go find a nice sixth grader! Because Kevin I am the Valerie of Now and now you don't interest me! Kevin, heed these words. (VALERIE *speaks the opening lines of "I Am Woman," up to the phrase, "And I know too much." She repeats the phrase.) And I know too much!* And I deserve better. (VALERIE *covers the phone with her hand and looks around.*) Sensing something, the Valerie of Now drops the phone, moves to her balcony and swings open her curtained window. Oh, my! She can't believe her eyes. Hello! There are these people—all different races and ages—millions and zillions of people. It's a candlelight procession and helicopters are in the air and planes are skywriting—and boys are hanging from light poles and they're all staring at me like I'm perfect. They're drooling—and there are fireworks and popcorn and dancing in the streets and I raise my hand to speak and there is *silence!* (*Silence. To the imagined crowd.*) Oh, boy. You see, it happens and you're different. Uhm. But you're not, you know? Thank you all for coming to my party! This is the best birthday ever! I will never forget this day! *I will never forget!*

(*Helen Reddy's version of "I Am Woman" comes up underneath the above text. Valerie is giggling, leaping about on the sofa, her arms extended in victory. As the music swells, the lights fade.*)

END OF PLAY

WE CANNOT KNOW
THE MIND OF GOD

Mikhail Horowitz

We Cannot Know the Mind of God was first presented as a staged reading by Actors & Writers at the Odd Fellows Theatre in Olivebridge, New York, on October 19, 2002. Directed by Sigrid Heath, it featured:

DAVIS HALL	God
JOE WHITE	Adam
SARAH CHODOFF	Eve
MARK CHMIEL	Brad
GRETA BAKER	Buffy
BRIAN MACREADY	The Angel of Death

The New York premiere was at the Makor-Steinhardt Center on August 1, 2004, with Dan Gallant directing. The actors were:

JOHN FITZ-MAURICE	God
MICHAEL LIDONDICI	Adam/Brad
LINDSAY HALLADAY	Eve/Buffy
SCOTT TARAZEVITS	The Angel of Death

CHARACTERS

GOD
ADAM AND EVE
BRAD AND BUFFY: Two of Adam and Eve's descendants.
THE ANGEL OF DEATH

Note: Brad and Buffy may be played by Adam and Eve.

Play opens with GOD *visiting* ADAM *and* EVE *in Eden.*

GOD: So let me get this straight: you've assigned a name to everything in the garden—appellated all of Creation, as it were—and now you're . . . bored?

ADAM: Well, at the risk of sounding ungrateful . . .

EVE: . . . or of insufficient intelligence to amuse ourselves in any meaningful way . . .

ADAM: . . . or, for that matter, in any unmeaningful way, since amusement, as we know . . .

EVE: . . . or *would* know, assuming we'd eaten from the Tree, but, uh, we haven't, so, uh, hey, scratch that . . .

ADAM: . . . since amusement, as I was saying, need not be instructive or edifying, but may simply be experienced for its own sake . . .

EVE: . . . but yes, in point of fact, and by no means do we intend this to be disrespectful, or in any way dismissive of your largesse . . .

ADAM: . . . but yes, now that you mention it, we are utterly, totally, absolutely bored.

GOD: Hmmm. Well, I did anticipate something of this nature.

EVE: (*Whispering, to* ADAM.) Well, like, *duh*, he is omniscient, right?

ADAM: (*Whispering harshly back.*) Ssshh! He's also omniaural, okay?

EVE: (*Whispering.*) Omni-what?

GOD: All-hearing, but let's pretend I didn't hear that. No, I did anticipate that protracted exposure to paradise would render it pedestrian, eventually . . . cause you to become a bit jaded with Creation. But I do have something in mind to make the time pass a little more swiftly, a little more engagingly. I propose we play a little game.

EVE: (*Warily.*) And, uh, this game is called . . .?

GOD: The game is called "I'm thinking of something." You see, I'll think of something, and you have to guess what it is.

ADAM: And, uh, the point of this being . . .

GOD: (*Sighs.*) The point of this being to provide a small diversion, since you and Eve have deemed such necessary, from the otherwise dreary and deadening perfection of your ideal existence in this flawlessly conceived, impeccably crafted habitat. Shall we begin?

ADAM: Uh, okay.

EVE: Hey, we'll give it a shot.

GOD: Very good. Now then: I'm thinking of something. Can either of you tell me what I'm thinking of?

ADAM: Is it . . . something having a nacreous color?

GOD: No.

EVE: Is it . . . something stridulating at the edge of a meadow?

GOD: No.

ADAM: Is it . . . something concealed in a bearded spruce?

GOD: No.

EVE: Is it . . . something phosphorescing on a jetty?

GOD: Uh-uh.

(*The Q&A gets faster.*)

ADAM: Something basking on a crag?

GOD: No.

EVE: Something squalling in a den?

GOD: No.

ADAM: Something swooping over a lake?

GOD: No.

EVE: Something whimpering in a ditch?

GOD: No.

ADAM: Is it something confectionery washing away in the rain?

GOD: No.

ADAM: (*Weakly.*) Something that . . . something that . . . say, why has my hair fallen out? And most of my teeth?

EVE: (*Drooping.*) I can't seem to keep my eyes open. And when did my back start hurting like this?

ADAM: Ack! I can barely raise my head. How long have we been playing this game?

GOD: Well, by your time, you've been playing this game for, oh, sixty years, eleven months, and seven days, and now you are both dying. I told you it would divert you!

ADAM: (*Very weakly.*) But . . . but we still haven't guessed . . .

EVE: Is it . . . something disturbingly out of place in a bowl of wonton soup?

GOD: Nnnnn-nupe.

ADAM: Something . . . that naps . . . in the shade of a . . . baobab . . .

(*Adam and Eve slump motionless to the ground. Enter* THE ANGEL OF DEATH.)

ANGEL: Sir?

GOD: Yes, Death?

ANGEL: We have innumerable descendants of Adam and Eve, sir, all waiting to play the game.

GOD: Very well. I suppose we've got to accommodate them all, to keep them from screaming bloody murder at contemplation of your blameless odiousness. Well, send them in, send them in. Who are these two?

ANGEL: Brad and Buffy Abramowitz, sir, from Bergen County, New Jersey.

(ADAM *and* EVE *awaken, rubbing their eyes; they are* BRAD *and* BUFFY.)

GOD: Thank you, Death. And shut the black hole on your way out.

ANGEL: Very good, sir.

(DEATH *exits.*)

GOD: Brad, Buffy, I'm thinking of something. Can either of you tell me what I'm thinking of?

BRAD: Is it . . . something that makes a crunchy, tart addition to a simple lettuce salad?

GOD: No.

BUFFY: Is it . . . something of faded radiance catching the eye from the bottom of a junk pile?

GOD: No, Buffy, but I like the cut of your jib.

BRAD: Is it . . . something rancid in an artist's refrigerator?

GOD: Sorry.

BUFFY: Is it . . . something described by an art critic as "a caravan of erratics deposited by a minimalist moraine"?

GOD: God no, but that's a good one!

(*Lights begin to fade.*)

BRAD: Wait, wait! Is it something . . . uh, is it something with a long, uh, you know, one of those whaddayacallums, you know, one of those?

GOD: Not even close.

(*Blackout.*)

END OF PLAY

THE TARANTINO VARIATION

Seth Kramer

The *Tarantino Variation* premiered at the Blueprint Theatre, New York, August–September 1997. Ted Brunetti directed the following cast: John Stonehill, J. Judah Collins, and Jeremy Guskin.

CHARACTERS

MR. MAUVE
MR. FUCHSIA
MR. PUCE
(3 MEN OR 3 WOMEN)

Three men in black suits, black ties, white shirts and sunglasses stand in a triangle. They are MR. MAUVE, MR. FUCHSIA, *and* MR. PUCE. *They each draw guns and stick them at each other's heads.* MR. MAUVE *at* MR. FUCHSIA, MR. FUCHSIA *at* MR. PUCE, *and* MR. PUCE *at* MR. MAUVE.

MR. MAUVE: Freeze!

MR. FUCHSIA: Don't move!

MR. PUCE: Hold it!

MR. MAUVE: Put it down.

MR. FUCHSIA: Not until he drops his.

MR. PUCE: No way.

MR. MAUVE: I mean it.

MR. FUCHSIA: So do I.

MR. PUCE: You're going to have to pry this gun out of my cold, dead hand.

MR. FUCHSIA: That can be arranged.

MR. MAUVE: Do it and I kill you.

MR. FUCHSIA: Not before I kill this guy.

MR. PUCE: You shoot, then I shoot.

MR. MAUVE: Okay, then.

MR. FUCHSIA: Your funeral.

MR. PUCE: Let's go!

MR. FUCHSIA: Fine.

MR. MAUVE: Fine!

MR. PUCE: FINE! (*Pause. Triangle shifts. Everyone looks at one another.*) This is a little awkward.

MR. FUCHSIA: I'm feeling a lot of tension here.

MR. MAUVE: I need to urinate.

MR. FUCHSIA: Piss and die!

MR. MAUVE: What?

MR. FUCHSIA: Squirt and you're dirt!

MR. MAUVE: But you're not even pointing your gun at me.

MR. FUCHSIA: So?

MR. MAUVE: So, you can't really threaten me.

MR. FUCHSIA: Fine, then I'll threaten him.

MR. PUCE: Hey, if the guy's gotta go . . .

MR. FUCHSIA: HE LETS ONE DROP OUT AND I'LL KILL YOU!

MR. MAUVE: I can hold it.

MR. PUCE: Hang on.

MR. FUCHSIA: WHAT!

MR. MAUVE: Why are you yelling?

MR. FUCHSIA: BECAUSE I'M . . . (*Beat.*) I'm a little nervous. Sorry. (*Beat.*) You got your gun to my head.

MR. MAUVE: I can relate.

MR. PUCE: Me too. (*Pause. Triangle shifts.*)

MR. MAUVE: You don't . . . *really* want to shoot me, do you?

MR. PUCE: Wanna bet?

MR. FUCHSIA: Go ahead, shoot him.

MR. PUCE: I will.

MR. FUCHSIA: So do it.

MR. PUCE: You don't think I got the guts?

MR. FUCHSIA: Naw, it's the BALLS you're missing.

MR. PUCE: I'll do it! I'll shoot this guy right in the head!

MR. MAUVE: Hey, hey, hey, hey, hey.

MR. FUCHSIA: What now?

MR. MAUVE: Why do you want this guy to shoot me?

MR. PUCE: Yeah, good question. Why do you want me to shoot him?

MR. FUCHSIA: So I can shoot you!

MR. PUCE: Oh.

MR. MAUVE: Oh. (*Beat.*) Well, what if I shoot you first?

MR. FUCHSIA: Shoot me first?

MR. MAUVE: Yeah, what if I blast you right through your eyeballs first?

MR. FUCHSIA: Then he'll smear your brains all over the pavement.

MR. MAUVE: You will?

MR. PUCE: I will?

MR. FUCHSIA: Absolutely, you will.

MR. PUCE: Absolutely, I will.

MR. MAUVE: Um, why?

MR. PUCE: Yeah, why?

MR. FUCHSIA: Because I have this gun to your head. BOOM!

MR. PUCE: BAM!

MR. MAUVE: KER-BLEWY! (*Pause. Triangle shifts.*)

MR. PUCE: All right, so let me see if I got this straight . . .

MR. FUCHSIA: Sure.

MR. MAUVE: Go ahead.

MR. PUCE: If I shoot you in the side of the head . . .

MR. MAUVE: Then I'm going to blow a big, huge hole through his skull . . .

MR. FUCHSIA: And I'm going to splatter your brains all over the ground.

MR. PUCE: So everybody dies?

MR. MAUVE: Yep.

MR. FUCHSIA: Looks that way.

MR. PUCE: And everybody's . . . okay with this?

MR. MAUVE: Can I say something?

MR. FUCHSIA: Absolutely.

MR. PUCE: Go ahead.

MR. MAUVE: I think I'm pointing my gun at the wrong guy.

MR. FUCHSIA: What?

MR. PUCE: You're joking.

MR. MAUVE: No, I think I'm pointing my gun at the wrong guy.

MR. FUCHSIA: That's great. That's just great.

MR. MAUVE: Sorry.

MR. FUCHSIA: Now is a hell of a time to say a thing like that. I mean, what exactly are we supposed to do now? Huh? You want to tell me?

MR. PUCE: Um . . . me too.

MR. FUCHSIA: (*Beat.*) No.

MR. PUCE: Yeah, me too.

MR. FUCHSIA: Okay, do we need to review who is supposed to be shooting who here?

MR. PUCE: Whom.

MR. FUCHSIA: What?

MR. PUCE: Who is supposed to be shooting WHOM here.

MR. FUCHSIA: Really?

MR. MAUVE: I think he's right.

MR. FUCHSIA: (*Yelling.*) I was never very good at grammar!

MR. PUCE: All right, WHO is supposed to be shooting WHOM?

MR. MAUVE: (*Gestures at* MR. PUCE.) Well, I need to shoot you.

MR. PUCE: And I want to whack him. (*Foot at* MR. FUCHSIA.)

MR. FUCHSIA: To be honest, I'd actually rather . . . (*Points at* MR. MAUVE. *Pause, everyone darts looks at one another. Beat. All three turn at the same time and point guns at the other guy.*)

MR. PUCE: All right!

MR. FUCHSIA: Let's go!

MR. MAUVE: Time to die!

MR. PUCE: I'm gonna blow you away, lie in your blood, and make snow angels.

MR. FUCHSIA: Yeah, well, I'm gonna smear your brains on the ground and throw them in the air like confetti.

MR. MAUVE: Not before I kill you, carve your body up with a knife, use your skin as furniture covers, make a necklace out of both your ears, and screw your skull through one of your eye sockets. (*Everyone makes gun-shooting sounds. It fades out.* MR. FUCHSIA *goes on a little longer then the others. Beat.*)

MR. PUCE: Damn.

MR. MAUVE: Well, that didn't solve anything.

MR. FUCHSIA: I'm starting to get a headache.

MR. PUCE: Anybody got any more bright ideas?

MR. MAUVE: Why don't we all put our guns away until we get this figured out?

MR. PUCE: How about on three?

MR. FUCHSIA: Fine.

MR. MAUVE: You start.

MR. FUCHSIA: Me?

MR. MAUVE: No, him.

MR. FUCHSIA: Why him?

MR. MAUVE: Why not?

MR. FUCHSIA: He's got a gun to my head.

MR. PUCE: Fine, you start.

MR. FUCHSIA: Me?

MR. PUCE: No, him.

MR. FUCHSIA: Why him?

MR. MAUVE: Oh, for God's sake . . .

MR. FUCHSIA: I just want to know why I can't start!

MR. MAUVE and MR. PUCE: Fine. You start!

MR. FUCHSIA: Okay, okay. (*Beat.*) One.

MR. MAUVE and MR. PUCE: Two. (*Beat.*) Sorry, go ahead. (*Beat.*) No, you. (*They gesture back and forth with little result. Eventually . . .*)

MR. MAUVE: Two.

MR. PUCE: Three. (*Of course nobody moves.*)

MR. FUCHSIA: Okay, we should have expected that.

MR. MAUVE: This time—for real, all right?

MR. PUCE: Yeah.

MR. FUCHSIA: One.

MR. MAUVE: Two.

MR. PUCE: Three! (*Beat, nothing.*)

MR. FUCHSIA: ONE.

MR. MAUVE: TWO.

MR. PUCE: THREE! (*Not a twitch. All three are totally exasperated, they fidget and exhale. A few ad lib groans and comments. All become still at the same time.*)

MR. MAUVE: We're gonna be here all day.

MR. PUCE: Let's just shoot each other and get this over with.

MR. MAUVE: I still need to take a squirt.

MR. FUCHSIA: Right, that does it! I've had it with you two. HAD IT!

MR. MAUVE: Be cool, be cool.

MR. PUCE: Don't do anything stupid!

MR. FUCHSIA: I mean, all this gun pointing and no shooting. It's pathetic. You're pathetic! You don't deserve to wear those cool black suits!

MR. PUCE: Hey, don't insult the dress code.

MR. FUCHSIA: I'm not spending another minute here. (*Gestures with gun.*) You see this? (*In a sudden move* MR. FUCHSIA *puts his gun to his own head.* MR. MAUVE *and* MR. PUCE *are surprised by this and train their guns on him.*)

MR. MAUVE: What do you think you're doing, man?

MR. FUCHSIA: This is my ticket out of here.

MR. PUCE: There's no need for this!

MR. FUCHSIA: And if either of you try and get in my way, so help me . . . (*Gestures at self with gun.*) I'll do it. I swear. I'm just crazy enough. I'll do it.

MR. MAUVE: Come on, man, point your gun back at me.

MR. PUCE: Or at me. You can point at me.

MR. MAUVE: Hey, I asked him first.

MR. PUCE: So what? I make a better target.

MR. MAUVE: Says who?

MR. PUCE: Says me! (MR. MAUVE *and* MR. PUCE *turn to each other and point their guns at each other's chests.*)

MR. MAUVE: All right then, Mr. Better Target, maybe I'll just blow a hole right through your chest.

MR. PUCE: Not before I blast one through yours.

MR. FUCHSIA: WILL YOU TWO STOP ARGUING! (MR. FUCHSIA *screams and draws a second gun, pointing one at* MR.

MAUVE *and the other at* MR. PUCE. MR. MAUVE *and* MR. PUCE *scream back and immediately respond in kind. Now everyone has two guns trained on everyone else. A good solid pause.*)

MR. MAUVE: Is anyone hungry?

MR. FUCHSIA: Starved.

MR. PUCE: You still need a bathroom?

MR. MAUVE: Yeah.

MR. FUCHSIA: You guys wanna get some Burger King?

MR. PUCE: How about McDonald's?

MR. MAUVE: I'm a vegetarian.

MR. FUCHSIA: B-K is closest.

MR. PUCE: McDonald's has got the best fries!

MR. MAUVE: Wendy's and the all-you-can-eat salad bar!

(*All three walk off, guns aimed at one another, arguing the whole way.*)

END OF PLAY

THE STATUE OF BOLÍVAR

Eric Lane

The Statue of Bolívar premiered on July 7, 2003, at the Makor/Steinhardt Center of the 92nd Street Y in the Festival of 'Wrights; Daniel Gallant, curator and producer. Nicole Quinn directed the following cast:

ELIZABETH	Melissa Leo
JEMMA	Siri Crane

CHARACTERS

JEMMA: A smart fourteen-year-old who has been ignored way too long.

ELIZABETH: A woman in her mid-thirties to fifties, well put together and trying a little too hard. She has experienced a few too many disappointments in her life and love, although trying to maintain a sense of hope.

SETTING

New York City. The statue of Bolívar. South entrance of Central Park at Sixth Avenue.

New York City. The statue of Bolívar. South entrance of Central Park at Sixth Ave.

JEMMA, *a fourteen-year-old, is seated on a bench.* ELIZABETH *stands. She looks off for her date, who is late. She fixes her lipstick.*

JEMMA: That shit'll kill ya.

ELIZABETH: Excuse me?

JEMMA: Lipstick. There are studies. Lab rats. The shit they developed, you don't wanna know.

ELIZABETH: You're right. I don't.

JEMMA: Government studies. Big bucks for putting Revlon on rat lips. Some world, huh?

ELIZABETH: I suppose. Look, do you know what time it is? (JEMMA *extends her arm, showing her watch.*) Thank you.

JEMMA: You like Bolívar?

ELIZABETH: (*Re watch.*) Yes, it's lovely.

195

JEMMA: Not the watch. The general. Simón Bolívar. (*Indicates statue.*) Big-ass statue and nobody even bothers. El Liberador. The George Washington of South America. Won independence for Bolivia, Panama, Columbia, Ecuador, Venezuela, and Peru. You want a Tic-Tac?

ELIZABETH: No thank you. If you don't mind . . .

JEMMA: I don't mind. What else I got to do?

ELIZABETH: I meant I'm waiting for someone.

JEMMA: He ain't showing.

ELIZABETH: That's a terrible thing to say.

JEMMA: True.

ELIZABETH: You don't know that.

JEMMA: I know.

ELIZABETH: You don't know that.

JEMMA: I know.

ELIZABETH: You *don't* know that!

(*A beat.*)

JEMMA: I know.

ELIZABETH: Why don't you go away?

JEMMA: Can't.

ELIZABETH: I'm sure there's another plaque somewhere in the park you can memorize. Bethesda Fountain or Cleopatra's Needle. A wealth of information for a young girl of your perspicacity.

JEMMA: Nah, I'm meeting somebody.

ELIZABETH: He won't show.

JEMMA: He's a she.

ELIZABETH: Either way. She's not coming.

JEMMA: You don't know that.

ELIZABETH: I know.

JEMMA: You don't know that.

ELIZABETH: I know.

JEMMA: You don't know that 'cause she's here.

ELIZABETH: Excuse me. Unless you're meeting some imaginary friend—

JEMMA: I'm Jem.

ELIZABETH: And . . . ?

JEMMA: (*Extends hand.*) Nice to meet you, Elizabeth.

ELIZABETH: Excuse me? How do you know my name?

JEMMA: Elizabeth M. Cunningham. The M's for Marie.

ELIZABETH: How do you . . . Who are you?

JEMMA: Jem.

ELIZABETH: Jem who?

JEMMA: Jem Hollingshead. Ring a bell?

ELIZABETH: Look, I don't know what you think you're—

JEMMA: My dad's your date. At least he was supposed to be. Nicholas I. Hollingshead. I for Ivan. Can you believe naming your kid Ivan? I don't have any kids. I'm not gonna. Fish is okay, but kids suck. I hate kids. I hate cheese. I hate jelly. And I really hate it when my food touches.

ELIZABETH: So where's your father?

JEMMA: Where's he always? Work. Too busy. Story of my life. Something came up, so guess who gets to go in his place. I mean, if you're gonna go to a benefit and buy all the raffle tickets, at least go out on the date when you win it. Instead of sending me.

ELIZABETH: Why would he buy all the raffle tickets and then send you?

JEMMA: He'd send me to take a crap for him if he could figure out how.

ELIZABETH: Well, thanks for the information and the apology.

JEMMA: You're better off. He's an asshole.

ELIZABETH: He's still your father.

JEMMA: He's still an asshole.

ELIZABETH: I tend to agree.

JEMMA: Like, if you're gonna bid on a date for some lame-ass charity, at least pick one with a decent T-shirt.

ELIZABETH: It's not lame-ass. It's a very worthy cause.

JEMMA: (*Rolls her eyes.*) Kidneys for Kids. Try wearing *that* to gym class. You don't look so good, you wanna sit down?

ELIZABETH: No, I'm fine.

JEMMA: You don't look fine. You look like somebody just gave you a big-ass wedgie and you're hoping nobody noticed.

ELIZABETH: I said I'm fine. Thank you.

JEMMA: So where are we going?

ELIZABETH: I don't know where *you're* going, but I'm heading home.

JEMMA: He'll cancel the check. If you don't take me.

ELIZABETH: He wouldn't dare.

JEMMA: You don't know him. Growing up with the middle name Ivan. That shit's deadly. He's probable to do anything. Trust me.

ELIZABETH: The date's off.

JEMMA: I'll tell.

ELIZABETH: Go ahead.

JEMMA: And some baby needing a new kidney instead's gonna wind up with monkey glands. What kinda shit is that to live with?

ELIZABETH: I'm sure they'll work it out.

JEMMA: I mean *you*. Knowing you coulda helped but turned your back at the exact moment of need. That's a heavy burden to bear.

ELIZABETH: I've borne worse.

JEMMA: Tell me about it. And cheese. Did I mention that? I hate cheese.

ELIZABETH: I hate your dad.

JEMMA: Welcome to my life. We could kill him.

ELIZABETH: Right.

JEMMA: Serious. I could. I'm still a juvenile. You could watch. There's no way you could've stopped me. You tried, but I was out of my mind. Years of neglect culminating in one final swipe of the ax.

(*She demonstrates giving him a whack with the ax.*)

ELIZABETH: You'd go to jail.

JEMMA: Good behavior, I'm outta there in no time. TV deal covers the legal fees. A TV movie. Drew Barrymore plays me.

ELIZABETH: Who plays me?

JEMMA: Susan Lucci.

(ELIZABETH *just looks at her.*)

Okay, Betty White. I don't know. Somebody. Who do you
want?

ELIZABETH: I have no idea.

JEMMA: C'mon, you must've thought about it.

ELIZABETH: Never.

JEMMA: Some night when you're lying in bed with your cat
between your legs and you can't fall asleep 'cause you keep
thinking about that asshole who stood you up—even though
you told yourself not to believe. Even though you knew it
wouldn't work, some part of you still hoping, believing that
maybe—

ELIZABETH: I don't have a cat.

JEMMA: No?

ELIZABETH: No. (*A beat.*) I have two cats.

JEMMA: Two cats and you never thought about who'd play you
in the TV movie? I find that hard to believe.

(ELIZABETH *just looks at her.*)

What?

ELIZABETH: Susan Sarandon.

JEMMA: (*Not quite buying it. Overarticulates each letter.*) O-K.

ELIZABETH: What?

JEMMA: Nothing.

ELIZABETH: Not nothing. I detect a certain air of sarcasm in your voice.

JEMMA: That's not sarcasm. That's life. So where we going?

ELIZABETH: How old are you?

JEMMA: Fourteen, but that's not my fault.

ELIZABETH: Fourteen. Jeez.

JEMMA: I won't ask how old you are.

ELIZABETH: No?

JEMMA: You'd probably make me guess, then get all offended and shit. No thank you.

ELIZABETH: That's what? Seventh grade.

JEMMA: (*Incredulous, corrects her.*) Eighth.

ELIZABETH: Eighth grade.

JEMMA: You like to row?

(ELIZABETH *just looks at her.*)

What? That's good exercise for you.

ELIZABETH: I'm not rowing.

JEMMA: Bicycle? We can rent them. Rollerblades? Merry-go-round?

(*No response.*)

That's okay. We can just sit here.

ELIZABETH: I'll give you ten minutes.

JEMMA: Two hours.

ELIZABETH: Ten—

JEMMA: You'd spend at least that with my dad, and he's a dick. (*A beat.*)

ELIZABETH: One hour.

JEMMA: One hour. Okay.

ELIZABETH: (*Looks at Jemma's watch.*) Starting now.

(*A pause. Neither speaks. After a moment:*)

ELIZABETH: How'd he do that? Bolívar. Win their freedom. (*Jemma shrugs.*) Wouldn't that be something?

JEMMA: What?

ELIZABETH: To do something so extraordinary that people build a statue.

JEMMA: Yeah, and pigeons shit all over it. (*Elizabeth looks at her, then laughs.*) What?

ELIZABETH: I think you're missing the point.

JEMMA: Which is . . .

ELIZABETH: Nothing.

JEMMA: Yeah. Nothing.

(*They sit together and look out. Lights fade.*)

END OF PLAY

MARS HAS NEVER BEEN THIS CLOSE

Warren Leight

Mars Has Never Been This Close premiered at The 24-Hour Plays, on September 15, 2003. It was directed by Andy Dorsen, starring Andre Royo as Gregory, Liev Schreiber as Sam, Griffin Dunne as Mark, Giancarlo Esposito as Earl, and Alan Cumming as Chris.

CHARACTERS

GREGORY: African-American, twenties, country club waiter.
SAM: Leading man type, thirties, straitlaced and straight, preoccupied.
MARK: White, forties, a louche, bitter, gay Peter Lawford.
DR. EARL CLEMENS: African-American, forties, articulate, reserved; Mark's long-term partner in a relationship that has seen better days.
CHRIS: Hip, thirtyish outrageous drunk (a lot). Omnisexual. Angry. The only guest at the wedding in a black leather jacket.

A wedding party at a Connecticut or Westchester Country Club, night. Downstage, at a table, drinking by himself, sits CHRIS. *Upstage, on one side of the deck, overlooking the bay,* SAM *looks up at the sky. Reflective.* GREGORY *comes up to him.*

GREGORY: Sir—

SAM: You know, Gregory, they say Mars hasn't been this close to the Earth in millions of years.

GREGORY: Yes, sir. I just wanted to let you know we are beginning to serve dinner.

SAM: Thanks, I'll . . . just be a minute.

(SAM *takes out a cell phone and dials someone.* MARK *and* DR. EARL CLEMENS, *on the other side of the deck.* MARK *has a drink in one hand, a small envelope in the other. He reads the small card that came from the envelope.*)

MARK: Table fourteen?

EARL: Let's don't.

MARK: It's Siberia.

EARL: Let's not.

MARK: Table fourteen? They . . . put us in the ghetto. You literally save her mother's life, and they put us—

EARL: Mark, let's just try to have a good time.

MARK: Do you think either of us would be allowed into this club if it wasn't a wedding?

EARL: We'd have no desire to be here if it wasn't Mary's wedding.

(MARK *sees* GREGORY *crossing past.*)

MARK: Oh, look, another person of color. How did that happen? (*Waves.*)

EARL: Mark—

(*Gregory comes over.*)

GREGORY: Can I help you find your table, sir?

(MARK *gives* EARL *a "what I tell you?" look.*)

MARK: We're at fourteen.

GREGORY: (*Underwhelmed.*) Fourteen? It's down those stairs.

MARK: Thank you.

GREGORY: (*Points.*) With that other . . . gentleman.

MARK: Thank you. Oh, I'll, uh . . . need a refill.

GREGORY: Yes, sir. Right away.

(EARL *reacts to* MARK'S *drinking.*)

MARK: (*To Earl.*) What? It's a Wasp wedding. When in Rye, drink it.

(*Before he can answer,* MARK *goes to the table, where* CHRIS, *also quite smashed, knocks back his drink.*)

Ahoy. Fellow outcast.

CHRIS: I prefer to think of myself as aloof.

MARK: Very Garbo.

EARL: (*Sits next to* MARK.) Garbo? You're dating yourself.

MARK: Somebody has to.

EARL: Not if this keeps up.

CHRIS: Okayyy. So are you two lovebirds friends of the bride or the groom?

MARK: Neither.

EARL: I'm Dr. Clemens, Earl, and—

CHRIS: Oh, yes, the one who saved Mary's mother.

EARL: I didn't really—

MARK: He did.

CHRIS: (*To* MARK.) An oncologist boyfriend. Your mother must be very proud.

MARK: I haven't had the heart to tell her about us yet. (*Whispers.*) He's not Jewish.

CHRIS: You saved her mother's life, and they seat you here. God, these people.

MARK: (*To* EARL.) I didn't bring it up.

CHRIS: It's all so . . . Connecticut Nazi. I think the only reason they don't make us wear yellow stars is it would clash with all the mint-green pants on the groomsmen . . . (*Off* EARL*'s lack of amusement.*) Doctor, is something wrong?

EARL: I just think it's a little facile to judge people on the basis of superficial choices. Or long-held traditions or—

CHRIS: Well, there goes my whole way of life.

(MARK *and* CHRIS *clink glasses.*)

SAM: (*Joining.*) Is this table fourteen?

MARK: Is the pope gay?

(SAM *not getting it, but laughing along.*)

SAM: I'm Sam. I guess we're the bachelor table tonight. Friends of the . . .?

MARK: bride-ish. I'm Mark. This is Earl. The bride's brother. Just kidding.

CHRIS: I dated the groom. Not kidding. (*Off of everyone's look.*) At Buckley.

MARK: Buckley. Oh, that doesn't count. That's called youthful experimentation.

CHRIS: We kept seeing each other, once in a while, up until a few months ago. He's insatiable.

SAM: (*Again, not getting it, but laughing.*) This is a funny table. You guys are funny.

MARK: (*To* SAM.) And what planet do you come from?

SAM: Finance, like everyone else.

MARK: What else is there, really?

GREGORY: Gentlemen. Your drinks.

CHRIS: Keep them coming. (*To the others.*) I have to make a toast to the happy couple.

GREGORY: Yes, sir. And will you be having the steak or the salmon?

EARL: Which do you recommend?

GREGORY: They're both very good, sir.

MARK: There's a surprise.

CHRIS: Do you know where the salmon comes from?

GREGORY: I imagine the ocean, sir.

CHRIS: (*Off of the others' looks.*) It actually matters. You know what they do to salmon these days. They ask the farmer what

color he wants it to be, they inject it with dyes. Then they let
them swim around in tanks filled with their own feces while
they feed them food laced with PCBs.

SAM: I'll have the salmon.

EARL: Sounds good.

MARK: Me too.

CHRIS: Make it four. And another one of these.

MARK: Two.

GREGORY: Very good, gentlemen. Four salmons.

MARK: Poor guy must go crazy working here.

SAM: Gregory's father's worked at the club for years. He's worked
his way up from ball boy.

CHRIS: What a success story.

EARL: (*Trying to change the subject, to* SAM.) Wasn't the bride just
absolutely stunning?

SAM: Totally.

CHRIS: She's not my type.

MARK: Sounds like she's not the groom's type either.

SAM: She's really helped him turn his life around.

EARL: Her mother tells me they are very happy.

MARK: Of course the wedding *was* postponed from the spring.

(*He looks at* CHRIS.)

SAM: Oh that. Mary got upset when she found his porno collection.

CHRIS: She what?

SAM: He tried to tell her it was no big deal. I mean, all guys have some, right. But I think she was upset . . . about the specifics.

MARK: Backdoor?

SAM: Actually (*Leans in.*) *Ghetto Booty, Part Two.*

CHRIS: Part two?

MARK: You should never get the sequels. They only make them for the money.

SAM: (*Not getting any of this.*) Mary was shaken up, but my wife finally told her the best thing was just to ignore it.

CHRIS: Your wife?

SAM: (*Again, not getting it.*) She couldn't make it.

MARK: That's his story, and he's sticking to it.

SAM: She's in the city. Chemo. Didn't feel up to traveling.

EARL: (*To* MARK.) Open mouth, take out Prada.

MARK: I'm sorry, I didn't know.

SAM: It's all right. She's going to be fine.

EARL: I hope so.

SAM: She will. She's a great gal. I called her from the deck, told her about Mars. How close it is. How it's a sign she can fight this thing.

EARL: Where is she being treat—

MARK: You're off-duty, Earl, remember?

(GREGORY *comes by, with drinks for* CHRIS, SAM, *and* MARK.)

Gregory, my good man.

CHRIS: You might as well bring me another with the salmon.

MARK: Me too.

(EARL *signals* GREGORY *no.* GREGORY *is unsure what to do.*)

EARL: Mark, it's a long drive.

MARK: For fuck sake, Earl, don't be such a fun cop. (*To* GRE- GORY.) Gregory, what are you waiting for? (*Pulls out a five- dollar bill.*) Hup hup.

GREGORY: Yes, sir. (*He goes.* MARK *looks at* EARL, *desperate for a reac- tion.* EARL *almost loses it.*)

EARL: That . . . was uncalled for.

MARK: Uncalled for? That's it? That's all you have to say. What is wrong with you, Earl? Don't you get it? You're never going to be one of them. You can save Mary's mother or maybe Sam's wife. It won't help. No matter how hard you work, no matter how hard you try to be perfect, as far as this world is concerned, the most you are ever going to be is hired help.

EARL: (*Gets up, angry, but restrains himself.*) I'm going to . . . get some air.

(*He walks out.*)

MARK: (*To* SAM *and* CHRIS.) Couple stuff. He'll be back.

SAM: You . . . you shouldn't take people for granted. You just . . .

(SAM *walks out, in* EARL*'s direction.*)

MARK: (*Faux sensitive.*) He's so right. (*To* CHRIS.) Now what?

(CHRIS *gets a big, kind of scary smile. He clinks a fork against his glass, slowly rises to his feet.*)

CHRIS: I'd like to propose a toast.

(*Lights.*)

END OF PLAY

SURPRISE

Mark Harvey Levine

Surprise was first produced by Theatre Neo (Los Angeles) in May 2000. It was directed by Loren E. Chadima, with the following cast:

WHITNEY   Carolyn Hennesy
PETER   Mark Harvey Levine
ESTHER   Sarah Nina Phillips

Surprise had its first Equity production as part of *Cabfare for the Common Man* at the Phoenix Theatre (Indianapolis, Indiana) in May 2005. Bryan D. Fonseca is the artistic director. It was directed by Bryan D. Fonseca, with the following cast:

WHITNEY   Sara Rieman
PETER   Jon Lindley
ESTHER   Deborah Sargent

A cheap all-night diner. PETER *studies his menu sheepishly.* WHITNEY, *much better put together, does not look at her menu, but stares at him, steaming mad.*

WHITNEY: Well, that's another evening thoroughly—

PETER: —ruined. I'm sorry, Whitney. Please don't—

WHITNEY: I can never see Jane and Margaret again. My only lesbian friends! I've lost my lesbians!

PETER: You haven't lost—

WHITNEY: I've never felt so—

PETER: —embarrassed, I know—

WHITNEY: (*Overlapping.*) —embarrassed in all my . . . Stop that! I hate when you—

PETER: —finish your sentences, I'm sorry.

WHITNEY: (*Overlapping.*) —finish my . . . yes!

PETER: I can't help it. You know I'm psychic.

219

WHITNEY: Yes, I know you're psychic, Peter. Everyone knows you're psychic. Jane and Margaret know you're psychic. Anyone forgets, wait five minutes, you'll remind them.

PETER: I knew you wouldn't understand.

WHITNEY: Ha-ha, very funny. God! You're not even an INTERESTING psychic. No, you're the ONE guy who's only psychic two minutes ahead.

PETER: I'm sorry. Are you ready to order?

(*As if on cue,* ESTHER, *the waitress, arrives at this moment.*)

ESTHER: Are you ready to order? Oh, hi, Peter.

WHITNEY: Does *she* know you're psychic? He's psychic, y'know.

ESTHER: I know.

PETER: I always come here when I'm about to be dumped. (*To* ESTHER.) I'll have the usual.

WHITNEY: Dumped?!

PETER: And she'll have the blueberry Belgian waffles. And we both want coffee.

WHITNEY: I'll order for myself, thank you very much.

(WHITNEY *grabs the menu, looks it over for a long beat.*)

I want the waffles. (*To* PETER.) Damn you, damn you.

ESTHER: I'll be back with your coffee.

(ESTHER *exits.*)

WHITNEY: So you know I'm going to dump you?

PETER: It's pretty obvious.

WHITNEY: In the next two minutes?

PETER: No, I think I've always known this day would come.

WHITNEY: We've only been dating three weeks.

PETER: Please don't break up with me, Whitney! I can't help myself! It's not easy being psychic! I had a terrible childhood.

(ESTHER *arrives with two cups of coffee as he speaks.*)

When Jimmy DeFornick would beat me up, I could feel each punch before it landed. Sometimes—you're going to burn your mouth—if I knew he was going to break my glasses I'd take them off and break them myself.

(*As* PETER *speaks,* WHITNEY *defiantly gulps her coffee and holds it in her bulging cheeks, glaring at him. Her mouth is frying.*)

(*Without pausing.*) He found that amusing. And I knew he would.

(WHITNEY *swallows, speaking funny at first due to her burnt mouth.*)

WHITNEY: Look, we all had louthy childhoodth, okay? Stacey Gerber used to stomp on my toes during baton practice. It doesn't give you the—

PETER: —I didn't!

WHITNEY: LET ME FINISH! Just once, just once in the final moments of this relationship, I would like to finish a sentence. Thank you. (*Pause, fuming.*) I forgot what I was going to—

PETER: "—the right to pick fights with your—"

WHITNEY: (*Overlapping.*) —with my friends! Yes!

PETER: (*Overlapping.*) And then I say "I didn't," and you say—

PETER and WHITNEY: (*Simultaneously.*) You most certainly did.

PETER: —and then I say—

WHITNEY: Stop that!

PETER: —and it's all so boring.

WHITNEY: Don't say things along with me!

PETER: Why bother having the fight if—

WHITNEY: You know I hate that!

PETER: All I said to them was the spinach mushroom lasagna was going to be dry and inedib—

WHITNEY: They *MADE* the spinach mushroom las—

PETER: How was I supposed to know?

WHITNEY: (*Banging table.*) BECAUSE YOU'RE PSYCHIC!

PETER: Look, I only know the next two minutes, okay? I can't tell who made dinner. I'm not a food psychic. Except ours is here.

(*Right on cue,* ESTHER *enters with their food: waffles for* WHITNEY *and a bowl of cornflakes for* PETER.)

ESTHER: Here ya go! Blueberry Belgian waffles and one "I'm Getting Dumped" Special.

WHITNEY: Cornflakes?! You go to a restaurant and order cornflakes?

PETER: (*Meekly.*) I like how they do them here.

ESTHER: Can I get you anything else?

PETER: We're fine. Just bring the towel.

(ESTHER *exits.*)

And the lasagna *was* dry and inedi—

WHITNEY: Of course it was! It always is! It's their specialty! That's why you go out to eat afterwards! And you don't have to be psychic to know when someone invites you over, they made the damn dinner!

PETER: I don't get invited over too much.

WHITNEY: Can't imagine why.

PETER: Well, people get freaked out just because I—

WHITNEY: Sarcasm! That was sarcasm! You know what? I want to thank you. I do. You've taught me the true meaning of hate. Oh, I thought I'd hated before. But I realize now it was a mere youthful dislike. Puppy hate. But with you, I finally know what it means to hate someone! I detest you with a passion I've never felt before! I despise you! I abhor you! Why, I think I loathe you! (*Pause.*) God, I hate you!

PETER: Doesn't surprise me.

WHITNEY: Aggggggggghhhh!

PETER: You missed.

(*She throws a waffle at him, missing him, of course.*)

WHITNEY: AGGGGGGGGGGGGGGGGGGGGGHHHH!

(*She throws her water at him, hitting him full in the face—precisely as* ESTHER *arrives with a towel.* PETER *dries off and tosses the towel to* ESTHER, *who catches it one-handed, hardly looking, as she passes by. They've obviously done this before.*)

WHITNEY: (*With great, but unsteady, calmness.*) Well, I think it is obvious that we are through, here, Peter. I feel no need to stay. (*To* ESTHER.) Could you bring us the—

ESTHER: —check?

WHITNEY: (*Going to pieces.*) Let me say it! LET ME SAY IT! Check! Check check check! In fact, never mind! He's going to pay! (*To* PETER.) But then you knew that, didn't you?!

(ESTHER *holds the door open for* WHITNEY *as she storms out.*)

PETER: (*To himself.*) Watch your step.

(*We hear a crash and a distant "Dammit!" from* WHITNEY *offstage.*)

   (*Sadly, to* ESTHER.) She was too good for me.

ESTHER: Are you kidding me? Honey, I've seen you get dumped by a lot of women, and she was definitely the worst of 'em.

PETER: She was my last chance. I'm never gonna f—

ESTHER: You'll find someone. You'll see. Someone pretty, smart, independent . . . who won't mind that you order cornflakes.

PETER: What are you, psy—

ESTHER: (*Overlapping.*) —pyschic? Nah. Let's just call it a hunch.

(*She grabs him and kisses him full on the mouth.* PETER *stands stunned for a moment.*)

PETER: . . . Didn't see THAT coming . . .

ESTHER: Surprise!

PETER: But . . . why didn't I know? Why couldn't I—

ESTHER: —tell? I guess some things even a psychic can't see.

PETER: Hey, you finished one of my—

ESTHER: —sentences. Do you—

PETER: —mind? No. No, I don't. So what happens—

ESTHER: —next?

PETER and ESTHER: (*Simultaneously, smiling.*) I don't know!

(*Blackout.*)

END OF PLAY

HOW WE TALK IN
SOUTH BOSTON

David Lindsay-Abaire

How We Talk in South Boston premiered at Theatre 40 One-Act Festival, Los Angeles, California, on January 1, 1999.

CHARACTERS

NORMAN: The father, in his fifties, has a strong Boston accent.
MARY: The mother, in her fifties, has a strong Boston accent.
MARTY: The son, in his twenties, has a strong Boston accent.
BARBARA: The daughter, in her twenties, has a strong Boston accent.
MARLON: An African-American man, in his twenties, does not have an accent.
PING: An Asian-American man, in his twenties, does not have an accent.
FRANKIE: A Native American man, in his fifties, does not have an accent.

Partial (Pah-Shel) Boston Glossary

BILL BUCKNER: Red Sox first baseman in the '86 World Series.
A BUM TICKA: A bad heart.
BRIGHAM'S: An ice cream store chain in Boston.
HARRY FRAZEE: Owner of the Red Sox in 1919.
JUDGE GARRITY: A prominent figure in Boston politics, instrumental in bringing forced busing to Boston's predominately segregated inner-city neighborhoods in the 1970s.
GOAHJIS: Gorgeous
HOODSIES: Small prepackaged cups of ice cream.
JIMMIES: Chocolate sprinkles put on ice cream.
KAH KEEZ: Car keys.
BOB KRAFT: Current owner of the New England Patriots.
PAHLAH: Parlor, a living room.
ROXBURY: A neighborhood in Boston, a primarily African-American community.
SOUTHIE: South Boston, a neighborhood in Boston, a primarily Irish Catholic community.
STAH MAHKET: Star Market, a supermarket chain in Boston.
SPUCKIES: Submarine sandwiches, also called grinders (grindas).

Accent Note

Practically everything in this play is written out phonetically, so anyone with a passing familiarity with a Boston accent should be able to figure out what's being said if it's not in the glossary list.

(*Lights up on a living room [parlor] in a blue-collar home in South Boston.* MARY *is making a latch-hook rug when her husband* NORMAN *enters with a car door. His arm is lodged inside it.*)

NORMAN: Muthah-ra-Gawd, look at dis. My ahm's cot in da kah dewah.

MARY: Doan bring dat hunka gahbitch into my pahlah, Nawman. Take it back outside and diddle inda gudda.

NORMAN: I ain't diddlin'. My ahm's cot.

MARY: Get owda heah. Ya ahm's cot? (*Calls downstairs.*) Hey, Mahdy, ya fathah's ahm's cot in the kah dewah. Cawl da fiah depahtmend. Tell 'em to get ovah heah befoah he gets dubbaya-dee-foddy on my latch-hook rug.

NORMAN: Dat's a nice rug yuh makin'.

MARY: Yuh like it? Thea havin' a time down at the VFW Post in Mahch, a bazah, like an ahts and craffs faih, an I dought I could sell my rugs.

NORMAN: Dat's a great idear, Meery.

(MARTY *enters.*)

229

MARTY: Yuh cawlin' me?

MARY: Yeah, wheah da frig whiryah?

MARTY: I coodin' heah ya. I was downsteahs ina cella.

MARY: Dis frickin' chowdah-head got his ahm cot in da kah dewah.

MARTY: How'd he get his ahm cot in the kah dewah?

NORMAN: I was fixin' da windah 'cause it was hahd to open, so I took da dewah apaht and was fiddlin' aroun' and my ahm got cot.

MARTY: Dat's wicket pissa. Whadda looza.

NORMAN: Get me owda heah. I gotta watch da Sox at fowah.

MARTY: I bet yaw cot in duh lockin' mechanism. I'll go get yaw kah keez.

(MARTY *exits.*)

NORMAN: D'jew buy me some beah, Meery? You know Hahvey and Kevin McCahthy ah comin' ova to watch da game.

MARY: Sully's not comin'?

NORMAN: Nah, Sully went to da dawg track with Fitzy an Beah-zo.

MARY: Okay. I went to Stah Mahket on Sadaday inny-ways. I bought beah and a pahty platta foah yis. I can cook up some budded con on da cob. An' I got some sub rolls so you can make spuckies.

NORMAN: D'jew get any tawnic? Cause Hahvey don't drink no mowah.

MARY: Yeah. I got two big bosses a' Pepsi. The three-leetah kind. And a box of hoodsies foah afta.

NORMAN: Aw, we should still have hoodsies left ova from lass Saint Paddy's Day.

MARY: Dose was hahd and freeza burnt. I trew 'em in da barrel. I didn't get no jimmies dough. You want me to run upta Brigham's?

(BARBARA, *their daughter, enters.*)

BARBARA: Ma, Dad, I have some wicket good news.

MARY: Bahbra. Ya fathah's ahm's cot in a kah dewah.

BARBARA: Whadda looza! Wanna heah my good news now?

(MARTY *enters.*)

MARTY: I gut da kah keez.

(*Holds up car keys.*)

BARBARA: Ma, Dad, Mahty, I'm gettin' married!

MARTY: No suh!

BARBARA: Ya-huh!

MARTY: No suh!

BARBARA: Ya-huh!

MARY: Oh my gawd, my dodda's gettin' meerried!

NORMAN: You know I got a bum ticka! I'm havin' a hahd attack heah! Gimme a hug!

(*Hugs her, but the car door makes it awkward.*)

BARBARA: Ahhh! Ya hit me wit da kah dewah, ya looza!

NORMAN: Sorry.

MARY: Wait a minute, Bahbra, who ah ya marion?

BARBARA: His name is Mahlin.

NORMAN: We don't know no Mahlins.

MARY: Shuwah we do. Mahlin Perkins. Da animal guy.

NORMAN: How come we neva herda dis Mahlin ya marion?

BARBARA: 'Cause I was afraid ya wooden likem.

NORMAN: Why wooden we likem?

BARBARA: He likes da Yankees.

(*There's a long, uncomfortable pause.*)

MARTY: Ya love 'em, Bahb?

BARBARA: Moah than my haht can beah.

MARTY: Den I ken accep' 'em, liddle sista.

BARBARA: Danks, Mahty. Ma?

MARY: I neva liked baseball. I doan kayah.

BARBARA: Dad?

(NORMAN *spits in her face.*)

BARBARA: Ya spit in my eye, ya looza!

NORMAN: You know about da curse, Bahb?

BARBARA: Yeah, but ya ain't gotta spit at me.

NORMAN: In nine-teen nine-teen, Babe Root was a Red Sox playah, an den Harry Frazee solt 'em to da Yankees, and da rest is history. Eva since den, my team has been cursed. In eighdy yeahs, we hahven won a Whirl Series. Shuwah, deer ah udda teams wit worse reckids, but nobiddy loses in such haht-breakin' ways. An' above all da teams in da leagues, da Yankees have been ah ahch enemies. Damn dat Harry Frazee. And damn all dose Yankees. Fenway Pahk shoulda been da house dat Root built. And now my ony dodda is gonna tell me she's marion a Yankee fan?

BARBARA: But I love 'em.

MARY: Da haht is a mysterious oahgan, Nawman. Dat I know.

NORMAN: So doan I! I know dat too, Meery!

BARBARA: Please, Daddy . . .

NORMAN: Awww, jeez. Alright. But nobiddy mention dat dis kid's a Yankee fan. Especially to Kevin McCahthy.

BARBARA: Oh dank you, Daddy!

(*Hugs him, but the car door gets in the way.*)

Ahhhh, dat damn kah dewah!

MARTY: I gut da kah keez!

(*Tries to unlock the car door.*)

MARLON: (*Offstage.*) Knock-knock. Anyone home?

BARBARA: In heah, honey! Dat's Mahlin. He was pahkin' da kah. Everyone be nice.

(MARLON *enters. He's a black man.*)

MARLON: Hello. I'm Marlon. I was parking the car by the bar on the far corner.

BARBARA: Dozen he tock funny?

(*They just stare at him blankly.*)

I just tolt 'em you was a Yankee fan.

MARLON: Oh, yeah? Sorry, I hope you don't hold it against me. Least I'm not a Mets fan. I was rooting for you guys in '86. Too bad about that Billy Buckner thing. Gimpy little ground ball down the first-base line. Right between Buckner's feet. World Series riding on that simple grounder. You must've been angry as heck. Kinda funny, though, right?

NORMAN: Funny?

MARY: Yoah black. Yourah black man.

MARLON: Yes, I know.

NORMAN: This is a black man, Bahbra.

BARBARA: Isn't he goahjis?

NORMAN: A black man who likes da Yankees and tinks Bucknuh is funny.

(*Spits in* MARLON'*s face.*)

MARLON: Eww. He spit at me.

MARY: Calm ya livva, Nawman.

NORMAN: Mahty, goto da stowah and get me a regulah coffee.

MARY: Anna cahtin a milk. Deah's money in my pockabook.

MARTY: I wanna stay.

NORMAN: We gotta talk to ya sistah.

MARTY: I'm gay.

MARY: What?

MARTY: I'm gay. Since youah so mad anyways and spittin' on evrybidy, I might as well tell yuhs.

NORMAN: Eura queeah, Mahty?

MARTY: Yeah, I'm queeah.

BARBARA: I knew he was queeah!

MARLON: What's a quee-ahh?

NORMAN: My own son is a fudge-packa.

(*Spits at* MARTY.)

MARTY: Ick, a loogy.

MARY: My heaht is breakin'.

MARLON: I support you, Marty. Be proud of your feelings.

NORMAN: Hey, da nigga's tellin' da queeah to be proud. Not in dis neighbahood, Sambo. Take it to da liberals ova da River at Hahvahd. Dale tellya to mahch in da parade ahm in ahm. Fuggin' outsidas.

BARBARA: Daddy . . .

MARY: He doan mean nuttin' by it. He was mugged by a black guy once.

MARTY: A *gay* black guy?

MARY: Shut up, Mahtty. Ya fathuh's upset.

NORMAN: You kids doe know about history. Dat's ya problem right deah.

BARBARA: I'm marion Mahlin whetha yis like it oah not.

NORMAN: Yaw ancestas came ova cuzza da famines in Iyaland in da 1850s. An you tink dose uppity Brahmin wannid 'em heah in Boston? No. Nobidy wannid a buncha imergrent Micks. So we found a liddle slice a land ona watah and made it ahrown. The Irish were discriminated against foh all dose yeahs, an now deah gonna tell us weah racist foah protectin' duh ony place dat's ahrown. Fuck dat.

MARLON: I can't understand a word he's saying.

NORMAN: Yuh stay wit yuh own kind. Dat's how God wants it.

(*An* ASIAN MAN *enters.*)

ASIAN MAN: I couldn't help overhearing the argument. I guess it's okay to come out now.

MARTY: Mom, Dad, this is Ping, my luva. He's been livin' inda basement wit me for tree months.

PING: It's a pleasure to meet you. Arm's caught in the car door, huh?

NORMAN: Whaddahell is goin' on heah? Did I raise yous kids to be freaks? Fuggin League a Nations in dis house! Dis ain't Greenwitch Village, Mahty!

MARY: It's dat tollarinse ting they been tocking about on da TV. Duh kids musta been watchin' da TV.

NORMAN: No tollarinse in dis house. Dis is Southie! We doan tolerate nobidy heah! Not da niggas, not da japs, not da chinks oah da spics, oah da fags, nobidy! Day all wanna take us ova. Duh fohced bussin' was da first step. Friggin Judge Garrity can suck my dick! Den da queeahs in da Saint Paddy's Parade! An remembuh when dat Hebe Bob Kraft tried to put the Pats Stadium in my backyahd? I don't tink so, Jew-Boy! We chased his Yiddish ass owda heah! I shoulda known he was no good, trying to move dat Jacksonville game so it wooden conflict wit Yom Kippa, whadeva da fuck dat is!

PING: I've never heard someone be so blatantly prejudiced.

BARBARA: Ain't he funny?

NORMAN: I ain't prejudiced!

BARBARA: See what I mean? Daddy, youah hilairy-us!

NORMAN: Don't laugh at me, Bahb!

MARLON: He's almost as funny as Bill Buckner!

NORMAN: Get outta my house!

MARY: You do look funny, Nawman! Ya face all red, ya ahm cot inda kah dewah!

(*They're all laughing at him now. He's so angry he can barely speak.*)

MARTY: Hey, Dad, live and let live, okay?

MARY: Nawman, I neva toldja I'ma Poahta Rican Lesbian!

(*Shrieks with laughter.*)

NORMAN: Go fuck yisself! Alla yis!

(*Sudden pain in his chest.*)

Ah! My haht! I hope yis ah happy! Alls I wanted was to watch duh Sox at fowah.

(*Falls to the ground in pain.*)

MARY: Ah you okay, Nawman?

PING: I'm a doctor. I can help.

NORMAN: No fuggin' way! Meery, call an American doctor. I doan need dis queeah gook puttin' his chinky hands on me.

(*Tries to spit, but dribbles on himself.*)

MARTY: Dad, he can help.

NORMAN: I doan need no help! I'm fine da way I am!

MARLON: Get him to my car. We'll drive him to City Hospital.

NORMAN: Youah not bringin' me to dat nigga' hospital in Roxbury!

BARBARA: But it's da closest, Daddy.

NORMAN: New England Medical is closa! I doan need yis help . . . I'm fine widout yis.

(*He crawls to the exit, the car door dragging.*)

MARY: Youah bein' very stubbin.

NORMAN: I doan needa tolerate nobidy . . .

(*He collapses.*)

Ahhhh . . .

(*He dies.*)

MARY: Muthah-ra-Gawd, he's dead.

BARBARA: My fathah is dead.

MARY: He wasn't really youah fathah anyways. Kids, I'd like you to meet Frankie Grey Hawk.

(FRANKIE *enters, an older man in full Native American regalia.*)

FRANKIE: How. Me smokum peace pipe.

MARY: Isn't he funny? Dat's duh ferse ting he says each mohnin' befoah he sneaks oudda da house. He's sucha joka.

FRANKIE: I'm actually a linguistics professor at Northeastern.

BARBARA: Youah ah fathuh?

MARTY: Dat explains Bahbra's terrible drinkin' problem.

BARBARA: And Mathy's dream to open a gamblin' casino!

FRANKIE: Kids, those are just racial stereotypes perpetuated by the white man to keep us down.

MARY and BARBARA: Sorry, Dad.

MARY: We gotta lotta catchin' up to do. Frankie's been hidin' inda attic foh twenny-eight yeahs.

MARLON: A regular Anne Frank. I hope that doesn't offend anyone.

EVERYONE: No, of course not.

(*They all laugh, then hock a loogy and spit at* NORMAN'*s dead body. Blackout.*)

END OF PLAY

THE ZIG-ZAG WOMAN

Steve Martin

The Zig-Zag Woman was originally presented in workshop by the New York Stage and Film Company with the Powerhouse Theatre in association with RJK Productions. The stage manager was Sandi Johnson; the director was Barry Edelstein. The cast included:

ROB CAMPBELL

BILL IRWIN

FRANK RAITER

KIMBERLY WILLIAMS

The Zig-Zag Woman's original New York production was by the New York Shakespeare Festival, George C. Wolfe, producer. The scenic design was by Thomas Lynch; lighting design was by Donald Holder; costume design was by Laura Cunningham; sound design was by Red Ramona; the production stage manager was James Latus. Barry Edelstein directed the following cast:

THE ZIG-ZAG WOMAN	Amelia Campbell
OLDER MAN	Nesbitt Blaisdell
MIDDLE MAN	Don McManus
YOUNG MAN	Kevin Isola

The curtain opens on a café set. Upstage center is a woman inside the magic effect The Zig-Zag Woman. It's as though a woman's head, arms, legs, and torso have been separated from one another.

THE ZIG-ZAG WOMAN: Maybe *now* he'll notice me.

(*An* OLDER MAN *walks out, with a chair. He sits alongside* THE ZIG-ZAG WOMAN.)

THE ZIG-ZAG WOMAN: What would you like?

OLDER MAN: I'll just have some coffee.

THE ZIG-ZAG WOMAN: Cream or black?

OLDER MAN: Don't care.

THE ZIG-ZAG WOMAN: Here you are, here's your coffee.

(THE ZIG-ZAG WOMAN *doesn't hand him the coffee; it just appears. A convention.*)

OLDER MAN: Thank you. (*He takes a sip of imaginary coffee. Pause.*) May I pay you a compliment?

THE ZIG-ZAG WOMAN: All right.

OLDER MAN: It's really nice the way your head is separated from your body like that.

THE ZIG-ZAG WOMAN: Thank you.

OLDER MAN: Most women, their heads are *on* their bodies. You don't often see one separated like yours.

THE ZIG-ZAG WOMAN: Well, thank you. (*To audience, pointing and gesturing with her exposed hands.*) You should know this is not the one. (*To* OLDER MAN.) Will there be anything else?

OLDER MAN: Could I ask you one more question?

THE ZIG-ZAG WOMAN: Please.

OLDER MAN: *Why* is your head separated from your body?

THE ZIG-ZAG WOMAN: I'm trying to meet someone.

OLDER MAN: In my day, they used Chanel Number 5. What's the reason for meeting this person?

THE ZIG-ZAG WOMAN: I want to be in love.

OLDER MAN: Ah, yes.

THE ZIG-ZAG WOMAN: All day long, I look into strangers' eyes and ask them what they want. I wait for them to ask me what I want, but they never do. I set the plates down in front of them, and for a second, I close my eyes and wait for a touch on the hand that never comes.

OLDER MAN: Just when you think love is dead, it is waiting for you like a crouching panther. But easy takes the step, easy takes the step.

THE ZIG-ZAG WOMAN: Yes.

OLDER MAN: Remember the dawn breaks.

THE ZIG-ZAG WOMAN: The dawn breaks?

OLDER MAN: The dawn breaks everything, including the mood from the night before.

THE ZIG-ZAG WOMAN: I see.

OLDER MAN: Would you like me to slide you back together?

THE ZIG-ZAG WOMAN: (*Looks offstage to see if anyone is coming.*) Maybe just for a minute.

(*The* OLDER MAN *stands up and slides her middle back together.* THE ZIG-ZAG WOMAN *gets out of the box and investigates her stomach.*)

THE ZIG-ZAG WOMAN: That feels better.

(THE ZIG-ZAG WOMAN *sets a candle on each of the tables and lights the candles.*)

OLDER MAN: The things you gals put yourselves through. Now, me? I've been in love with the same woman my whole life. She's gone now, but not a day goes by that I don't think about her.

THE ZIG-ZAG WOMAN: What was she like?

OLDER MAN: Well, she had a laugh that could spin your head around, and a personality as unpredictable as a ricochet. She could write, sing, and draw, and she issued a declaration of independence every time she entered a room. She was smart as a whip, yet could sit down intensely with the morning crossword and not get one. She brightened my life in a way I never could for myself. Her hair was practically edible. Joy issued from her eyes and hands and her walk, and she could sit like Buddha and speak to the fourth place in your heart.

THE ZIG-ZAG WOMAN: You must miss her.

OLDER MAN: I do.

THE ZIG-ZAG WOMAN: How long has she been gone?

OLDER MAN: Twenty-three years. (*Pause.*) Divorced me, married an actor. In the beginning of something, its ending is foretold, and we met in an elevator going down. After she left, in my travels I would sit in hotel lobbies expecting her to appear; telling me what a mistake she'd made. I would land at airports, thinking that she got my flight number and would be waiting for me. When I went to a show, I would buy two tickets in case she had found out where I was and quietly joined me, nothing having to be said. I never figured out why she went away, but I did figure out this: Love is a promise delivered already broken.

THE ZIG-ZAG WOMAN: I should go back in the box.

OLDER MAN: Here, let me help.

(*The* OLDER MAN *helps her back into the box. While the box is in the closed position, he opens the stomach window and tickles* THE ZIG-ZAG WOMAN. *She laughs.*)

THE ZIG-ZAG WOMAN: Just slide my middle out.

(*The* OLDER MAN *does this.*)

THE ZIG-ZAG WOMAN: Thank you.

(*A second man, the* MIDDLE MAN, *enters. Mid-thirties, brassy and loud. Texan. He sits.*)

MIDDLE MAN: Oh, hell with it, I'll have a piece of pie.

THE ZIG-ZAG WOMAN: (*Quickly.*) Here you are.

MIDDLE MAN: Today is my anniversary.

THE ZIG-ZAG WOMAN: Mine, too. Two years with nobody. How about you?

MIDDLE MAN: Twelve years. Twelve years with the wifey. She recently cut her hair short. Looks good. Last night I put my head between her legs, and it was still paradise. I hope I didn't offend you.

THE ZIG-ZAG WOMAN: (*To audience.*) By the way, this is not him either.

MIDDLE MAN: Tough debate. Married or single. Single brings a sadness, but sadness has its own perfection. Marriage brings a misery of a rare kind, the kind that loves company. (*He looks at* THE ZIG-ZAG WOMAN.) You look like a girl in a fix.

THE ZIG-ZAG WOMAN: A bit of one. The four-wall kind.

MIDDLE MAN: What do you mean?

THE ZIG-ZAG WOMAN: The staring-at-four-walls kind.

MIDDLE MAN: Well, you've got to get it together, babe. There's no four walls inside your head. You just get yourself a person-ality, that's all. You put two women next to each other, one with a personality and one without, you go for the one with the personality every time. Unless the other one is wearing a red dress. But that's the mistake a lotta guys make. I mean, that red dress comes off. The personality doesn't. So here's what you do: You get yourself one of those self-help books. You know, nine ways to do this, seven ways to do that. You memorize that stuff, tell it to people, and they think you're a genius. They think *you live by it*, but really you're just going home and whacking off to a record, banging your head against a headboard as the TV sends numbing rays to your groin.

THE ZIG-ZAG WOMAN: Have you noticed that I'm ripped apart?

MIDDLE MAN: Oh, yeah, but I didn't know if it was some cosmetic surgery or what. You know, the latest thing. Didn't know if I should mention it. At the parties I go to, you could spend all night not mentioning things. At the parties I go to, there's enough hacked-off flesh to create another party somewhere else. Probably a more fun party, since all that flesh would have to be reanimated by some scientist using pig brains, which would create at least *something*. Is this some kind of beauty thing, like a nose ring?

THE ZIG-ZAG WOMAN: This is just a displacement of the heart.

MIDDLE MAN: Ah yes. But that can be beautiful too. (*He opens the stomach window in the Zig-Zag box and tickles her.*) Here, let me be a momentary salve. (*He slides her middle; she gets out of the box.*) Take the first wife. Crazy as a map of London. Her heart was displaced into the next state. Made her attractive. Every night was like drawing to an inside straight: all or nothing. Ecstasy or agony. She shot herself with a twenty-two. Dumb. Took nine days to die. If you're going to shoot yourself, you gotta use something big like a cannon. Otherwise, you could lay around for years on your own bathroom schedule. Anyway, she lay there comatose, then suddenly popped into consciousness and told me this. I mean these were her dying words; she looked me straight in the eye and said, "I would assign every lie a color: yellow when they were innocent, pale blue when they sailed over you like the sky, red because I knew they drew blood. And then there was the black lie. That's the worst of all." She said, "A black lie was when I told you the truth."

THE ZIG-ZAG WOMAN: How can the truth be a lie?

MIDDLE MAN: That's what I asked her, and here's what she said: "I told you the truth not to tell you the truth, but because I knew the truth would hurt you." By the way, this is so typical of her. You didn't get dying words; you got a dying essay. Then I asked her why did she do it, why did she shoot herself, and she said, "The joy of life juts out of me like the Matterhorn, but the pain of life looms over me like Everest." Then she dropped her head down on the pillow dramatically, like she died. I thought she died too, but they told me she actually died three hours later. Not from what you think. Diabetes. They said she could have lived with the bullet in her head. In fact, it was lodged in the right side of her brain, and they said the only consequence was it would probably make her draw better. Drama queen. Am I talkin' too much?

THE ZIG-ZAG WOMAN: More pie?

MIDDLE MAN: Pie. Pie. That reminds me of something. I don't know why. (*He stands, lost in his memory.*) I was eighteen. I was traveling in Italy with my girlfriend. She was seventeen. She was *seventeen*. We had about six months of experience between us. We had no money. I can't remember how we got there. But can you imagine? Eighteen in Italy with nothing but T-shirts and a bag. Not one word of Italian. One watch between us. No tickets, no reservations. A compass. A compass . . . we thought that would be useful. Like we would suddenly be helped if we knew north. It was August like nobody's business. So hot you could fry eggs in the *air*. We decided to sleep in a park next to the Colosseum. Cars all night long. We went to an Italian market and bought a bottle of white wine. Screw top. We drank it; it tasted bad, but we got drunk, drunk in the park. Sleeping bags, love. Love. The night. Eighteen. We saved the bottle, kept it with us, took it back with us. Later we were told it was olive oil. (*A* YOUNG MAN *enters, full of fire.*)

YOUNG MAN: I'll have six cheeseburgers, five Cokes, one Sprite, two shrimp salads, four iced teas, and three bags of fries.

THE ZIG-ZAG WOMAN: To go?

(*The* YOUNG MAN *never looks at* THE ZIG-ZAG WOMAN.)

YOUNG MAN: No, I'll eat it here.

THE ZIG-ZAG WOMAN: Here you are.

(*The food appears.*)

YOUNG MAN: American food. Yes! I just came back from Italy? I was with a girl; she's seventeen. She went to Italy to get a face-lift and abortion. Plus they can do a twelve-step program there in eight steps. She got busted coming back trying to take a gun on the plane. They let me get on 'cause they couldn't link me to her, even though she was staring into my face and screaming my name in the waiting lounge. I got bumped up to first class on the way back, so all in all, it was a pretty good trip. But I did learn this, though: no more girl-friends that I meet on the street. Hey, guess what? I woke up the other day and had a brilliant flash of insight.

(*The* YOUNG MAN *finds this amusing, then goes back to eating.*)

OLDER MAN: (*After a pause.*) Well, what the hell was it?

YOUNG MAN: Sorry?

OLDER MAN: What was the insight?

YOUNG MAN: Oh, well, here goes. I figured this: I'm twenty-one years old.

OLDER MAN: I know what you mean.

MIDDLE MAN: Keep talkin', kid.

YOUNG MAN: And how much could I really know.

OLDER MAN: Very wise.

MIDDLE MAN: A wise old owl at twenty-one.

YOUNG MAN: I figure a lot. I probably know a lot.

(*The* OLDER MAN *and the* MIDDLE MAN *look at each other.*)

OLDER MAN: He doesn't understand.

MIDDLE MAN: No way.

YOUNG MAN: I came up with this: Every emotion is consumed by its opposite. Every ounce of pleasure is balanced by an equal amount of disaster. Generosity breeds contempt; power breeds weakness. Agony leads to a greater appreciation of bliss. You love your friends, they start dying; when your friends start dying, you take more chances with your own life. Every ache you feel makes its inverse more possible. And that is the ecology of joy and pain.

THE ZIG-ZAG WOMAN: (*To audience.*) You should know that this is him.

MIDDLE MAN: (*Snaps his fingers.*) Her nickname was Pie. That's what reminded me of her. Sorry, go ahead.

YOUNG MAN: (*Stands, goes downstage of the Zig-Zag box.*) I'm tryin' to combine the both. The full life. The good with the . . .

(*The* YOUNG MAN *indicates the others to finish his sentence.*)

MIDDLE MAN: Bad.

YOUNG MAN: The dark with the . . .

OLDER MAN: Light.

YOUNG MAN: The yin with the . . .

(*There is a long pause while the* OLDER MAN *and the* MIDDLE MAN *look at each other.*)

OLDER MAN: Good?

YOUNG MAN: The yin with the . . .

MIDDLE MAN: Uh . . . yellow?

YOUNG MAN: The yin . . . with the . . .

OLDER MAN: Hey, you, bub?

YOUNG MAN: The yin with the . . .

THE ZIG-ZAG WOMAN: Yang.

(*The* YOUNG MAN *snaps his fingers and points, but does not look at her.*)

YOUNG MAN: Right-o.

THE ZIG-ZAG WOMAN: What about love?

YOUNG MAN: Love? When I feel myself falling in love, I go buy a boomerang instead. At least with a boomerang, something comes back to you. Unless, of course, she were zig-zagged. If she were zig-zagged, there you go, that would be a girl I could love forever.

(*The* OLDER MAN *and the* MIDDLE MAN *look at* THE ZIG-ZAG WOMAN, *who is out of her box. She and they rush into the box. The* YOUNG MAN *still faces forward but won't look.*)

YOUNG MAN: No middle . . . arm a mile from her torso . . . now we're talkin'. We'd walk down the street side by side by side. We'd live in a little cottage with a fireplace; just her and me and three little zig-zag babies . . .

MIDDLE MAN: Hello?

THE ZIG-ZAG WOMAN: Hello?

OLDER MAN: Hello?

YOUNG MAN: Not right now, I'm thinkin' about the Zig-Zag Woman.

OLDER MAN: What it takes to turn someone's head today.

(*The* OLDER MAN *opens his suitcase and retrieves the Twister: the Twister is a magician's trick where a person's head appears to twist fully around. He walks over to the* YOUNG MAN *and puts it on his head.*)

YOUNG MAN: Excuse me?

OLDER MAN: Excuse *me.*

(*The* OLDER MAN *then twists the* YOUNG MAN*'s head around, 360 degrees. The* OLDER MAN *realizes he's twisted it too far and moves the* YOUNG MAN*'s head around again to 180 degrees. Now the* YOUNG MAN *stares directly at* THE ZIG-ZAG WOMAN.)

THE ZIG-ZAG WOMAN: Hi.

YOUNG MAN: Hi. My God, you're coming apart.

THE ZIG-ZAG WOMAN: You're twisted.

(*The* YOUNG MAN *walks toward her—backward, of course.*)

MIDDLE MAN: My wife has no head. And you know what, she gets around just fine.

OLDER MAN: My wife could eat fire, and I loved her for it.

YOUNG MAN: Would you like to go to a movie?

THE ZIG-ZAG WOMAN: Yes, I would.

YOUNG MAN: How would we do that?

MIDDLE MAN: Here.

(*The* MIDDLE MAN *walks over to the* YOUNG MAN *and untwists his head, leaving the Twister box on him.*)

YOUNG MAN: Man, that was invigorating.

(*The* YOUNG MAN *takes the* WOMAN*'s zig-zagged hand and starts to push her off the stage, leaving the two other men alone.*)

YOUNG MAN: Want to get a snack first?

THE ZIG-ZAG WOMAN: (*As they exist.*) I could go for some pretzels.

OLDER MAN: In the beginning of something, its ending is fore-told.

MIDDLE MAN: How do you think they will end?

OLDER MAN: That's an easy one.

(*The* OLDER MAN *waves his hand over the candle; there is a small explosion of fire.*)

MIDDLE MAN: Well, good night.

(*The* MIDDLE MAN *exits. The* OLDER MAN *sits a minute, then brings the* MIDDLE MAN'*s chair over to his table. He adjusts it, so a second person could join him. He sits carefully back in his own chair, adjusts the second chair again, then hopefully looks offstage toward the door and waits. Slow fade to black.*)

END OF PLAY

THE WAY OF ALL FISH

Elaine May

The Way of All Fish is the first part of *Power Plays*, three one–act plays by Elaine May and Alan Arkin. It was originally produced in New York City by Julian Schlossberg, Meyer Ackerman, Ben Sprecher and William P. Miller, and the Manhattan Theatre Club, Lynne Meadow, artistic director; Barry Grove, executive producer; on April 14, 1998. The set design was by Michael McGarty; costume design was by Michael Krass; lighting design was by Adam Silverman; sound design was by Andrew Keister; the production stage manager was Andrew Neal. Alan Arkin directed the following cast at the Promenade Theatre:

MS. ASQUITH   Elaine May
MISS RIVERTON   Jeannie Berlin

An office, richly furnished: wood paneling, suede sofa, Persian rugs. MS. ASQUITH, *perfectly groomed and expensively dressed, sits behind an impressive desk.* MISS RIVERTON, *her secretary, much less expensively dressed, stands in front of her.*

MS. ASQUITH: Miss Riverton.

MISS RIVERTON: Yes?

MS. ASQUITH: Do you remember my distinctly telling you that I wanted nothing thrown out?

MISS RIVERTON: Yes.

MS. ASQUITH: Well, you've thrown out my exercise elastic.

MISS RIVERTON: Oh, I don't think so.

MS. ASQUITH: Well, here it is—in the wastebasket and I didn't put it there.

MISS RIVERTON: Oh, is *that* your . . . Oh, forgive me. I thought it was a piece of old rubber.

MS. ASQUITH: It doesn't *matter* what you thought it was. The point is—you threw it out.

259

MISS RIVERTON: Well, yes . . . because I thought it was rubbish.

MS. ASQUITH: Miss Riverton, I didn't ask you to use your best judgment. I didn't say, "Throw out what you think is rubbish and keep the rest." I said, "Don't throw anything out."

MISS RIVERTON: Well . . . but what about rubbish?

MS. ASQUITH: Rubbish is not your affair. I have a maid who deals with rubbish.

MISS RIVERTON: Yes, I see.

MS. ASQUITH: Your job is to see that my life runs smoothly and my appointments are kept. You are my secretary, not my housekeeper.

MISS RIVERTON: Assistant. Yes, of course.

MS. ASQUITH: You are not my assistant, Miss Riverton. You are my secretary.

MISS RIVERTON: All right.

MS. ASQUITH: I don't like to call something something else just because it's politically correct. A secretary is a perfectly fine thing to be.

MISS RIVERTON: But I do assist you.

MS. ASQUITH: Yes, you do. And so does a secretary.

MISS RIVERTON: But . . . isn't an assistant closer to what I do?

MS. ASQUITH: No, it isn't. It just uses the verb *assist* as a noun. You don't assist me in altering my clothes or cutting my hair or doing my nails. You assist me in the way a secretary does, a word that, you may be interested to know, originally meant *desk*.

MISS RIVERTON: Yes, I see.

MS. ASQUITH: Thank you. That will be all. (*She rises, goes out, comes back.*) Where am I going?

MISS RIVERTON: When?

MS. ASQUITH: Now.

MISS RIVERTON: Nowhere.

MS. ASQUITH: Nowhere? That's impossible. It's Friday night.

MISS RIVERTON: Yes, I know.

MS. ASQUITH: Well . . . how did this happen?

MISS RIVERTON: You had an engagement with Nelson Miles and then the Stradners invited you for a sail around East Hampton with Princess Agnelli and Ralph Lauren, so you canceled Mr. Miles. Then the Stradners canceled because of the weather and it was too late to get Mr. Miles back, so you placed a call to your son so you could invite him to dinner, but he told me he was going out of town with his father and stepmother on a long weekend to visit her parents' dairy farm. Then it was today.

MS. ASQUITH: You know. Miss Riverton, when you place a call for me, I would appreciate it if you didn't discuss the purpose of my call with the person I'm calling. You shouldn't have asked my son if he was free for dinner on Friday. I didn't ask you to do that.

MISS RIVERTON: Yes, but he said, "What does she want?"

MS. ASQUITH: It doesn't matter what he said. *You* should have said, "One moment and I'll put her on."

MISS RIVERTON: You were on another call.

MS. ASQUITH: It doesn't matter.

MISS RIVERTON: It's just that I thought you were busy.

MS. ASQUITH: I was busy. I am busy. I'm a busy woman. But it still doesn't matter. My son lives in a dorm. It takes time to get him on the phone. Time you save me by instituting . . . I'm not going to be made to feel guilty because I don't personally dial every member of my family.

MISS RIVERTON: I assure you I had no intention of making you feel guilty.

MS. ASQUITH: Well, I *am* guilty. So it doesn't take much.

MISS RIVERTON: I'm sorry. It's just . . .

(MISS RIVERTON *breaks off.*)

MS. ASQUITH: What?

MISS RIVERTON: Nothing, really. It's not important.

MS. ASQUITH: Miss Riverton, please finish your sentence. It drives me crazy when you do that. What? I want to know. What? (MISS RIVERTON *shakes her head.*) Oh, *don't* make me go through this. WHAT?

MISS RIVERTON: Well, it's just that your son . . . has said . . . a few times he's said . . . that . . . he's said that it's rude to call some-

one and then make them wait while you—not you, anyone—
come to the phone. It's like knocking at the door and then
leaving a sign saying, "Back in a minute—stay right there."

MS. ASQUITH: (*After a moment.*) He's right.

MISS RIVERTON: He says no matter how fast someone gets
there . . .

MS. ASQUITH: No, no, no, he's right, he's absolutely right. I *do* do
that. All the time. No wonder I'm guilty. Of course, it would
just cut my day in half if I dialed all those numbers and then
had to wait for a secretary to answer and tell me whether or
not someone could come to the phone . . . and half the time
they couldn't . . . and then I had to leave a message that I
called . . .

MISS RIVERTON: Perhaps if you just did it with family and close
friends . . .

MS. ASQUITH: Yes. That's a good idea. Remind me to do that.
Did he ask to talk to me? My son?

MISS RIVERTON: No. He said he knew you were busy.

MS. ASQUITH: (*Sighs.*) What a lousy week.

MISS RIVERTON: It *has* been complicated.

MS. ASQUITH: Awful. The worst. First the root canal and then
this hideous haircut and then I got on the scale this morning
and I'd gained three pounds—because I couldn't find my
exercise elastic and I was just too irritated to work out. Thank
God the mammogram turned out all right. I have to keep
things in perspective.

MISS RIVERTON: I'm sorry about the elastic.

MS. ASQUITH: Well . . . these things happen.

MISS RIVERTON: Tomorrow night is Lincoln Center. You've been looking forward to that.

MS. ASQUITH: Tomorrow night is twenty-four hours away. (*After a moment.*) What are *you* doing tonight, Miss Riverton?

MISS RIVERTON: Me? Nothing.

MS. ASQUITH: Well . . . would you care to come home with me and have dinner?

MISS RIVERTON: Thank you, but . . . the cook and maid are off tonight.

MS. ASQUITH: WHAT!

MISS RIVERTON: You told me . . .

MS. ASQUITH: Oh, *no*!

MISS RIVERTON: . . . they wouldn't be needed because of the Stradner dinner party . . .

MS. ASQUITH: But the Stradners canceled.

MISS RIVERTON: Yes, but they didn't cancel until Thursday night and I didn't get the message until this morning and by then the cook and the maid were gone.

MS. ASQUITH: Oh, shit! It's just the fucking end of the world.

MISS RIVERTON: I'm sorry.

MS. ASQUITH: Don't be silly. How could you know the Stradners would cancel.

MISS RIVERTON: I was thinking about the exercise elastic. It's so awful to gain weight.

MS. ASQUITH: Forget the exercise elastic. The exercise elastic is past. The exercise elastic is just something to sustain me between sessions. The important thing is—what are we going to eat. (*Looks at her watch.*) It's too late to get into a really decent restaurant. Even for me. Oh, *God*. Can we order in?

MISS RIVERTON: Yes. What would you like.

MS. ASQUITH: I don't know. Pasta? Fish?

MISS RIVERTON: Perhaps Japanese. You like Japanese.

MS. ASQUITH: Yes. Japanese would be good. Order Japanese (*As* MISS RIVERTON *picks up the phone and dials.*) Order something I like. But nothing raw.

MISS RIVERTON: Nothing raw.

MS. ASQUITH: I'm afraid of parasites.

MISS RIVERTON: Well, would you like . . .

MS. ASQUITH: Don't ask me what I'd like. I'm no good at that. You pick it.

MISS RIVERTON: (*Into phone.*) Yes, I'd like to place an order—322 Madison Avenue . . .

MS. ASQUITH: Order shumai . . .

MISS RIVERTON: . . . The penthouse . . .

MS. ASQUITH: Ask if they have soft-shell crab.

MISS RIVERTON: . . . Asquith Enterprises. Do you have soft-shell crab? . . .

MS. ASQUITH: Roll. Hand roll.

MISS RIVERTON: One soft-shell crab roll hand roll. One shumai.

MISS RIVERTON:	MS. ASQUITH:
. . . one California roll . . . two shumai . . . one Manhattan roll— *three* shumai . . . and three soft-shell crab roll . . . No, that's two beside the last one. Three all together. Two shrimp teriyaki. Another California roll and extra brown rice and saki.	Maybe two shumai— but they're small . . . three shumai . . . and three soft-shell crab rolls . . . and shrimp teriyaki. . . . Did you tell him shrimp teriyaki? And maybe two California rolls . . . no—yes—two. And rice, extra rice, brown rice and saki. Plenty of saki.

(MISS RIVERTON *hangs up.*)

MS. ASQUITH: Perfect. Oh, yum. Get some plates and we'll set the desk . . . (*Calling, as Miss Riverton runs off.*) . . . and I opened two excellent bottles of wine for lunch before that barbarian, Charles, said no alcohol—what assholes accountants are. Now . . . Let's see—where's the wine . . . the wine . . . Ah! Here it is. And two glasses.

(MISS RIVERTON *comes back in carrying plates, napkins, and silverware and heads for the desk.* MS. ASQUITH *continues as she pours the wine.*)

MS. ASQUITH: Oh, this is going to be such fun. Just like a picnic. Perhaps we should set the coffee table instead of the desk. More picnic-y.

(MISS RIVERTON *stops and heads for the coffee table.*)

MS. ASQUITH: But it's low.

(MISS RIVERTON *stops again.*)

MS. ASQUITH: Maybe the desk *is* better.

(MISS RIVERTON *heads back for the desk.*)

MS. ASQUITH: Oh, what if it *is* low. We'll sit on the floor. Here.

(MISS RIVERTON *heads back to the coffee table.*)

MS. ASQUITH: (*Holding out a glass.*) Just put the plates down anywhere and try some of this.

MISS RIVERTON: (*Setting the plates on a chair.*) Yes, Miss Asquith.

MS. ASQUITH: Perhaps you should call me Margaret for tonight.
Well . . . perhaps not. (*Holds out a glass.*) Well, what shall we
drink to?

MISS RIVERTON: To your having a wonderful time at Lincoln
Center tomorrow night.

MS. ASQUITH: Lovely.

(*They clink glasses and sip.*)

MISS RIVERTON: Oh, this *is* good.

MS. ASQUITH: Isn't it? I'm glad you appreciate it. So many people have no understanding of wine.

MISS RIVERTON: I know. Long ago I made a pact with myself never to drink wine unless it was very, very good. This is excellent.

MS. ASQUITH: Really. That's fascinating. How did you develop such an interest in wine?

MISS RIVERTON: My father was French.

MS. ASQUITH: Ah. Enough said.

MISS RIVERTON: Oh, this is *very* good.

MS. ASQUITH: Hmm. *So* good. Such clarity.

MISS RIVERTON: And subtlety. The wine presents itself but not boldly. Delicately, innocently.

MS. ASQUITH: Well put. Very well put. (*Pouring more wine.*) I guess I'll be having a few additional sessions with my trainer next week.

MISS RIVERTON: May I suggest . . .

(*She breaks off.*)

MS. ASQUITH: Yes? Oh, please. Please finish your sentence. It just drives me up the wall when you do that. This is a social evening. All the rules are changed. You just say whatever comes into your mind.

MISS RIVERTON: Well, all I was going to say is—I wonder if your trainer does quite enough aerobic work with you.

MS. ASQUITH: You think I'm fat?

MISS RIVERTON: No, no. I'm just talking ... healthwise, weight control-wise.

MS. ASQUITH: He does half an hour.

MISS RIVERTON: Well ... sometimes not a full half hour. And is a half hour on the trampoline enough?

MS. ASQUITH: You don't approve of the trampoline?

MISS RIVERTON: Oh, I do. It's just that so much of the movement is momentum. Fast walking or jogging is much more effective.

MS. ASQUITH: How do you know so much about this?

MISS RIVERTON: I'm very interested in the body.

MS. ASQUITH: You're in wonderful shape.

MISS RIVERTON: Thank you. I'm very strong for a woman.

MS. ASQUITH: You look very strong.

MISS RIVERTON: Too strong?

MS. ASQUITH: Don't be silly. You can't look too strong. The appearance of strength is the appearance of power. Do you know the real difference between men and women, Miss Riverton? (MISS RIVERTON *shakes her head.*) Strength. Sheer physical strength. Do you know that there are male fish that actually change sex when a bigger fish comes along because only the biggest fish can be male. All the rest of the fish are his harem.

MISS RIVERTON: You're joking.

MS. ASQUITH: Absolutely not. And these fish have it down to such a science they don't even have to fight—they just measure. The fish that seems most likely to inflict injury wins.

MISS RIVERTON: Well, it's . . . it's certainly . . . certainly a man's world if you're a fish, isn't it?

MS. ASQUITH: That's not my point, Miss Riverton. My point is that it's not whether you're a man or a woman that determines who's world it is, it's how strong you are that determines whether you're a man or a woman. Metaphorically, of course.

MISS RIVERTON: Of course. I see. Well . . . I'm very strong.

MS. ASQUITH: Yes, I've seen you carry those file boxes. (*Pours more wine.*) You know, Miss Riverton—Jane—you're the best secretary I've ever had. I can't tell you the idiots I had to put up with until you came along. I don't think I could get along without you, Jane.

MISS RIVERTON: Joan. Well . . . thank you. I try to do my job.

MS. ASQUITH: Joan? Oh, what a fool I am.

MISS RIVERTON: No, no, no.

MS. ASQUITH: This is so embarrassing.

MISS RIVERTON: Not at all.

MS. ASQUITH: To have had you as my secretary for so long and not know your first name.

MISS RIVERTON: Well, you don't call me by my first name. And you were very close. Jane . . . Joan.

MS. ASQUITH: I'll bet you know my first name.

MISS RIVERTON: Well, yes. But I make out all your checks and handle your mail.

MS. ASQUITH: There's that. But no—that's the easy way out. I don't know your first name because I don't notice anything. That's a terrible failing of mine. I don't really notice people unless they're directly in my line of vision, part of what I'm focusing on. That was one of the reasons for my divorce. One day I handed my husband an envelope and said, "Mail this for me." And he said, "Can't your secretary mail it?" and I said, "Oh, I'm sorry, darling. I didn't realize I was talking to you."

MISS RIVERTON: That doesn't seem so awful . . . I mean, awful enough for a divorce.

MS. ASQUITH: Well—it wasn't just that . . . that discussion. It turned out he'd been very miserable for a very long time. But of course I didn't notice. I'm very insensitive. And everyone has to forgive me. Until they don't.

MISS RIVERTON: I think you're wonderful.

MS. ASQUITH: Well . . . thank you, Joan. But it's a shortcoming— being blind to others. Power in a relationship belongs to whoever wants to leave first—and you can't anticipate that unless you notice the other person. The irony is that I wondered for years if I didn't make a mistake marrying him, if I couldn't have done better, if it wasn't a waste of my time—all those vacations, and dinners, and preludes to sex. And the minute he said he wanted a divorce I realized that I loved him madly. Madly. And it was too late.

(*There is a brief pause.*)

MISS RIVERTON: Shall I get the other bottle of wine?

MS. ASQUITH: Yes. Thank you. (*Watching* MISS RIVERTON *rise.*) You know, Joan, I'm having just a wonderful time. I'm *glad* the Stradners canceled.

MISS RIVERTON: This is very pleasant.

MS. ASQUITH: So you're from France.

MISS RIVERTON: No. I'm from Michigan. My father was from France.

MS. ASQUITH: Michigan! I've heard so much about Michigan. We always went to Italy or the South of France. But I wish we'd gone to Michigan. It sounds lovely.

MISS RIVERTON: And I wish we'd gone to the South of France. Life is funny.

MS. ASQUITH: Very.

(MISS RIVERTON *pulls the cork out of the second wine bottle with a pop.*)

MISS RIVERTON: Good sound. That's very important. My father taught me that. He was a room service waiter in Cannes. He started the same year as the film festival.

MS. ASQUITH: How interesting.

MISS RIVERTON: It was all before I was born, of course.

MS. ASQUITH: Of course. That's when everything interesting happens.

MISS RIVERTON: But seeing the South of France and Italy . . . that must have been interesting . . .

MS. ASQUITH: It wasn't. Not to me. I'll tell you a secret that no one else knows. I was a fat child.

MISS RIVERTON: No!

MS. ASQUITH: And a fat teenager. I went to school in Switzerland and Swiss food is just butter looking for a reason. By the time I was thirteen I was so fat they called me *petite vache yanquee.*

MISS RIVERTON: *Petite vache yanquee?*

MS. ASQUITH: "Little Yankee cow." Switzerland can be very cruel.

MISS RIVERTON: Oh, Miss Asquith, underneath everything I think you're a very vulnerable woman.

MS. ASQUITH: Well, I'm not. I can't tell you how much I hate that word. I have no idea why everyone thinks it's so special to be vulnerable. It's a self-pitying, time-consuming preoccupation and everyone has it. Hitler was vulnerable. He sobbed on Mother's Day. What does that tell you?

MISS RIVERTON: I didn't know that about Hitler. Well, that changes things. I always thought he was just this awful man.

(MS. ASQUITH *stares at her . . . then laughs.*)

MS. ASQUITH: Very good. I must remember that. (*Slugging back her wine.*) So tell me more about Michigan.

MISS RIVERTON: Well, there's not a whole lot more to tell. It was very cold. In the winter. And then in the summer it got hot. Not a good climate.

MS. ASQUITH: No. (*She pours more wine.*) So you came to New York.

MISS RIVERTON: Yes. That's right.

MS. ASQUITH: Wonderful story. Well, I can tell you I'm hungry.

MISS RIVERTON: It's a pretty boring story.

MS. ASQUITH: No, no. Not at all.

MISS RIVERTON: I've had a pretty boring life.

MS. ASQUITH: Nonsense. With a father who worked in Cannes and traveling from Michigan to New York . . .

MISS RIVERTON: When I was young I so wanted to be someone special.

MS. ASQUITH: Well, you are someone special.

MISS RIVERTON: I mean, you know, someone special, who everyone knows is special. I guess what I'm saying is I wanted to be famous.

MS. ASQUITH: Ah, well.

MISS RIVERTON: Because being famous is . . . like being immortal, isn't it?

MS. ASQUITH: Well—only if you're very famous for a very long time.

MISS RIVERTON: But you can be. Anyone can be. And I know how. You know how? You can kill someone famous. Of course, it has to be someone *really* famous and people have to be convinced that you're not part of a conspiracy. And meeting someone famous isn't so easy. When I was younger that's all I thought about—who can I kill who's famous and how can I meet him. Probably I should have been thinking how can I meet who's famous and how can I kill him—but I was just a kid. (*She pours some wine.*) I thought of killing the president, but everyone who tries to kill the president is such a slug. I mean, I made a list of successful presidential assassins who still had some kind of stature, and you know who there is. Booth. Because he killed Lincoln. And where are you going to find another Lincoln? And—I don't know—it just seems like such a failure of imagination to go right to the president: kill someone famous—kill the president. Duh. Of course, Jack the Ripper is still famous and he just killed a lot of totally unknown prostitutes. But that may be because no one knows who he really is. And Charlie Manson is still famous and he just killed a starlet and some hairdressers. But who knows if he'll stand the test of time. I mean, you can easily kill someone and just be overlooked—unless you kill a lot of people, or kill a few people but in a really ghastly way—but it would have to be so ghastly.

MS. ASQUITH: You . . . you've given this a lot of thought.

MISS RIVERTON: I have. I mean, if there was another way—but I *can't* write a novel, I *can't* become a movie star, I can't invent a vaccine because I have no talent. Not that talent is any guarantee of fame, but with talent I'd have had a shot at it, an honest shot. And I'd have taken it. I didn't want an easy way out. I didn't *want* to resort to murder. But fame is fame. The important thing to me is not to . . . just pass through. To leave a mark. To change the world. To have people's consciousness enlarged to include me. And it wasn't for material gain, I didn't want to get rich. I wasn't going to live well from my crime. If I got caught I'd probably be electrocuted. So in a way, I would have been sacrificing my life for immortality— just like an artist or a scientist does. I would have been driven to kill not for the reward, but because there was nothing else I could do to fulfill myself—the same reason an artist creates.

My curse has always been that I'm a special person with no special ability.

MS. ASQUITH: Yes. That . . . is a problem.

MISS RIVERTON: And then, as the years passed, I realized how hard it is to meet someone famous and I thought maybe if I just killed someone rich and important or socially prominent. But by then I knew I was compromising. I was just after fame, not lasting fame. I told myself some fame is better than no fame (*Shrugs, sighs.*), and I was probably right.

MS. ASQUITH: Well . . . not . . . not necessarily. Lasting fame is . . . is by far . . . but why all this talk about fame. There's . . . there's so much more. To life. Than fame. There's . . . self-esteem, how well you've done with what you've had . . . love. Love is important.

MISS RIVERTON: That's just what Oprah said.

MS. ASQUITH: Did she? Well, she's a very wise woman in many ways.

MISS RIVERTON: She's very famous.

MS. ASQUITH: Yes, indeed.

MISS RIVERTON: She'd be a good one to kill.

MS. ASQUITH: Excellent. Yes. You'd want someone that famous.

MISS RIVERTON: Sometimes that backfires.

MS. ASQUITH: Hardly ever.

MISS RIVERTON: Oh, yes. The celebrity of the victim is so great it overshadows the assassin. That was the real triumph of

Charles Manson. He killed people who were just rich and famous enough. That, of course, was what I didn't realize when I was a kid. I aimed too high.

MS. ASQUITH: You know, Joan—may I call you Joan?—

MISS RIVERTON: Of course, Miss Asquith.

MS. ASQUITH: Margaret, please. You know, Joan, things don't always work out as happily as they did for Charlie Manson. Sometimes there's a terrible murder and it's fun for a while and then people forget, or there's another, worse murder and they're distracted. And meanwhile, the poor murderer is imprisoned or electrocuted with no real reward for his crime. What was so important to him—or her—has been forgotten by everyone else. How far away is this restaurant you ordered from? Tokyo? Just joking. But it has been a long time since you ordered.

MISS RIVERTON: I've made you nervous, haven't I?

MS. ASQUITH: What? Not at all.

MISS RIVERTON: Yes, I have. I've ruined everything. We were having such a nice time, one of the nicest times I've ever had and I ruined it.

MS. ASQUITH: Nonsense. You've ruined nothing. Talking about murder is . . . just a little . . . always a little . . . edgy . . . but it's been such a long day . . . and I'm sure we're both . . . Would you like some music? Why don't I put on some music? (*She rises.*) That's interesting. I can't move my legs. I have no feeling from the waist down. Something very strange is happening to me . . .

MISS RIVERTON: Miss Asquith . . .

MS. ASQUITH: . . . It's as though somebody has put something in my food or drink . . .

MISS RIVERTON: Miss Asquith! You've had half a bottle of wine on an empty stomach. And I've had the other half. We're both going to feel strange.

MS. ASQUITH: Oh, yes. I forgot about the wine. How quickly the brain cells die. Now let's see—the music. (*She staggers over to the remote, presses it, and "Night on Bald Mountain" blares out.*) Wrong music. (*She presses the button again. "Death and Transfiguration" comes on, then a Philip Glass piece.*) Don't I have one fucking song in this whole stupid collection?

MISS RIVERTON: You asked me to get classical. You said it would serve the clients better.

MS. ASQUITH: Oh, of course. I was just talking to myself.

MISS RIVERTON: Oh, Miss Asquith, I think I should go. I've really upset you. Your hands are shaking.

MS. ASQUITH: Well, I haven't eaten and it's late . . . so you might want to go . . . because it's late. But you certainly shouldn't go because you think you've upset me.

MISS RIVERTON: You know, this was just a hypothetical discussion. It's not like I would really kill someone. I'm not like some madman who gets fired from the post office and shoots everyone for revenge. I have no reason to do anything bad to anyone.

MS. ASQUITH: That's right. And you never will.

MISS RIVERTON: I'm just this little secretary who makes thirty thousand a year and that's all I'll ever be. Because that's all I'm worth. I've accepted that.

MS. ASQUITH: No! Joan! What are you talking about. You're worth . . . everything.

MISS RIVERTON: But you're only paying me thirty thousand and I don't think you'd pay me less than I'm worth.

MS. ASQUITH: I . . . I . . . would . . . pay you more . . . if I could . . .

MISS RIVERTON: But why should you? I make so many mistakes . . .

MS. ASQUITH: Well, now, Joan, that's true, isn't it?—a little true. You do make mistakes. So I tell you what—when you stop making so *many* mistakes—I'm going to give you a very nice raise.

MISS RIVERTON: Oh, Miss Asquith . . . do you think . . . maybe someday I can become an assistant?

MS. ASQUITH: Yes! Well! How about today?

MISS RIVERTON: Do you mean it?

MS. ASQUITH: Absolutely. I'm not going to pay a mere secretary more than thirty thousand a year—and that's what you'll be getting when I give you your raise—more than thirty thousand a year.

MISS RIVERTON: How much more?

MS. ASQUITH: We'll see.

MISS RIVERTON: Some secretaries make a hundred thousand a year.

MS. ASQUITH: Very, very few.

MISS RIVERTON: I . . . I wish I could be sure you're not doing this because . . . in some way . . . I made you nervous. I would feel so awful if you were just being nice to me as . . . a kind of . . . out of fear.

MS. ASQUITH: Don't be ridiculous. Do I seem to you to be the kind of person who would be intimidated into giving an employee a raise? And why would you make me nervous? Because when you were younger you wanted to kill someone famous? Hey! Who hasn't wanted to . . . pick up a gun and shoot a few famous people . . . at one time or another . . .

MISS RIVERTON: Actually, I was only going to shoot a man. If it was a woman I was going to stab her or strangle her. Weaker victim, lighter weapon.

MS. ASQUITH: So many rules. And so fair.

MISS RIVERTON: Oh, yes. Of course it's risky to be fair. If you try to stab or strangle a woman and her strength is too close to yours she can inflict so much injury you won't get the knife in. That's one of the reasons I got so strong.

(*The phone rings.* MISS ASQUITH *leaps up.*)

MS. ASQUITH: I'll get it. (*Snatching up the phone.*) Hello? . . . Hi, Charles. How are you. Where are you? . . . Martha's Vineyard? What fun. . . . Miss Riverton and I are just finishing the wine you wouldn't let me drink this afternoon. We're having dinner together. In the office. Just the two of us.

(*There is the sound of a buzzer.*)

MISS RIVERTON: That'll be the food.

MS. ASQUITH: (*Into phone.*) And the deliveryman is here and Miss Riverton is just going out to get our food now. She's walking out of the room . . . she's . . . (As MISS RIVERTON *exits* MS. ASQUITH *whips up the remote and turns the music on again; then speaks softly under it.*) Charles! Miss Riverton is psychotic. She just told me she wants to kill someone famous—but now she just wants to kill someone important to be famous—she's just terrifying. . . . No, no, no, I can't fire her. She's talking about the post office. I'd have to spend the rest of my life with a bodyguard. . . . I want you to give her a raise. Give her a raise! She's playing some kind of Machiavellian game with me, some kind of brilliant cat and mouse game, but I think I'm safe if I just do whatever she says . . .

(*She breaks off as* MISS RIVERTON *enters with the food.*)

MS. ASQUITH: I have to hang up now, Charles. Miss Riverton is back and I don't want to keep her waiting.

(MISS ASQUITH *hangs up and clicks off the stereo.* MISS RIVERTON *begins unloading the food.*)

MISS RIVERTON: We have everything! Everything we could ever want.

MS. ASQUITH: It smells very good.

MISS RIVERTON: This is so nice, isn't it? I mean, this means so much to me. Well, I don't want to embarrass you.

MS. ASQUITH: (*Studying her.*) No.

MISS RIVERTON: Here's to a whole new . . . what?

MS. ASQUITH: You name it.

MISS RIVERTON: Oh, I'm so bad with words.

MS. ASQUITH: I think you're pretty good.

MISS RIVERTON: Well, thank you. (*She looks up.*) You're looking at me . . . so . . . so hard.

MS. ASQUITH: Well, you're in my line of vision.

MISS RIVERTON: Ballgame! Is that a good word?

MS. ASQUITH: Excellent. That's an excellent word. And now that you're in my line of vision . . . I begin to see . . . how very clever you are.

MISS RIVERTON: Careful—or I'll ask for that raise now.

MS. ASQUITH: How very, very clever. Miss Riverton, you're fascinating. This is fascinating. This is almost relaxing.

MISS RIVERTON: Is it?

MS. ASQUITH: Oh, yes. Because there's nothing I can do, is there?

MISS RIVERTON: I think . . . I'm not following you too well.

MS. ASQUITH: I mean once someone wants something more than life—they win. There's nothing you can threaten them with.

MISS RIVERTON: Like the Arabs who blow themselves up so they can go straight to paradise.

MS. ASQUITH: Yes. See? You are following me, after all. We all have our version of paradise, Miss Riverton. Yours is fame. And mine is to live. I'll do anything to live. So I lose.

MISS RIVERTON: Maybe you should eat something before you drink the saki.

MS. ASQUITH: I wonder if this is what Dostoyevsky meant when he wrote about the voluptuousness of surrender. Have you ever read Dostoyevsky's journals, Miss Riverton?

MISS RIVERTON: Who's Dostoyevsky? Stalin?

(*There is a stunned pause.*)

MS. ASQUITH: What?

MISS RIVERTON: Is Dostoyevsky Stalin?

MS. ASQUITH: No. He's Dostoyevsky.

MISS RIVERTON: Oh, I just thought . . . you were talking about Hitler before. So I thought . . . maybe Dostoyevsky is Stalin.

MS. ASQUITH: Then who would Stalin be?

MISS RIVERTON: I don't know. I thought maybe that was his real name—Stalin's. Like Tito was only a nickname for . . . whoever Tito was. So I thought maybe Stalin was a nickname for Dostoyevsky.

MS. ASQUITH: No.

MISS RIVERTON: Well . . . I didn't know. I don't think that's such a big mistake—not knowing who Dostoyevsky is. I know who Stalin is—and he's the famous one.

MS. ASQUITH: Miss Riverton, I don't think I can submit to you if you go on with this.

MISS RIVERTON: What do you mean?

MS. ASQUITH: I mean, I can't play cat and mouse with a bimbo.

MISS RIVERTON: Please don't call me a bimbo, Miss Asquith. That really upsets me.

MS. ASQUITH: Well, what else can I call you when you suddenly sound like every chauffeur I've ever been to bed with. It just makes me wonder if you're really as crazy as you pretend to be. Or as strong.

MISS RIVERTON: I don't know what you're talking about.

MS. ASQUITH: I'm talking about your strength, Miss Riverton, this strength with which you're going to strangle or stab a woman. And I'm wondering if the idea of presenting yourself as strong didn't come from my saying that the appearance of strength is power. And then . . . just building from there . . .

MISS RIVERTON: I'm not presenting myself as anything. (*Rising.*) I'm not a bimbo. And I'm very strong.

MS. ASQUITH: As strong as I am?

MISS RIVERTON: As strong as you are? (*She laughs.*) Oh, I think so!

MS. ASQUITH: But you also think Dostoyevsky is Stalin, so your opinions aren't as informed as they might be.

MISS RIVERTON: You saw me carry the file boxes.

MS. ASQUITH: No, I didn't.

MISS RIVERTON: You said you did.

MS. ASQUITH: I lied.

MISS RIVERTON: Well . . . I carried them.

MS. ASQUITH: Really? So did I.

MISS RIVERTON: You carried file boxes?

MS. ASQUITH: Yes.

MISS RIVERTON: How many.

MS. ASQUITH: How many did you carry?

MISS RIVERTON: When?

MS. ASQUITH: Any time. The time you carried the most.

MISS RIVERTON: Six.

MS. ASQUITH: So did I.

MISS RIVERTON: You carried six file boxes?

MS. ASQUITH: Absolutely.

(MISS RIVERTON *studies her for several moments . . . then drops to the floor.*)

MISS RIVERTON: Can you do this?

(MISS RIVERTON *does several marine push-ups.*)

MS. ASQUITH: Yes.

MISS RIVERTON: Let's see.

MS. ASQUITH: Take my word for it.

MISS RIVERTON: You can't, can you? I'll bet you don't have the strength to do even one.

MS. ASQUITH: Sheer physical strength isn't that necessary, Miss Riverton. Will counts, too.

MISS RIVERTON: No, it doesn't. Because a strong person can make a weak person do something *against* his will. He can destroy a weak person's will by using physical force. And then the weak person is always in his power.

MS. ASQUITH: Isn't that just a wee bit dramatic for what is, essentially, a push-up contest?

MISS RIVERTON: Get down on the ground and try a push-up, Miss Asquith. I challenge you.

MS. ASQUITH: I don't accept challenges. It would mean I have something to prove.

MISS RIVERTON: You'll accept this one. It's time for us to measure. (*Taking a step toward her.*) I'm afraid I have to insist.

(MISS RIVERTON *takes another step.*)

MS. ASQUITH: (*Quickly.*) Well, if it's that important to you . . .

(MISS ASQUITH *gets slowly down, brushes away some dust on the rug, sits back up.*)

MISS RIVERTON: See? You can't do it. But don't give up trying. Keep using that will of yours. You see? . . . (*She picks up the exercise rubber.*) This is trash. I put it right where it belongs. In the trash basket. It doesn't do anything. It doesn't make you strong. It's just a toy that gives you the illusion of strength—a personal trainer's silly invention for silly rich women. You know what makes you strong? Carrying file boxes, climbing three flights of stairs to a walk-up so you can afford to live in Manhattan, lugging groceries, walking miles to save money on subways, doing your own housework, wheeling your mother around when you visit her because you can't afford a nurse, painting your own ceiling, fixing your own pipes because the plumber costs so much. Hard, terrible labor—that's what makes you strong. And it's insane to think that God would create a world so lopsided that a multimillionaire who hires a trainer to get her little hour of physical labor would be as strong as someone who actually . . .

(MISS RIVERTON *breaks off as* MS. ASQUITH *suddenly rises up in a marine push-up . . . and then another . . . and then another . . . and then another.*)

MS. ASQUITH: You're right! It's not will. But it *is* that personal trainer. And I've been skipping sessions. (*Exultantly.*) It would be very hard to get that knife in me, Miss Riverton, I'd inflict a lot of damage—if you were looking for a victim, I mean. You'd have to stab me in the back and break your rules—and I know you wouldn't do that. You see, Jane, I'm afraid God *did* create a lopsided world. In that way he's very much like Tito. (MISS RIVERTON *turns away.*) Well now, don't cry. That's no way to end a contest. Don't cry. It's not so bad. Although that walk-up doesn't sound wonderful. But look at those leg muscles. Oh, that food smells so good. (*She sits down and pats the sofa;* MISS RIVERTON *rises obediently and sits down beside her.*) Think of it this way. Everything's just the same as it was this morning. And you weren't crying then. Now let's have our picnic, shall we? It's getting late. And get my exercise elastic out of the trash.

MISS RIVERTON: You're not going to fire me?

MS. ASQUITH: Never. You're going to be the reason I stay in shape.

END OF PLAY

THERE SHALL BE NO BOTTOM

(A BAD PLAY FOR WORSE ACTORS)

Mark O'Donnell

There Shall Be No Bottom was presented at Playwrights Horizons on November 14, 2005, directed by the author, with the following cast:

JEFF   John Bedford Lloyd
JOE   Christopher Evan Welch
JANE   Mia Barron
JED   Nat DeWolf

(*We hear eight bars of Handel's* Water Music *or any baroque brass voluntary to indicate classy theatre is afoot. Lights come up on* JEFF, *the actor who is playing the indolent, slightly overaged young heir in this drawing room drama. He sits reading an upside-down newspaper, fitfully stealing glances off, since he expects another actor to enter.* JEFF's *main problem, we shall see in time, is a moronic tendency to misdeliver his lines, changing their meaning. He wears a secondhand smoking jacket.* JOE, *the actor who plays the Sherlock Holmes–like inspector, appears, looking menacing, he hopes. He is a smooth, ominous hero/villain, but his main problem as an actor is a tendency to skip large portions of the script. He presses an imaginary or prop doorbell several times, to no effect.*)

JOE: (*Hissing stage whisper.*) Sound cue!

(*Finally he covers the error awkwardly.*)

    Ahem . . . bing-bong!

(JEFF *jumps up promptly. He overdoes the jaunty cad act.*)

JEFF: Ah! The doorbell! That will be all, Wickersham. Inspector Billingsgate! At last you're here!

JOE: (*Crisp, formal, mysterious.*) I'm here, that is true.

JEFF: (*Sunny as only the guilty can be.*) Yers, quite here! I think it's topping of you to come to our lovely summer home, which I shall inherit in the fullness of time.

JOE: (*Doesn't give an inch.*) Do you? (*Pause.*) Where is your only sister, Fanny?

JEFF: In the garden, I expect—though I'm so indolent and destined for a bad end, I scarcely keep track of details! Do come, in? (*This last line has been oddly delivered.* JOE *eyes him hatefully, but goes to center stage.*)

JOE: Than . . . (*He crosses, sits, and elaborately crosses his legs.*) . . . Kyou.

JEFF: (*Whose back has been turned briefly.*) Have a sea . . . (*He turns, sees his error, and corrects it hastily.*) I see you're sitting, Inspector. How elegant. A drink, perhaps, or two? At once? Ha-ha?

(*Pause.*)

JOE: (*Coolly.*) You're nervous, Fenton. (*Pause. Now he makes his first attack.*) Do the words *millizend aspimoza* mean anything to you?

JEFF: (*Panicked; they clearly do have meaning.*) No! No! Why should they?

(*Pause.*)

JOE: I was just testing you. They're nonsense words, you're quite right.

(JEFF, *as Fenton, nervously leans on the fireplace mantel, imaginary or not. In any case it seems awkwardly high.* JEFF's *arms are at head level, so his attempted insouciance seems strained.*)

JEFF: (*In pain.*) Would you care for a cigarette? Or two at once, ha-ha? They're here on the mantel in this silver box . . .

(JOE *as Billingsgate regards* JEFF *contemptuously.*)

JOE: You make me laugh, Fenton.

JEFF: No, you make *me* laugh, Inspector!

(*There follows a brief hot uncomfortable, slightly crazed "laughing" contest.*)

BOTH: Ha-ha, ha-ha-ha, ha-ha-ha-ha—

(*It ends abruptly.*)

JOE: How little you've changed since your boyhood!

JEFF: Time is a bitter artist, Inspector. Cigarette?

JOE: (*Glowering.*) I've already said no.

JEFF: No you haven't.

JOE: (*Overlooking this.*) Have you ever known a man named Cinnamon Boris?

JEFF: (*Suavely.*) Certainly not. I've never even been to that part of town.

JOE: (*Relentless.*) But you know him well enough to borrow money of him!

JEFF: (*Confused.*) Of him?

JOE: (*Annoyed but accommodating.*) From him!

JEFF: Ahh!

(*He adopts an attitude of well-bred boredom, but then misdelivers his line like an "Is so!" school yard taunt.*)

Really, Inspector! . . . This IS SO fatiguing!

(*Beat. He realizes this didn't sound right, and corrects this delivery.*)

This is SO fatiguing!

JOE: You're complacence itself, aren't you? Even if the Bluebottle fortune hangs in the balance?

(JEFF *misinterprets the word* afraid *in the following line by trembling and speaking with cartoonish fearfulness.*)

JEFF: I'm afraid! . . . (*Now lackadaisical again.*) . . . I can't help you, Inspector. I think you're mistaken in your suspicion.

JOE: Do you?

JEFF: (*Breezily, automatically.*) Yes, I do. I so very do!

(*That isn't the next line, so* JOE *pointedly cues him again.*)

JOE: That's not right. So you do, do you?

(JEFF *regards him blankly. He's forgotten where they are in the script, and this throws both of them.*)

JEFF: Do I?

JOE: Do you? (*Aside.*) What's the next line? (*He covers ineptly and in a panic.*) Answer me, do you?

JEFF: (*Unhappily, also panicking.*) Yes, I do!

JOE: (*Still stuck, agonized, helpless.*) Do you?

JEFF: (*Tears and anger about to surface.*) As I've said, yes!

JOE: (*Trying to stall, a shambles.*) Do you?

JEFF: (*Resentful and near hysteria.*) Yes I do, if you want to know the truth!

JOE: (*In a tiny, miserable voice.*) Do you?

JEFF: (*Desperately takes over.*) But what's this you were about to tell me, Inspector, about my sister being in grave danger?

JOE: (*Relieved, hectic.*) Oh, that's right, thanks! (*Now, as* BILLINGS-GATE.) She is! That's right! Grave danger!

(JEFF *recoils at the news he himself has just revealed, and considering the next line, ill-advisedly puts his hands on his hips.*)

JEFF: Danger? My Fanny in danger? (*He takes one step back.*) I am taken aback! (*He turns and calls offstage.*) Fanny, enter right, quickly! (*Now he turns his hate on the Inspector, but the actor again mispronounces his line.*) You dog! You cure!

(FANNY *enters, an ingenuous bauble of a girl, played by a smart if also overaged actress named* JANE.)

JANE: Fenton, I've been dressing for simply hours! Kendall will be here at any moment! We're going to the Sophomore Ambassador's ball! Tell me, do you think the Count likes pearls on women?

JEFF: (*Frisks her from head to toe.*) Fanny, you're in no danger!

(*He turns on the Inspector angrily, in a comically overdone pivot.*)

You lied to me! And you didn't tell me the truth!

JOE: (*Implacably.*) She is in no grave danger, it is true. I did lie. I was just . . . testing you. No, it is not Fanny who is in grave danger, but her child!

JEFF: Child! Fanny!

JANE: (*With cardboard pathos.*) I am underdone!

JEFF: (*Mangling his delivery.*) Fanny, what? Have you and Kendall *been* to each other? (*He realizes his error and corrects it.*) Fanny, what have you and Kendall been to each other?

JANE: (*With painful periphrasis.*) He . . . had his way with me.

JEFF: (*Solicitously, but increasingly eager and turned on*) You mean . . . he worked his will upon you?

JANE: (*Simply.*) He pressed the advantage.

JEFF: He led you down the path of dalliance?

JANE: He made a dishonest woman of me.

JEFF: (*Slavering.*) He enjoyed your sweet favors?

JOE: (*Intervening curtly.*) That's quite enough, Fenton.

JEFF: Sorry.

JOE: (*Significantly.*) So you mean to say you've risked the family fortune on a racehorse, just to ransom Fanny's little Charlie?

JEFF: (*Boggled.*) Uhhh . . . (*Improvises.*) You read my mind, Inspector! (*With a sting.*) Like a man who has skipped many pages ahead in the script! (*He turns to deliver an entrance cue.*) But I say Hang It All to Blazes! (*Wheels again to face an expected actor, who isn't there.*) And as for you, Kendall! Uh, sorry, I thought I heard someone come in. Kendall, in fact. (*Now louder.*) Hang it all to blazes!

JANE: (*Gamely trying to cover.*) Why, I hear gravel crunching in our driveway . . . er, footpath now! (*Silent terror onstage.*) I'm sure someone is about to enter as if on cue!

JOE: (*A bad improviser, he addresses empty space with fury.*) So! You thought you were pretty clever, didn't you?

JANE: (*Again trying to help.*) Yes, er, that's right, Kendall! Hide behind the drapes like the coward you are!

JEFF: (*Actor to actor.*) Good cover!

(*Suddenly a breathless boob stumbles on, carrying the script and a clipboard. It's the stage manager, JED, headset and all, covering for an absent actor. He's no performer and reads tonelessly from the script.*)

JED: "I—don't ka-now . . ." Whew, sorry! Jarrod's stuck in traffic! "I"—*gasp*—"I don't know what—you're insinua—"

(*Pause as he noisily turns the page of the script and resumes.*)

". . . ting, Inspector!"

JANE: Kendall! Is it really you?

JED:(*Jaunty monotone.*) "I—don't—give—a—twirl—Inspector. I'm—sure—she's—no—better—than—she—should—be."

JEFF: So, Kendall! You spit in my face behind my back!

JED: (*Cheerfully, like a happy pitchman.*) "Take that, and that and that!"

(*Suddenly understands what the line means.*)

Oh.

(*A bad fight ensues, with punches faked to the stomach met with recoiling heads and vice versa.*)

"Take that! And that! And . . ." (*Noisily turns page again.*) ". . . that!"

JEFF: (*Unconvincingly.*) And several of these!

JOE: (*Causes the fighting to freeze with this sudden exclamation.*) What do you mean, Captain's Folly has won the race? That means the fortune is saved!

JEFF: You read *his* mind now, Inspector. (Again *with a sting and no English accent.*) Again, like a man who has skipped many pages ahead in the script!

JOE: (*The actor.*) Sorry, I sometimes have this problem with premature ejac—

JED: (*Loudly and out of it.*) "He—crosses—left—smiles—broadly— and pours—a drink—"

JANE: Oh, Fenton! And Mother!

JEFF: (*Trying to straighten the keel.*) Married? How absolutely rather!

JOE: (*Helplessly.*) Have we skipped to the end?

JED: (*Befuddled, sloppily consults script.*) What, to where it says blackout?

(*An unseen technician misunderstands and obligingly provides an instant blackout.*)

ALL: (*In darkness, together.*) Hey!

END OF PLAY

CHECK, PLEASE

Jonathan Rand

Dedicated to Christy

For your free consulting services,
breathtaking vocal stylings,
and your friendship

CHARACTERS

GIRL	PEARL
GUY	TOD
LOUIS	SOPHIE
MELANIE	BRANDON
KEN	LINDA
MARY	MANNY
MARK	MIMI

SETTING

A restaurant.

TIME

Now.

PRODUCTION NOTES

I originally wrote this play with the intention of having the same two actors play the roles of GIRL and GUY, and having thirteen different actors play the rest of the roles. Another fun option would be to cast the play using four total actors, with all twelve characters split between two quick-change artists. The other option (which I least prefer) would be to cast every scene with a different pair of actors. While this would be a great opportunity to get heaps of people involved in the production, it does cheapen the conclusion of the play.

Every scene is a pairing of male vs. female. I wrote it this way simply because I have firsthand experience only with heterosexual dating. Should your production group wish to mix and match the characters' genders, I absolutely approve of it (though Scene 9 would have to remain male vs. female).

I envision the stage setup as two small dinner tables at opposite sides of the stage, with GUY and GIRL facing away from each other. I also imagine there would never be a need for a full blackout—just a quick lighting switch at the end of each scene to move from GIRL's table to GUY's table, and so on. If full blackouts make more sense to your production, then by all means, blackout away.

SCENE 1

LOUIS: Hi.

GIRL: Hi there.

LOUIS: It's great to meet you.

GIRL: You too.

LOUIS: So how long have you lived in the city?

GIRL: Oh, eighteen months? I think? It doesn't feel like it's been that long.

LOUIS: I've been here three years. It's a great city.

GIRL: Oh, definitely. What do you like most about it?

LOUIS: What do you like most about living here?

(*Pause, as* GIRL *is only slightly noticeably confused.*)

GIRL: Well . . . I love walking my dog in the park. Especially on a pretty day.

LOUIS: Yeah? Is that the truth? I love to ride my bike around the city—when the traffic is light, of course.

(*He chuckles.*)

GIRL: Same here.

LOUIS: Oh and also—and this may just be me—but I have this thing for walking my dog in the park on a pretty day.

GIRL: No, I like that, too. I said so earlier.

LOUIS: So do you like watching TV?

GIRL: No.

LOUIS: Me too! I love it!

(*Pause.*)

GIRL: (*Curious.*) Are you listening to me at all?

LOUIS: Sometimes I like to curl up with a bag of popcorn and just chow down while I watch *Home Improvement.* Do you like *Home Improvement*?

GIRL: You really aren't listening to me.

LOUIS: Me too! That's a riot. Tim Allen just cracks . . . me . . . up.

GIRL: This is ridiculous . . .

(*Throughout the below monologue, GIRL gradually tries out different tactics to see how self-centered and nonreactive LOUIS truly is. She tries saying things to him like "pardon me" and "hi"; she tries whistling at him a little; she even tries touching his nose with her index finger or a spoon for a few seconds. No matter what she does,* LOUIS *just keeps on trucking, as if she wasn't there.*)

LOUIS: I mean, his comedy is just choice. It's like his comic timing was a gift from the gods, you know? You know what I'm talking about? Man . . . I'm just blown away every time I see the show, or one of his movies. Did you see *The Santa Clause?* Ah! If you haven't, go and rent it *right away.* That is one funny guy. He reminds me of me, actually. We have the same sense of humor. My old roommate Bill? He says I'm the funniest guy he's ever met. Hey—he's entitled to his opinion, right? Anyway, I've got my personality flaws. Sometimes I'm too funny. People don't realize it when I'm being serious!! Do you believe that?! But jeez, enough about me. I'm talkin' like a motormouth here! Tell me about you.

GIRL: Or we could just end the date right now, since you're the biggest tool I've ever met.

(*A slightly long pause; we assume he is going to break.*)

LOUIS: I'm a Capricorn myself.

(*Scene.*)

SCENE 2

(*This next scene will work best if* MELANIE *is truly sweet, innocent, and adorable when she's focused on the date.*)

GUY: Hi.

MELANIE: Hi.

GUY: It's so great to finally meet you.

MELANIE: Same here!

GUY: So . . . What do you—

MELANIE: Wait, before you . . . sorry. (*Meekly.*) This is so rude, but the Bears game is on right now? You don't mind if I check the score . . .

GUY: Oh, sure. Totally.

MELANIE: (*As she pulls out her cell phone to check her web browser.*) Thanks. I know this is such an awful thing to do on a first date, but it's late in the fourth quarter, and it's do-or-die if we wanna make the playoffs.

GUY: It's no problem at all. Really.

MELANIE: Thanks. (*As she checks.*) I love the Bears. They're really strong this season. (*Sees score; reacts a little.*) Okay, I'm done. (*Cheerily.*) That wasn't so bad, was it?

GUY: What's the score?

MELANIE: Packers by seven.

GUY: Uh-oh.

MELANIE: Nah, it's no big deal. It's just a game, right? So, c'mon, enough about football. Let's hear about "Mister Mystery." Harriet's told me tons about you.

GUY: Man . . . The pressure's on now.

(*They laugh together genuinely.* MELANIE'*s laugh then fades directly into her next line, which is suddenly serious.*)

MELANIE: I'm just gonna check on the game one more time.

(She digs into her purse.)

GUY: *(Smiling.)* No worries.

MELANIE: Is it all right with you if I put on this little earpiece
thingy? It won't be distracting, I promise.

GUY: Sure.

MELANIE: *(As she puts the earpiece in her ear.)* I'm making the worst
first impression, aren't I?

GUY: Not at all.

MELANIE: It's just because it's for the playoffs. I'm usually pretty
normal.

GUY: It's really no—

MELANIE: *(Throws her hands up.)* Ah!

GUY: What?

MELANIE:: Oh. Nothing. The line only gives A-Train this huge
running lane, but he fumbles after two yards. The ball rolled
out of bounds, so we're cool, but come on—it's for the play-
offs. You don't just drop the ball like that, you know? Now
you're third and long, and the whole season is riding on one
play.

GUY: That's—

MELANIE: WHAT?!

GUY: What?

MELANIE: PASS THE BALL!!

GUY: What's wrong?

MELANIE: Miller! He doesn't pass it. The man refuses to pass the ball this season. It's third and long—who hands it off on third and long? Is he suddenly AFRAID OF HIS RECEIVERS?!

(GUY *looks around subtly at the other patrons.*)

Oh my God, I'm sorry. I'm being loud, aren't I.

GUY: (*Trying hard to be convincing.*) No . . .

MELANIE: Oh, I am. I'm so sorry. Look, how about this: I'll make it up to you. After dinner I'll buy you dessert at this tiny little bistro on 11th that nobody knows about. It's gotta be one of my absolute favorite places to go. It's so precious. I think you'll just—PASS THE BALL!! Jesus, people! This is FOOTBALL, not FREEZE TAG. It's FOURTH DOWN— pass the FRIGGING BALL!

GUY: Listen, we could go to a bar or something if you want— watch the game on TV.

MELANIE: Oh please, no. I wouldn't do that to you. The game's basically over. (*She takes a deep breath and is now very calm.*) Okay. I'm done. I got a little carried away there, didn't I? Let's order.

(*They peruse for a moment, as if nothing has happened.*)

GUY: Oh. (*Indicating the menu.*) Harriet said we should definitely try the—

(MELANIE *suddenly lets out a bloodcurdling shriek and rips the menu in half. Beat.*)

GUY: Or we could order something else. (*Beat.*) Your menu tore a little.

MELANIE: (*Downtrodden.*) They lost . . .

GUY: Oh. Oh, I'm sorry.

MELANIE: (*Starting to tear up.*) They lost. They just blew the play-offs.

GUY: Well, I—

(MELANIE *breaks down, bawling.* GUY *thinks for a moment, then takes out a handkerchief and offers it to* MELANIE. *She uses it to blow her nose.*)

GUY: I'm so sorry. Can I do anything to help?

MELANIE: (*Still weepy.*) The Bears suck . . .

GUY: Aww, no. They don't suck.

MELANIE: They do . . . They suck.

GUY: They're probably just having a bad season—

(MELANIE *grabs his collar, pulls him extremely close, and speaks in a horrifying, monstrous, deep voice.*)

MELANIE: THE BEARS SUCK.

GUY: (*Very weakly.*) The Bears suck.

(*Scene.*)

SCENE 3

GIRL: Hi.

KEN: Hello.

(*He kisses her hand, lingering there a second too long.*)

GIRL: It's great to meet you.

KEN: The pleasure . . . is all mine.

GIRL: So . . . where are you from? I can't place the accent.

KEN: I was raised in the mountains of Guam . . . and was born . . . on the shore of New Jersey.

(*Beat.*)

GIRL: Do you want to order some appetizers?

KEN: Anything . . . which will ensure happiness for your beautiful lips.

(*He looks at the menu, unaware of her subtle look of disbelief. She finally looks down at her menu.*)

GIRL: Ooh! The shrimp cocktail looks good.

KEN: Shrimp . . . a creature of the ocean. The ocean . . . which is not nearly as lovely as the ocean of your eyes.

(*Pause.*)

GIRL: Listen, can I ask you sort of a . . . barbed question?

KEN: Anything which your heart desires will be—

GIRL: Yeah, yeah. So—are you going to be doing this for the rest of dinner?

KEN: Whatever do you mean?

GIRL: All of this . . . sketchy, provocative garbage?

(*Pause.*)

KEN: Yes.

(*Scene.*)

SCENE 4

GUY: Hi.

MARY: Hi.

GUY: It's so great to finally meet you.

MARY: Same here! Listen: I was wondering if you were free next Friday.

GUY: Ah, I think so. Why?

MARY: Well, if dinner goes well tonight, I wanted to go ahead and line up a second date.

GUY: Oh. Okay, sure.

MARY: See, 'cause here's the thing: My parents are having a housewarming party at their new place on August second, and if you and I hit it off tonight and end up seriously dating, that party would be the perfect opportunity for you to meet my parents. So naturally I'd like to squeeze in several healthy-sized dates before then. If we don't, my parents might be a little bit skeptical of our relationship, which could in turn be disastrous for our future when you eventually pop the question. Not only would it make my whole family uncertain and uncomfortable during the ceremony, but it would also most likely carry over during our sixteen-day honeymoon in St. Martin. Even more importantly, it would be just awful if you had to deal with skeptical in-laws during the years down the road, and all because of a little thing like not setting aside fourteen healthy-sized dates before the housewarming party. Think about how a family conflict like that could upset Jocelyn.

GUY: Jocelyn?

MARY: Our little darling. Middle child. Bryan first, then Jocelyn, and of course little Madison.

(*Pause.*)

GUY: Wow . . .

MARY: What? What is it? You don't like the name Madison?

GUY: What? No. I mean, yes. No, that's a great name.

MARY: Something's on your mind. Honey, you can tell me. You're talking to your little sugar pumpkin, remember? Tell me.

GUY: Well, it's just—You just seem to have our whole relationship figured out—and we just met thirty seconds ago. (*Chuckling a little.*) I mean, you've got everything pinned down but the wedding dress.

MARY: Does that make you uncomfortable?

(*Beat.*)

(*As she withdraws several boxes.*) Because if it does, we can pick it out now.

(*Scene.*)

SCENE 5

(*Lights up to* MARK *dressed in nothing but a burlap sack. He's looking at the menu, as if nothing is out of the ordinary.* GIRL *is looking at him, expressionless. After several moments, he folds the menu, his dinner decision made. He looks up. Pause.*)

MARK: (*Innocent.*) What?

(*Scene.*)

SCENE 6

GUY: Hi.

PEARL: Hi.

GUY: It's so nice to meet you.

PEARL: Same here. Julia's told me a lot about you.

GUY: She's a great girl.

(*The moment* GUY *begins speaking the above line,* PEARL *quickly and slickly steals a fork.* GUY *thinks he saw wrong.* PEARL *continues on as if nothing has happened.*)

PEARL: Yeah. So much fun to be around. We've been friends for something like, oh, I don't know . . . six years?

GUY: (*As* PEARL *quickly steals the rest of the utensils.*) Where'd you two meet? In school?

PEARL: Yeah. We played soccer together. Both second stringers, keeping the bench nice and toasty for the rest of the team.

(*They laugh together. During their laugh,* PEARL *swipes her napkin.*)

Honestly? Julia is one of my favorite girlfriends. And she's got great taste, so when she told me about you, I was definitely all about it.

(*The moment* GUY *begins speaking the next line,* PEARL *swiftly and deftly removes the flower from the vase, pours the contents of her glass into the vase, pockets the glass, and replaces the flower in the vase.*)

GUY: That's very—sweet . . .

PEARL: No, I'm serious. I've been looking forward to this for a while now.

GUY: (*As* PEARL *takes the flower.*) I'm flattered.

PEARL: So . . . you hungry? I'm about ready.

(PEARL *picks up her menu;* GUY *does likewise. The moment* GUY *begins speaking,* PEARL *slides the menu into her jacket.*)

GUY: I'm pretty hungry, too—you know, I can see that you're stealing. You don't have to play it off like you're not.

PEARL: What? What are you talking about?

GUY: (*As* PEARL *steals a plate.*) I'm sitting right here. See? There. You just stole a plate.

PEARL: I don't understand. That's such a cruel accusation.

GUY: (*As* PEARL *steals sugar holder.*) Accusation?! I'm watching you steal those sugar packets right now? How can you honestly believe I don't notice?

PEARL: (*Starting to leave.*) Look, I don't know what your beef is with me as a person, but this is really insulting. I think we'll have to do this another time.

GUY: Wait. Listen. This is really silly. If you'll stop stealing things, I won't insult you. That's all. Then we can have a perfectly normal dinner. Okay?

(*Resolved,* PEARL *collects herself and moves back toward the table.*)

GUY: Great, so—

(*She whips the tablecloth off the table and starts stuffing it down her pants. Halfway through, she looks up at* GUY's *reaction.*)

PEARL: WHAT NOW?

(*Scene.*)

SCENE 7

(GIRL *is sitting across from* TOD, *a little boy—regardless of the age of the actor portraying this role, it should be immediately and abundantly clear that* TOD *is far too young for* GIRL. *A long pause.*)

GIRL: This may sound insensitive, but . . . how old are you?

TOD: What's yer favorite animal?

GIRL: No, no. I'm serious. I really want to know your age.

TOD: I like elephants.

GIRL: I think there's been a misunderstanding. See, when Christy said that you were still in school, I assumed she meant—

(*She is suddenly interrupted by* TOD*'s elephant impression. Beat.*)

GIRL: That's very . . . lifelike.

TOD: Do you have a scar?

GIRL: No.

TOD: I have a scar! Do you want to see it?

GIRL: No, that's all right.

(*Before she can finish her thought,* TOD *throws his leg up on the table, rolls up his pant leg, and shows the scar on his knee.*)

TOD: I got it from kickball. Do you see it?

GIRL: No.

TOD: It's right there.

GIRL: Oh, I trust you.

(*He removes his leg from the table.*)

GIRL: Honestly, how old are you?

TOD: (*A quick display on his fingers.*) This many. Will you be my girlfriend?

GIRL: Your girlfriend.

TOD: 'Cause Katie Johnson always brings a boring lunch to school and Courtney Shuler smells like horses.

GIRL: You've got a lot of girlfriends.

TOD: Yeah, will you be my girlfriend?

GIRL: (*Sarcastically giving in.*) Sure, why not . . . I'd be honored to be one of your girlfriends. But only if you pay for dinner.

TOD: Okay.

(*He produces a huge piggy bank and begins emptying change. Scene.*)

SCENE 8

(SOPHIE *enters the restaurant. She is a very old woman, edging toward the table in a walker.* GUY *just stares. Scene.*)

SCENE 9

(BRANDON *and* GIRL *are in mid-laugh.*)

BRANDON: I didn't even—

GIRL: —I know, I know—

BRANDON: —I mean, seriously! Jeez!

GIRL: —I know, right?

(*They settle down from the laughter.*)

BRANDON: So listen—all joking aside . . . this is fun! I'm really loving hanging out with you!

GIRL: Me too! This has been really, really great.

BRANDON: Hasn't it? Neat.

GIRL: Uh! There's a fly in my water.

BRANDON: Gross. Here, take mine. (*To offstage.*) Waiter? Can we get another water here?

GIRL: You are so—sweet.

BRANDON: Ah, c'mon.

GIRL: No, really.

BRANDON: Anyone would do that.

GIRL: Actually, you'd be surprised. With the luck I've been having lately with dating . . .

BRANDON: Really? But you're so fun. And beautiful.

GIRL: Oh, please.

BRANDON: No. I mean it.

GIRL: You are just too good to be true.

BRANDON: Oh, Terry, stop.

(*Pause.*)

GIRL: What?

BRANDON: What?

GIRL: Who?

BRANDON: What?

GIRL: Who's Teri?

BRANDON: What do you mean?

GIRL: You just called me Teri, who's Teri?

(BRANDON *fidgets*.)

GIRL: Is it your girlfriend?

BRANDON: Nooo! No.

GIRL: Who is she?

BRANDON: He.

(*Beat.*)

GIRL: He?

BRANDON: He.

GIRL: You're gay?

BRANDON: No! Well, yes. But Terry is my agent. (*Beat.*) I'm an actor.

GIRL: You're gay.

BRANDON: Yeah.

(*Pause.*)

GIRL: And why am I on a date with you?

BRANDON: Okay . . . I'm sorry I didn't tell you this sooner, but it would've totally backfired if I did. Here's what's going on: I'll be playing Stanley in a local production of *Streetcar*, and since I'm a method actor, I won't be able to get the part down until I method–act straight.

GIRL: Method–act.

BRANDON: Yes. I can't be Stanley Kowalski until I truly experience what it feels like to woo a woman.

(*Pause.*)

GIRL: So you're telling me you asked me out on a date, had me get dressed up for a nice dinner, drive myself all the way downtown, and then completely get my hopes destroyed after thinking I had finally met a decent guy—all so you could get a better feel for being straight?

(*Beat.*)

BRANDON: Yes. I hope that wasn't unfair to you or anything.

(*Pause. She takes her glass of water and douses his face. Pause.*)

BRANDON: Oh, my God. That was perfect! The ultimate heterosexual dating moment! I've got it! I'm in! I'm straight! STEL-LAAAAAAAAAAA.

(*She grabs the other glass of water and douses his face again.*)

BRANDON: I deserved that.

(*Scene.*)

(*Note: The character of* BRANDON *should NOT be played as flamboyantly gay; the audience should be made aware of that fact only when he explains it during the date. The actor should play the part completely straight throughout.*)

SCENE 10

LINDA: Hi.

GUY: Hi.

LINDA: I've been looking forward to this for a while.

GUY: Me, too. Sorry about all the rescheduling.

LINDA: Pssh, whatever, it's cool. Oh, shoot. Hold on. I forgot to—

(*She starts rummaging through her purse, and after a couple of seconds, starts removing objects: compact, lipstick, etc.*)

GUY: What's up? What's wrong?

LINDA: Oh, it's this silly thing. I've got this pill I need to take or else I get all weird. (*Back to her purse.*) I know I brought them. They've gotta be—You know, whatever. I'll be fine.

GUY: You sure? I could drive you to a pharmacy or something.

LINDA: Nah, it's no big deal. It's just a precautionary drug, you know? It won't kill me if I don't take it for one night. I just may be a little out of whack. You probably won't even be able to tell. Whatever. So—anyway.

GUY: (*Smiling.*) Anyway.

LINDA: It's nice to finally meet you.

GUY: The feeling's mutual.

LINDA: (*Suddenly sarcastic, morose, in a monotone voice.*) Oh, yes. It's so wonderful to finally put a name with a face. How wonderfully fascinating.

GUY: Heh. Yeah. Seriously.

LINDA: (*Giggly/bubbly.*) Hee hee hee. You're funny. You're cute.

GUY: Oh—

LINDA: (*Gruff.*) He's not cute. You just haven't been out in a while.

(*Snobby.*) That is NOT TRUE. He is GOOD-LOOKING.

(*Bashful.*) No . . . No . . . He's—

(*Sensual.*) Oh, you are absolutely right. He is a hunk of man.

(*Jittery.*) Shhhhhhhh . . . You're embarrassing yourself . . .

(*Gruff.*) Quit freaking out, man.

(*Easily offended.*) Wha? Wha? Why are you jumping all over me? I—

(*Little girl.*) She started it!

(*Motherly.*) Girls, please don't fight. What would your father say.

(*Fatherly.*) Oh, let 'em fight. Builds character.

GUY: Excuse me. Are you gonna be okay?

LINDA: (*Pissy, to* GUY.) You stay out of this!

(*Reasonable.*) Hey, leave him alone. You just met him.

(*Gruff.*) Oh, he can take care of himself

(*Monkey.*) Ooh ooh, ah! ah! ah!

(*Pissy.*) All right, who brought the monkey?

(*Easily offended.*) I didn't, did you?

(*Assertive.*) No.

(*Little girl.*) No.

(*French.*) Non.

(*Innocent.*) No.

(*Pushover.*) I did. It's my fault. I'm so sorry.

(*Snob.*) Idiot!

(*Gruff.*) A monkey? Come on!

(*Sarcastic.*) Way to ruin a magical evening.

(*Sensual.*) Mmmmm . . . The evening's about to get a lot more magical.

(*Motherly.*) You'd better behave yourself, young lady, or you're grounded.

(*Fatherly.*) Get off her case, woman! She ain't a child.

(*Monkey.*) Ooh ooh ooh ooh.

(GUY *notices a bottle under a napkin and shows it to* LINDA.)

GUY: Hey, are these the pills?

LINDA: (*Cheery.*) There they are!

(*Pissy.*) Yeah, too little too late.

(*Sensual.*) You are so sweet to find them!

(*Peppy.*) Yeah! YEAH!

(*Sarcastic monotone.*) Whoop-dee-doo.

(LINDA *swallows the pill.*)

GUY: Is everything all right?

LINDA: (*Mostly back to normal, but woozy.*) Whoa. Uh. Okay. Okay. It's starting to kick in.

GUY: Great.

LINDA: In a couple of seconds, the medicine'll take effect and I'll settle into a single personality. But don't worry—like, ninety-nine times out of a hundred, it's one of the normal ones.

GUY: But with my luck—

(LINDA *suddenly lets out a monkey shriek, grabs some bread from the table, sniffs it voraciously, stuffs it in her mouth, and lumbers offstage. Pause.*)

GUY: She was nice.

(*Scene.*)

(*Note:* LINDA's *personality switches should be fast. Each personality should be a different level—her voice and demeanor should be changing dramatically throughout.*)

SCENE 11

GIRL: Hello.

MANNY: Hi.

GIRL: It's nice to meet you.

MANNY: You too.

GIRL: Do you want to order? I'm starved.

MANNY: Yeah, me too. Let's go for it.

GIRL: Jeez. This menu's enormous! It's got everything.

MANNY: Seriously. I can never decide when the menu's so big. I'm so picky when it comes to ordering.

GIRL: Oh, I'm sure you'll find something. (*Beat.*) Ooh! I'm definitely getting the brisket. What about you?

MANNY: I don't know. I don't think I want any of this.

GIRL: Are you kidding? This menu's got everything. Why don't you tryyyy—the roast chicken.

MANNY: Naaahhhh. Too dry.

GIRL: Okay. How about . . . the filet mignon.

MANNY: Too moist.

GIRL: Oh.

MANNY: I actually have a tiny case of hygrophobia.

GIRL: Hygrophobia?

MANNY: It's an innate fear of dampness or moisture.

GIRL: Okay. How about . . . the French onion soup?

MANNY/GIRL: Hygrophobia.

GIRL: Right. Oh, let's see . . . You could get the potatoes.

MANNY: Too much fiber.

GIRL: Ummmm, the eggplant Parmesan?

MANNY: Porphyrophobia. Fear of the color purple.

GIRL: What about desserts? You could have the banana split.

MANNY: Coprastasophobia.

GIRL: Fear of—

MANNY: —constipation.

GIRL: How about the sushi?

MANNY: Japanophobia. (*Beat.*) It's the—

GIRL: Yeah, I got it. What about this? It's that Hawaiian fish my dad loves. Lemme see if I can say it right: humu-humu-nuku-nuku-apuaa. Yeah, there we go. You should get that.

MANNY: That actually sounds delicious.

GIRL: Great!

MANNY: But I suffer from a rare case of hippopotomonstros-esquippedaliophobia.

GIRL: Which is—

MANNY: Fear of long words.

GIRL: Okay! I've got one! And it never fails: peanut butter and jelly sandwich.

MANNY: Sorry.

GIRL: What could possibly be wrong with peanut butter and jelly?

MANNY: I recently developed arachibutyrophobia.

GIRL: Fear of sandwiches?

MANNY: Fear of peanut butter sticking to the roof of my mouth.

GIRL: So what can you eat?

MANNY: Not much. I do have sitiophobia. (*Beat.*) Fear of food.

GIRL: Right. Look, since you have all of these dietary issues, maybe you shouldn't have asked me to "dinner."

MANNY: Huh.

GIRL: Look, how about we just skip this and go to a hockey game or something.

MANNY: Oooh, can't. I'm a pacifist.

GIRL: Play minigolf.

MANNY: Asthma.

GIRL: See a musical.

MANNY: Depends.

GIRL: On what?

MANNY: I have ailurophobia.

GIRL: (*Overlapping.*) Fear of—

MANNY: Cats.

(*Pause.*)

GIRL: Well, what do you want to do?

MANNY: Well, I have one or two ideas.

GIRL: Sounds great. Let's do it.

MANNY: But I have decidophobia.

GIRL: Okay, I'll decide for you. How about I go home, and you go home?

MANNY: I can't.

GIRL: Why not?

MANNY: Nostophobia.

GIRL: What's that? Fear of staying single for the rest of your life?

MANNY: No! That's anuptaphobia. I have that, too. But no, nostophobia is the fear of returning home.

GIRL: I see.

MANNY: Honestly, a lot of these phobias flare up on account of my deipnophobia.

GIRL: And that is—

MANNY: Fear of dinner conversations.

(*Beat.*)

GIRL: I think it's time I head out.

MANNY: Why, what's wrong?

GIRL: I recently developed a phobia of my own and it's really flaring up.

MANNY: Yeah? What's it called? Maybe I have it, too!

GIRL: Phobophobia.

(*Beat. Beat.*)

MANNY: I don't have that.

GIRL: (*Overlapping.*) No.

(*Scene.*)

SCENE 12

(GUY *is sitting across the table from a fully outfitted mime,* MIMI, *who throughout the scene is extremely over-the-top and exuberant, as stereotypical mimes are. I hate to add to the mime bigotry out there in the world, but someone's gotta tell it like it is. The scene begins with* MIMI "leaning" on "something." Mimed actions in this scene will be indicated with brackets. A few moments pass as we get a feel for the ridiculousness of the scenario.)

GUY: So what do you do for a living?

(*Beat.*)

MIMI: [Pulling something heavy with a rope.]

GUY: You pull rope. (*Pause.*) Look . . . I respect your profession and all? I think it's noble what you do. . . . The world needs more people who . . . climb invisible ladders and pull imaginary ropes. But I really don't see how it's appropriate to bring your work to a date.

MIMI: [Battling against harsh winds.]

GUY: Oh, yeah, quite a storm in here. Listen, I'm gonna go ahead and order.

(GUY *opens his menu and reads.* MIMI *gets past the storm and mimes picking up an imaginary menu, proceeding to peruse it far too elaborately, turning page after page.* GUY *looks up. There is silence as he watches* MIMI *do her thing for a few moments.*)

GUY: Hey, I'm gonna go . . . use the restroom.

(GUY *gets up, takes his jacket from the back of the chair.*)

MIMI: [You're leaving? Driving away? Far? Bye-bye?]

GUY: No, I'm not leaving. I'm taking my jacket with me because . . . it might get cold in the men's room.

MIMI: [Cold like me in this wild blizzard?]

GUY: Yeah, exactly like that.

(GUY *starts to leave.* MIMI *follows close behind, maybe as an airplane pilot or a bus driver.*)

GUY: No, you stay here. You—

MIMI: [Let me feed some chickens. Awww, those chicks are adorable. I love petting these lovely animals.]

GUY: I don't know what that is. . . . Look, I have to—

(*An idea dawns on* GUY. *The following is an extremely loud and animated sequence of events—very frantic for* MIMI; *sarcastically frantic for* GUY.)

GUY: (*Looking up.*) Oh my God! A BOX!

MIMI: [Where? Where?]

GUY: A huge glass box, falling from the sky!

MIMI: [Oh no! Oh no! I can't see it! What in heaven's name will I do? Help me, Lord!]

GUY: Noooooooo!

(GUY *follows "the box" with his finger as it plops directly on the frantic* MIMI, *who is now very much "trapped." Scene.*)

SCENE 13

(*Lights up to* MARK *in his burlap sack. He is reading the menu. Long pause.*)

GIRL: Why don't you just give up?

MARK: If you've got a bone to pick with me, why don't you just come out and say it?

GIRL: You're wearing a burlap sack.

(*Pause.*)

MARK: That's your opinion.

(*Pause.* GIRL *stands and takes her jacket.*)

GIRL: I need to go powder my nose.

(*Beat.*)

MARK: Nice jacket.

GIRL: You, too.

(GIRL *exits toward* GUY's *table. The lights on* GIRL's *table remain up as lights come up on* GUY's *table.* MIMI *is still in her box, but not so as to distract from the action center.* GIRL *and* GUY *bump into each other.*)

GIRL: Oh, sorry.

GUY: No. My fault.

(*A short moment of instant chemistry. Then* GUY *shakes it off, as does* GIRL.)

GUY: Well, good night.

GIRL: Good night.

(*They start to go their separate ways.*)

GUY: Wait a second. (*Pause.*) This may sound like a really random question, but . . . do you like football?

GIRL: A little. (*Beat.*) Do you own any burlap?

GUY: No.

(*Beat.*)

GIRL: Do you wanna go and get some ice cream?

GUY: Yes.

GIRL: Let's go.

(*They exit together. A few moments pass.* MIMI *finally finds a "key" in her "pocket," unlocks the "door" to the "box" and exits. She moves to* MARK, *"spits" in her hand exuberantly, and extends it to him for a handshake.* MARK *looks up and notices what is going on in front of him. Beat. Beat.*)

MARK: (*Deadpan.*) Check, please.

END OF PLAY

CONTROLLING INTEREST

Wayne Rawley

Controlling Interest premiered under the title *Terms of the Agreement* on July 17, 2003, at 14/48: The World's Quickest Theater Festival. Brian Faker directed the following cast:

JACK	Mark Fullerton
BRAD	James Lapan
DAVID	James Garver
STEVEN	Seanjohn Walsh
ASHLEY	Susanna Burney
BETHANY	Amber Hubert

CHARACTERS

JACK: An eight-year-old boy.
BRAD: An eight-year-old boy.
DAVID: An eight-year-old boy.
STEVEN: An eight-year-old boy.
ASHLEY: A nine-year-old girl.
BETHANY: An eight-year-old girl.

SETTING

JACK's office. In the office is both hard and soft seating. JACK's desk and chair, plus a chair next to JACK's desk. The soft seating is a small couch and coffee table. JACK's office should be tidy, as JACK is a tidy kid.

NOTE: These characters should be played by adult actors of any age. These characters should speak in tone and manner as if they are adults. No kid voices. At some points the kid in them comes out, but at all times their actions and mannerisms are adult. At no point do the characters become children.

COSTUMES

The boys should be dressed for a day at the office. If they are not wearing suits they should be wearing khakis and polo shirts. They should look like smart, wealthy urban professionals.

The same for the girls. They should be dressed very professionally, in business suits, with some allure.

At rise, JACK *sits at his desk wearing a telephone headset. The phone rings.* JACK *answers.*

JACK: This is Jack. Yeah . . . Yeah, what can I do for you, Fred? I've got a meeting starting here like right now. Uh-huh. Uh-huh. Fred, Fred, Fred—honestly, let me stop you right there, I don't know if you're ready. Uh-huh. Well, we're gonna swing. Yes, Fred, on the swings—that *is* where you swing, see? That's what I'm talking about—Well, let me ask you this: Can you pump?

(BRAD *enters.*)

BRAD: Jesus Christ, Jack, we're getting creamed out there.

(JACK *holds up his hand as if to say "I'm on the phone."*)

BRAD: Oh, sorry.

JACK: (*To* BRAD.) It's okay, have a seat. (*To* FRED.) Yes, Fred, pump. Pump. Can you propel the swing back and forth under your own power without having to be pushed by a second party? Don't mess with me, Fred, you know what it means. (*Motions to* BRAD: *"Can you believe this guy?"*) Okay, look, Fred, I have to go. You come around lunch recess, we'll give you a go, but listen to me, Fred, I don't want to see you eat-

337

ing your boogers because we're not doing that anymore. We're eight now. Okay, well, okay. See you then. (*He hangs up. To* BRAD.) Dude still eats his boogers.

BRAD: Gross.

JACK: What's up?

BRAD: We're getting cremated out there, Jack. They got ghost runners on every base, and they keep changing where second is. One minute it's the garage door, the next minute it's the side hedge. It's like they're just making it up as they go along.

JACK: They're Big Kids, Brad, it's important we give them the impression that we are happy they're even letting us play.

(DAVID *and* STEVEN *enter.*)

DAVID: I'm telling you, Steven—

STEVEN: I'm sorry, that sounds extreme.

DAVID: I'm telling you. Ask Jack.

STEVEN: Jack, I'm sorry, I missed last week. Is it true we aren't eating our boogers anymore?

JACK: It's true, we're not.

STEVEN: That sounds extreme.

JACK: If you want a voice, come to the meetings. Sit down.

STEVEN: So what are we supposed to do with them?

BRAD: We don't know yet. For now, just leave them in there.

DAVID: We're looking into it. I'm talking to an eleven-year-old, says you can flick them on people.

STEVEN: Who the hell here has got that kind of hand-eye coordination?

JACK: Gentlemen, enough. We aren't here to discuss old business.

BRAD: What *are* we here to discuss, Jack?

DAVID: You know, I'm scheduled to smash an anthill today.

JACK: I know.

STEVEN: And I'm supposed to meet Gary for a late Lunchable at three. One thing I don't need in my life is more meetings, Jack.

JACK: I know, fellas. Listen, your time is valuable, I understand that. I have something very important I need to discuss with you. I've been thinking about this since, like, this morning.

BRAD: (*Concerned, this is important.*) Jesus, Jack.

DAVID: I'm sorry, um, wasn't this morning, like, a bazillion years ago?

JACK: I know. Yes, it was. That's why I asked you guys to come over to play today. I've been thinking—I've been thinking about this and . . . I want to discuss the possibility of . . . of us . . . liking girls.

BRAD: NO WAY!

DAVID: GROSS!

STEVEN: (*Pointing at* JACK.) FAG! FAG! FAG!

JACK: Hey hey hey. Hey now. We don't . . . Okay? We don't need that kind of insensitive talk around here, Steven. Please. Let's be kids about this. Besides, and I think I will have the support of the membership here when I say, you're the fag.

STEVEN: You're the fag.

JACK: You are the fag.

STEVEN: Nuh-uh!

JACK: Yes-huh.

BRAD: Gentlemen, please. You know, we've run around this pole before and I have a feeling we aren't going to come to any real concrete decisions about it today. While you both make excellent points on the other person being the fag, I think we should stick to the issue on the table—namely, Jack's proposal that . . . what I'm hearing you say, Jack, is that we somehow stop hating girls and begin, what? Liking them?

JACK: Yes, Brad, thank you.

DAVID: Okay, um, I'm uncomfortable with this and I'll tell you why. Number one, there is the whole size thing. I mean, they are just bigger than we are, physically taller, and that, that's new, okay, that's a recent thing and it frightens me. And number two, they seem to be—what's the word?—smarter than we are. More advanced somehow.

STEVEN: Not to mention the whole cootie issue.

JACK: That is unsubstantiated.

STEVEN: Says who, Jack? Unsubstantiated? Says who? Where is this coming from?

JACK: Look, I know this is new territory for all of us, but David, look at it this way, okay? Your mommy. You know your mommy?

DAVID: (*Not sure where this line of questioning is headed.*) Yes, Jack, I know my mommy.

JACK: Okay, well, your mommy is a girl, right?

DAVID: Um . . . I don't know that.

JACK: Well, she is. Trust me. She is.

BRAD: It's true, David. Her boobies make her a girl.

DAVID: (*Cornered.*) What's your point, Jack?

JACK: My point is that I have a feeling they may have something to offer us. And I think we ought to hear them out.

STEVEN: Hear them out?

JACK: They've sent representatives, two representatives, to discuss what would be involved. They are in the outer playroom right now.

DAVID: I am *very* uncomfortable with this.

STEVEN: You're setting us up.

BRAD: Guys, come on. We can do this. I believe in Jack. This is the guy who taught us how to make a shadow on the ceiling that looks like a butt—using only a flashlight and our knuckles. Huh? Now, we run this block and we have all day. We can do this. This is easy. Game face. Come on.

(*Pause. They agree by their silence.* JACK *speaks into a speaker on his desk.*)

JACK: Send them in.

(ASHLEY *and* BETHANY *enter. As they do,* BRAD, STEVEN, *and* DAVID *all shift to the other side of the room and stand in a clump.*)

ASHLEY: Good afternoon, gentlemen.

JACK: Afternoon, ladies, please come in, welcome to the play-room. Can I get you some Legos or something?

ASHLEY: Thank you, no. My name is Ashley with an *e-y*, my daddy's a policeman, and I'm nine. This is my associate, Bethany.

BETHANY: I can do short division.

(*The boys are impressed by this but try not to show it.*)

JACK: Please sit down.

(*The girls sit on chairs between the desk and the clump of boys.* STEVEN *immediately reaches over and tugs on a piece of* BETHANY's *hair.*)

BETHANY: (*Whirling around.*) Hey! Knock it off!

STEVEN: What? Wasn't me! Wasn't me! (*The boys snicker.*)

ASHLEY: (*Standing.*) Very good. Have a nice day, gentlemen.

JACK: Wait! Hold on. Steven! Dammit! Please! Um, please, let's not step off on the wrong foot here. That won't happen again. Will it? Please don't go. We would like to talk.

(ASHLEY *looks at* BETHANY. BETHANY *nods.*)

ASHLEY: We understand you are interested in liking us?

JACK: We are interested in exploring that possibility, yes.

ASHLEY: And you are ready to discuss terms?

JACK: That is why we're here.

ASHLEY: Excellent. Bethany?

BETHANY: (*Pulling a document from her clipboard.*) I know how to type.

ASHLEY: (*Taking the document.*) Thank you.

BETHANY: And I speak French.

JACK: So what do you want?

ASHLEY: Your complete and undivided attention.

JACK: Well, you've got it.

ASHLEY: (*Smiling.*) Ah, yes, of course I do. Um, no, no. I mean your complete and undivided attention until the end of time.

DAVID: Uh-oh.

JACK: Excuse me?

ASHLEY: In accordance with the terms of the agreement, we will be occupying your every thought, motivation, and decision-making process from the moment you wake up in the morning until the moment you fall asleep at night, at which point we will play a major role in nine out of ten of your dreams.

We do allow one wild-card dream, usually a sports dream or flying dream of some type, that is completely up to you, of course. But everything else becomes, for all intents and purposes, about us.

BETHANY: Love.

ASHLEY: Right. Until, of course, you actually fall in love with one of us. Then we get pretty much ten out of ten.

DAVID: Yeah, um, I'm sorry . . . I'm not falling in love with anybody.

ASHLEY: Right. Bethany, am I missing anything?

BETHANY: Stop doing stupid stuff.

ASHLEY: Right. And you will have to stop doing stupid stuff. Like playing Star Wars and making laser-beam noises with your mouths.

DAVID: Yeaaah, okay, I'm very sorry, I'm just not comfortable with this.

STEVEN: (*Scared.*) Okay, so what if I don't even care? I mean, like, what if I don't even want to stop playing Star Wars? What if I don't even care if I think about you or not, like if I say, like, I don't even care?

ASHLEY: I'm afraid that won't be possible.

BRAD: All right then, so what's in it for us? Right? I mean I'm just thinking out loud here at this point, but it seems like you're asking a lot, with all that thought time and no Star Wars and everything, so, like, what is in it for us? Exactly?

ASHLEY: Knowledge, mostly.

BRAD: But we already know everything.

ASHLEY: Right. So let me ask you a question then. Do you ride the school bus?

BRAD: (*This is easy!*) Yeah.

ASHLEY: Where do you get off?

BRAD: I get off in front of my house.

ASHLEY: You do?

BRAD: Yeah.

ASHLEY: You get off in front of your house?

BRAD: Yeah!

(BETHANY *begins to snicker.*)

ASHLEY: You *get off* in front of your house.

BRAD: What? Yes!

DAVID: Dude, you get off in front of your house?

BRAD: What? I mean . . . the bus! What?

STEVEN: Dude gets off in front of his house!

JACK: Wait a minute, wait a minute, wait a minute. Am I crazy or did you just get Brad to admit, in front of all of us, that he masturbates, in public, outside of his own house?

(ASHLEY *shrugs like it wasn't anything.*)

JACK: And you can teach us stuff like that?

ASHLEY: That was just a parlor trick.

BRAD: Oh, yeah? So what? Like you're so smart? What else? What else do you know?

BETHANY: (*Looking right into their very souls.*) We know where babies come from.

(*The boys are stunned.*)

DAVID: (*Defiant but timid.*) Y-yeah? S-so? So what? Everyone knows where babies come from. They . . . they come from the Garden. With the morning dew.

(ASHLEY *and* BETHANY *shake their heads a very definitive no.*)

DAVID: Jack, I'm very uncomfortable with this.

STEVEN: This is out of control, man. This is out of control!

BRAD: I meant get off the bus.

JACK: Yeah, ladies, I think we are going to need some time. To think. This is a lot to consider. And wow, we really do appreciate you coming by—

ASHLEY: Oh, and of course there is the possibility—no guarantees, of course—but if you play your cards right, there is the possibility that someday you might possibly be able to see one of us without a shirt on.

(*The boys stop cold. Long pause as they contemplate this. Finally.*)

BRAD: You mean, um, you mean, like, right in front of us? Like, right there in person or, like, pictures in books or what?

ASHLEY: Well, you will probably start out with pictures in books, but someday, who knows?

(*The boys look at one another. Defiance is gone. The negotiation is over.*)

BETHANY: (*Writing on her clipboard.*) Steven, Jack, David, Brad.

ASHLEY: Yes, well, gentlemen, thank you for your time. We will definitely be in touch.

BETHANY: I can write cursive.

(ASHLEY *and* BETHANY *exit. The boys stare vacantly for a beat. Then suddenly, as if slowly waking from a daze.*)

DAVID: Um, Jack? Say, if it is all the same to you, I think I'm going to skip smashing that anthill today.

JACK: Um, yeah. Yeah, David, that would be fine. Take the rest of the day off.

DAVID: Good thing we stopped eating our boogers, huh?

JACK: Yeah, yeah. Good timing on that.

STEVEN: Um, I have to go home and comb my hair. And lose some weight.

(STEVEN *and* DAVID *exit.* BRAD *moves to the door. He stops.*)

BRAD: Jack, how long do you think it will be? Before we, you know, actually get to see 'em without shirts on?

JACK: I don't know, Brad. I wish I could tell you. But I just don't know.

BRAD: Yeah, I don't even care.

JACK: I know. Me neither.

(BRAD *exits.* JACK *stands at his desk for a beat, then brings his hand up to his mouth to check his breath. Lights down.*)

END OF PLAY

2B (OR NOT 2B)

Jacquelyn Reingold

This play is for Rich.

2B (*or Not 2B*) had a staged reading in Acts of Love, a benefit for Cure Autism Now at the Canon Theatre in Beverly Hills, on October 20, 2003. David Tochterman directed the following cast:

FRANNY   Julie Warner
DAVE THE BEE   Patrick Warburton

2B (*or Not 2B*) was first fully staged at the Actors Theatre of Louisville on February 2, 2005. Sets by Brenda Ellis; costumes by Kevin Thacker; lights by Matt Cross and Katie McCreary; props by Joe Cunningham and Deanna Hilleman; dramaturg, JoSelle Vanderhooft. Erica Bradshaw directed the following cast:

FRANNY   Anna Bollard
DAVE THE BEE   Ian Frank

CHARACTERS

FRANNY: A woman in her thirties.
A BEE: A male bee named Dave.

TIME

Now.

PLACE

Franny's studio apartment in Upper Manhattan.

(FRANNY, *upset, disheveled, in her studio apartment, on the phone, and waxing her legs. She talks fast.*)

FRANNY: I know you told me it was over and I respect that. I mean, I understand it and I know you don't want to see me again and I know I was not very nice to you at times, and I just want to say that I've had a—well, a complete not-nice-ostomy and a total unlike-ectomy, I've had all the not-nice unlikable parts removed, so if you call me, I'm sure we can work it out. (*She hangs up. She tears a strip of wax from her legs.*) AH! (*She cries. She dials. She holds the receiver to her leg. She rips wax.*) Ah! I'm waxing my legs. I know you hated my hairy legs, so I'm waxing! I can't believe you haven't called me back. (*Hangs up. Rips off more wax.*) Ah! (*Dials.*) I heard you asked out my friend Eleanor, and I thought you'd like to know she has the papilloma virus—*in her vagina.* And in her mouth. On her tongue. In case you happened to have kissed her already. Wouldn't worry about it, though, I'm sure it's fine. Okay, well, thanks for breaking my heart. And I still really love you and if you want to change your mind and give it another try, let me know. (*Hangs up. Cries. Rips wax.*) Ah!

(*A human-size bee appears.*)

AHH!! (*She hides her head; she looks.*)

Ohmigodohmigodohmigod!

(*She tries to hide. The bee is huge. There's nowhere to go. She runs into a corner.*)

Ohmigod. Okay. Could you just go? Please. Um. Shoo. Go. (*He doesn't budge.*) Look, the park is a few blocks away. If you could just fly over there, I'm sure you'd be happier. (*He doesn't move. She crouches to the floor or hides under the bed.*) Or or in the back, there's a garden. With, uh, plants. Or my neighbor downstairs, she has these window boxes: geraniums, impatiens. I'm sure you're in the wrong place.

BEE: Is this 2B?

FRANNY: What?

BEE: 2B or not 2B?

FRANNY: It's a joke, right?

BEE: I wouldn't make a joke like that.

FRANNY: Okay, this is 2B, but I'm sure it's the wrong building.

BEE: 344 West 188 Street?

FRANNY: (*Grabs her bag and tosses it at the bee.*) Okay, take whatever you want. I only have ten dollars, but I'll write down my PIN number. My bank's on the corner, you can have it all.

BEE: I don't want your money.

FRANNY: Then take the TiVo. Or the organic honey, okay?

BEE: I don't want that.

FRANNY: Look, I'm possibly allergic. And my EpiPen will not be of much use in this case, 'cause you are ohmigod so fucking big. You are the biggest bee I have ever seen. I can't believe this is happening. (*She grabs the phone.*) Frank. Help! There's a giant bee in my apartment. Could you come over? Please!

BEE: He's a jerk. Forget about him.

FRANNY: What?

BEE: You deserve better.

FRANNY: Well, thank you, I will consider that. Now please, go away. Or I'll call the police.

BEE: I don't think they'll come for a bee.

FRANNY: I am really afraid of you. I mean, really afraid. Bees are my . . . well, thing. You know, some people it's snakes or heights or whatever, but me, it's bees.

BEE: I won't hurt you.

FRANNY: Well, that's nice to hear but . . .

BEE: Why would I hurt you?

FRANNY: I don't know. Because you're a bee.

BEE: Have you been hurt before?

FRANNY: Yes.

BEE: Yellow jackets.

FRANNY: No, bee. Bees. I've been stung. So I am sure you are in the wrong apartment.

BEE: It's the right apartment.

FRANNY: Then it's the wrong species. I'm a human, a female human, and you're not invited.

BEE: How's that going for you?

FRANNY: What?

BEE: Being a female human?

FRANNY: It's fine. It's just fine.

BEE: Work and love, it's all good? How's your job?

(FRANNY *sneaks toward the window while talking.*)

FRANNY: Fine. I'm a receptionist. It's a career change. I used to be a painter. Very cutting edge, I didn't even use paint, I used body fluids. But um, it didn't work out because several others already claimed that niche. You wouldn't believe what some people do with their menstrual blood. So now I, uh, have a job and a boss and uh— (*She can't get out the window.*)

BEE: And your human female love life?

(FRANNY *crawls all around the room, heading toward a certain cabinet while talking.*)

FRANNY: Well, my first relationships were with typical self-involved commitmentphobes when I was between the ages of, say, five and twelve. Then junior high was alcoholics; high school was drug addicts; college, gay men, a guy who owned a duck, then a physically challenged interpretive ice skater, meaning you know an amputee who'd skate with a kind of stick with a blade at the bottom. Then I married a guy who liked to put garlic in his ears, but I went away a lot with my boyfriend, who was a puppeteer for the blind. Then my husband fell for a woman with small limbs, and I got pregnant but lost the baby and the father, well, he was a midwesterner. So then I had a slew of Internet dates with incredibly boring men, which is I guess a sign of getting older. The men tell long stories that sound like intricate recipes on how to marinate poultry.

(FRANNY *has snuck around to her cabinet, pulled out a can of bug spray, and points it at the bee.*)

Okay, get out. Or I will spray you with this deadly spray.

(*She sprays. The can is empty. She shakes, tries again, nothing.*)

Damn.

(*She runs for the door. It won't open.*)

BEE: You like flowers, don't you, Franny?

FRANNY: How do you know my name?

BEE: (*Pulls out a bouquet.*) And tulips are your favorite, aren't they?

FRANNY: How do you . . . Okay, thanks for the delivery. You can put those down over there. And now you can go.

BEE: Do you know how intoxicatingly beautiful you are?

FRANNY: Now, *that's* a joke.

BEE: We find you unbearably sexy.

FRANNY: Who's we?

BEE: We know you haven't even begun to tap into your erotic capacity.

FRANNY: What's that smell?

BEE: That's my nectar.

FRANNY: Mmm. Not bad.

BEE: Franny Dambrose, you are wonderfully demanding, fascinatingly moody, exquisitely impossible to please.

FRANNY: Well . . .

BEE: Complicated, codependent, and controlling. Perfect in all ways.

FRANNY: Well . . .

BEE: We want to give you everything you always wanted, but thought you couldn't have: love, fulfillment, hot sex; we will serve your every need.

FRANNY: Well . . .

BEE: We want you to be our Queen.

FRANNY: What?

BEE: We've watched you. We've chosen you. We know you.

FRANNY: What is this?

BEE: You can run, but you can't hive. We even have a sense of humor.

FRANNY: Hardly.

BEE: Just think: You wouldn't have to work. You'd have plenty of time: to read, to lounge, to do your art. Think what you could paint with pollen.

FRANNY: That's very nice of you, but hey, why don't you get, um, a real bee? I know you could find one in, um, the park.

BEE: We had a bad experience. She was a . . . killer. So we've opted for this scientifically advanced entomologically evolutionary revolutionary solution. We find a very special human female and offer her a better life. Works well for all involved.

FRANNY: If it works so well, what happened to your last one?

BEE: She fell in love with a wasp. Not recommended. The children will be confused.

FRANNY: Okay.

BEE: Franny, imagine yourself as Queen. You'd never be alone again on a Friday night. You'd be serving the greater good by helping to cross-pollinate. Not to mention, we will please you in every way. Have you ever thought about being with more than one male and their only pleasure is your pleasure?

FRANNY: Well, um, look, it's nothing personal, but I find you, I'm sorry to say, physically, uh, repulsive.

BEE: Oh, I think that could change.

FRANNY: And I'm human.

BEE: That too can change. Amelia Earhart? She didn't disappear. She made a choice. So can you.

FRANNY: But what's wrong with being human?

BEE: Have you read the paper lately? Your species isn't exactly living up to its potential.

FRANNY: Amelia Earhart?

BEE: I don't want to rush you, Franny, except that my brothers and cousins are eagerly waiting and time is quickly running out. Don't you want what I've offered? What is it you're reluctant to give up?

FRANNY: Well, my apartment.

BEE: A studio in Inwood?

FRANNY: It's near the subway.

BEE: You'd have your own hive.

FRANNY: My job.

BEE: That job sucks.

FRANNY: There are perks.

BEE: Like what?

FRANNY: Uh . . . frequent flyer miles.

BEE: You won't need those.

FRANNY: And there's Frank.

BEE: Frank is a fly, a gnat, a roach. Besides, he's an actor. Forget Frank.

FRANNY: Believe me, I've tried.

BEE: Franny, oh, Franny, have you looked at your life lately?

FRANNY: I prefer not to.

BEE: All of your qualities that absolutely don't work as a female human will work like gangbusters as a bee.

FRANNY: Things'll get better.

BEE: How long have you been saying that?

FRANNY: Time heals all wounds.

BEE: Then why are you still hurting? And why are you inflicting excruciating pain on your lovely legs? We like fuzzy!

FRANNY: Really?

BEE: Really. Weren't you the queen in your grade school play? Didn't you enjoy it?

FRANNY: I loved it. But I didn't get to keep the crown. I wanted that crown.

BEE: You could have a crown.

FRANNY: But still, I'm terrified of you. I see a bee, I flee. It's a kind of a flight-or-flight kind of thing. I don't go on picnics, I avoid practically the entire outdoors because of you.

BEE: What exactly are you afraid of?

FRANNY: Pain, death, dying alone, that sort of thing.

BEE: Touch my stinger.

FRANNY: What?

BEE: Touch it.

FRANNY: No.

BEE: Don't you think it's time to change?

FRANNY: That's a pretty big change.

BEE: I know you, Franny Dambrose. The reason you're afraid of me is because you *are* me. In your heart, you're a bee. Touch it.

(*She touches it, pulls her hand away twice. Touches it.*)

FRANNY: Oh. Oh. It's—it's nice.

BEE: Isn't it?

FRANNY: It's, mmm, warm.

BEE: Yes.

FRANNY: Powerful.

BEE: Yes.

FRANNY: It's . . . growing.

BEE: Yes.

FRANNY: And that smell. Your . . . nectar.

BEE: Yes.

(*A musical humming is heard. Lights change.*)

FRANNY: That sound. What is it?

BEE: My cousins and brothers. Here to serve you.

FRANNY: Oh my. (*She feels them all over her body.*) What are they doing?

BEE: Touching you, tickling you, trying to please you.

FRANNY: Oh. Oh. (*The* BEE *puts yellow stripes on her.*) What're those?

BEE: Your stripes.

FRANNY: They're so . . . soft. (*He puts antennae on her.*) Oh. (*He puts wings on her.*) Oh, they're beautiful. Oh.

(*The* BEE *kisses her.*)

FRANNY: I can't believe I kissed a bee. I feel . . . different. What's your name?

BEE: Dave the Bee.

FRANNY: Hi, Dave.

(*The phone rings.*)

BEE: Let it ring.

FRANNY: But . . . (*Rings.*)

BEE: Forget it.

FRANNY: But (*Rings.*) it might be my boss.

BEE: It's time.

FRANNY: But . . .

BEE: Let's go.

FRANNY: What if it's Frank? (*She answers the phone.*) Hello?
Frank?

(*The lights change. The humming stops.*)

I'm glad you called. What? You want me to stop calling?
You're really happy since we broke up? You're still seeing my
friend, Eleanor? You've asked her to marry you? Great. That's
just great.

(*As* FRANNY *is about to burst into tears and launch an attack, Dave
puts a crown on her head. Voilà. She is transformed. She nearly drops
the phone.*)

Frank, remember the Don't Bee and the Do Bee? Well, you
are most definitely a Don't. And when it comes to you and
your kind, I am done. (*She hangs up. She dials again.*) Buzz off!
(*She hangs up.*)

(*Humming sounds. Lights change. Music. She kisses Dave.*)

FRANNY: Okay, boys, let's fly.

END OF PLAY

POPS

Edwin Sánchez

Pops was originally performed at Primary Stages in 2003 with Michael Ray Escamilla in the role of Tomás and directed by Tyler Marchant. It was performed a year later at Town Hall as part of an evening commemorating 9/11 presented by Brave New World. That performance was directed by Dennis Smith and featured Ivan Davila in the role of Tomás.

(The theme to I Love Lucy *plays in the background. The volume comes up, then disappears.* TOMÁS, *sixteen, stands center stage.)*

TOMÁS: Can I just say, I hated Lucy. I used to have to watch it all the time with my Pops. He would call her La Colora, the Redhead. He thought she was so funny. He'd come home late at night from work, sneak me out of bed, and we'd watch *I Love Lucy* reruns. Now, that was kinda cute when I was a kid, but the older I got, the more tired it got, you know what I'm saying? When my father wanted to be funny he'd walk around the house saying *(Thick Desi accent.)*, "Lucy, 'splain." My father's English was pretty bad as it is. "Lucy, 'splain." Funnee, Pops. Laugh riot. Parents should never be allowed to try to be funny. So one night he drags me out of bed again, and I'm so not in the mood, I don't even remember why, and we're sitting there watching Lucy and my father is laughing as loud as Ricky would. You know, almost like he's pronouncing "Ha-ha-ha." And I couldn't take it anymore and I snapped, "Man, why do you think that's still so funny? You've only seen it, like, a hundred times." My father got real quiet after that and I felt terrible. So I started laughing really hard, trying to make it up to him, you know. But he didn't dare laugh anymore. I think my father thought I was smarter than him, so if I told him he shouldn't laugh, then he shouldn't laugh. He went to bed early that night. He was a busboy and

he had a breakfast shift the next day at the restaurant where
he worked. Windows on the World at the World Trade Center. He didn't come home the next day. Or ever. I had to go
with my mother to all these agencies to translate for her, but
no one could help us. "He was a busboy, not a citizen." I tried
to explain it to my mother in Spanish, but she would just
look at them and say, "Please, 'splain." And people would roll
their eyes, or try to be nice or get impatient and try to get us
out of whatever office we were in. "Busboy, not a citizen."
We had the wake in our apartment. We didn't have a body, of
course, just a picture of my Pops. He was smiling in it. All
our relatives and neighbors were there, and the priest came
by. I stood in a corner, facing away from his picture. From
the laugh I had silenced. I could see my mother on the sofa,
crying quietly, people trying to comfort her. I turned then
and walked up to my father's picture, and outta nowhere, it
started. (*In perfect Lucy.*) "Are you tired, run-down, listless?
Do you poop out at parties?" The room fell to a dead hush.
(*Lucy-like.*) "The answer to all your problems are in this bid-
dle lottle." (*Quickly corrects himself as Lucy did.*) "Little bottle!"
My cousins started to scream with laughter, my uncle looked
like he wanted to kill me, and my mother just stared at me.
But I couldn't stop. I was by Lucy possessed. I started doing all
her bits, I was, like, "Lucy's Greatest Hits." Lucy trapped in
the icebox, Lucy as a showgirl with a heavy headdress, Lucy
in the chocolate factory. Pretty soon everybody is laughing
so loud you can barely hear me. The priest calls out "Do
Lucy in the wine vat!" Like now I'm getting requests? I look
at my mother and she is laughing so hard tears are flowing
down her cheeks. And when I finally break, when I can't
take it anymore, I cry like Lucy did when Ricky caught her
doing something she shouldn't have. (*Lucy-like.*) "Wah!!!!!!!"
(*Changing to real pain. Silence.*) My mother now has to work
two jobs, she wanted us to stay in the U.S. because that's what
my father wanted. The busboy, not the citizen. He never got
a plaque and no one mentions him or nothing, so I like to

think that every time there's an *I Love Lucy* rerun on, it's a tribute to my father. And baby, that Colora, she is on twenty-four hours a day.

(*Theme to* I Love Lucy *returns.*)

END OF PLAY

FORTY TO LIFE

Nina Shengold

FORTY TO LIFE

Forty to Life was first performed as a staged reading at Actors & Writers in Olivebridge, New York. The New York premiere was at the Makor/Steinhardt Center's Festival of Wrights, July 7, 2003. Nina Shengold directed the following cast:

SUSIE WISMER	Melissa Leo
SGT. LORRAINE FREUD	Nicole Quinn
PAUL KAPLOWICZ	David Smilow
THE EX-BOYFRIENDS	Ted Cancilla, Daniel Gallant, Michael Gallant, Eric Lane, John Seidman

CHARACTERS

LORRAINE FREUD: Over thirty, preferably African-American or Latina.

SUSIE WISMER: Mid-forties New Yorker.

PAUL KAPLOWICZ: Mid-forties New Yorker.

THE EX-BOYFRIENDS: Three or more, as diverse as possible.

Setting: Minimal indication of a precinct house in Hell's Kitchen. SUSIE
WISMER *rushes in. Mid-forties, wild-eyed, dressed for a date.*

SUSIE: HELP!!!

(*Desk sergeant* LORRAINE FREUD, *urban, seen it all, barely looks up
from the counter.*)

LORRAINE: Wanna get more specific?

SUSIE: I'd like to report a . . . a theft. I was robbed! At a restau-
    rant, that sidewalk café on the corner . . . called Bangkok
    Delight.

LORRAINE: (*Interested now, on the case.*) What exactly was stolen?

SUSIE: My sense of hope.

LORRAINE: Poof?

SUSIE: Thin air.

LORRAINE: What did it look like?

SUSIE: Um . . . maybe six-two, intelligent, kind, sense of
    humor . . .

LORRAINE: (*Nods grimly, identifying the code.*) Someday My Prince Will Come?

SUSIE: He doesn't have to be a *prince*.

LORRAINE: Yes he does.

(*Stands.*)

We've been seeing a rash of these lately. I'm going to ask you to look at some possible suspects. Don't worry, it's one-way glass.

(*A Law & Order–style "Ka-chung" as a height chart drops in from above.* SUSIE's EX-BOYFRIENDS *file in and stand in a sullen line, holding cards with numbers against their chests.*)

SUSIE: Oh my God. Where did you dig them up? That's everyone I've ever dated!

LORRAINE: We'll find your perp. One of these men made you sob in your pad thai and he's gonna pay. Atten-HUT!

(*The* EX-BOYFRIENDS *straighten reluctantly.*)

Step forward one at a time and repeat this phrase: "Hey, it's been great, but . . ."

EX 1: (*Stepping forward.*) Hey, babe, let's both be adults here, okay?

(SUSIE *shakes her head. He steps back.*)

LORRAINE: Next!

(*The* EX-BOYFRIENDS *step forward in turn. Three, four, or six actors can play all parts, each moving down to the end of the line and flipping his number to become a new character.*)

EX 2: Two roads diverged in the woods, man. It isn't a fault thing.

EX 3: This just isn't fair to you. Or to my wife, or the twins.

EX 4: I'm not going to deal with your shit anymore. And hey, hello, I'm not the bad guy here. *You* made this happen. Your anger, your mood swings, your PMS—

LORRAINE: Back in line, bozo!

(EX 4 *gives her the finger and stomps back to lineup.*)

EX 5: You deserve more than I'll ever be able to give you. I'm setting you free.

EX 6: (*Second grader.*) Mary Jo gave me candy, not just a dumb card.

EX 7: Leaving? Whoa, hold it, who said anything about *leaving*? No. No. No. You're putting words in my mouth. You're making . . . no, see, that's exactly why—I did *not* use that word, I said . . . You need to listen! I am *not* being passive-aggressive!!!

EX 8: I'll never forget you. You taught me to brush my tongue.

EX 9: It isn't the sex, it's your cats.

EX 10: You're so good my pants hurt.

LORRAINE: How'd *he* get in here?

SUSIE: Wait.

EX 10: It's not that contagious, I swear. It's like no worse than crab lice.

EX 11: It has nothing to do with you gaining that weight.

(EX 12, PAUL KAPLOWICZ, *steps forward, opens his mouth, then starts suddenly, pointing at* SUSIE.)

PAUL: *She's* the one! Stop, thief!

SUSIE: What?

PAUL: She ransacked my id! I have witnesses!

SUSIE: (*To* LORRAINE.) I thought you said it was one-way glass.

LORRAINE: It usually is.

SUSIE: I don't even remember him.

PAUL: (*Struck to the heart.*) AAAAAUGH!!!

LORRAINE: This looks bad.

(*Grilling* SUSIE.)

Where were you on the night of December fourteenth, 1969?

SUSIE: I was in junior high school!

PAUL: Geometry!

SUSIE: Paulie? Paul Kantrowitz?

PAUL: Kaplowicz!

SUSIE: How did you find him? We went out *once!*

PAUL: Twice!

SUSIE: Your bar mitzvah does not count!

PAUL: It counted to me! I've had three broken marriages. Systemic acne. A retrograde colon. My life is in shards because you, you, YOU threw me over for Julius Pitzkoff!

EX 8, JULIUS PITZKOFF: Hey!

PAUL: That bottle was pointing at *me*!

SUSIE: I don't believe this.

PAUL: And you kissed that . . . weasel. You frenched!

SUSIE: Thirty years ago!

PAUL: Thirty-two!

LORRAINE: Okay, you're under arrest.

SUSIE: But I didn't—

PAUL: *She wrecked my life!*

LORRAINE: Both of you. (*Whipping out handcuffs.*) You have the right to remain celibate. Any sex you indulge in may be held against you.

PAUL: I want a divorce lawyer!

LORRAINE: You should've thought about that in geometry class.

(*She handcuffs them back-to-back.*)

SUSIE: You can't do this to me! I'm the *victim*!

LORRAINE: We're all victims, lady.

SUSIE: But how about my hope?

LORRAINE: He's it.

SUSIE: Paulie Keplovitch?

PAUL: Kaplowicz!

LORRAINE: This is as good as it gets.

SUSIE: *Junior high school?*

LORRAINE: Take it or leave it. The jig is up.

SUSIE: Can't I at least have a grown-up?

PAUL: I've grown up!

SUSIE: Like hell. You're still rehashing your first spin the bottle game. *He* had potential.

(*She points at* EX-BOYFRIEND 5, *pulling* PAUL*'s hand with hers in the handcuffs.* EX-BOYFRIEND 5 *shakes his head violently.*)

LORRAINE: No plea bargains. You two are stuck with each other. Forty to life. The rest of you guys are free to go back on the street and start dating.

(*The other* EX-BOYFRIENDS *file off, lighting cigarettes, flipping sarcastic salutes, etc.* LORRAINE *faces* SUSIE *and* PAUL.)

Okay, now you're gonna do serious time.

SUSIE: But—

LORRAINE: Shut up. Quit whining. He did this, she said that, boo fucking hoo. You're not going to find perfect mates, okay?

Ever. You're forty-five. Nobody scarred you for life. No one saves you. There's no shining armor, no dream girl. You'll have to do. (*Exhales hard.*) I need a fuck and a cigarette.

(*She stomps offstage.*)

PAUL: HEY! You can't—

LORRAINE: (*Offstage.*) Watch me.

PAUL: Don't I get a phone call?

(*No answer. He and* SUSIE *stand back-to-back, handcuffed.*)

SUSIE: These *hurt.*

PAUL: I'm allergic to metal.

SUSIE: Move *over*, for God's sake.

(*They glare at each other over their shoulders.*)

So what have you done with yourself for the last thirty years?

PAUL: Thirty-two.

SUSIE: Three failed marriages? That took some work.

PAUL: Better than not getting married at all. Least I tried.

SUSIE: Oh, I tried, buddy. God knows I tried.

PAUL: With *that* pack of losers?

SUSIE: I'd like to see wives number one, two, and three!

PAUL: No, you wouldn't.

(SUSIE *pulls his arm upward.*)

What are you doing?

SUSIE: I have an itch. Right behind my ear.

PAUL: May I?

SUSIE: What, scratch me?

PAUL: We're chained to each other. Here?

(*He scratches her gently behind the ear.*)

SUSIE: Bit higher. Farther left. Ooh.

PAUL: Too hard?

SUSIE: (*Surprised to enjoy his touch.*) . . . No, it feels kind of . . . mmm, that's so—Watch it!

PAUL: What?

SUSIE: Handcuff. Stuck in my hair.

PAUL: Should I—

SUSIE: NO! DON'T MOVE!

PAUL: Don't go berserk. I'll just—

SUSIE: HELP!

LORRAINE: (*Offstage.*) WORK IT *OUT.*

PAUL: If I just pull my hand around . . .

(*He does, inadvertently spinning her in a sort of swing-dance move. They're now face-to-face.*)

Better?

(SUSIE *nods, a bit breathless.*)

SUSIE: Were you always this tall?

PAUL: I shot up four inches at Camp Winnebonka. You've still got those eyes.

SUSIE: Tinted contacts.

PAUL: Bifocals. They're inside my briefcase.

SUSIE: You've still got your hair, though. Well, some of it.

PAUL: At least I don't dye it!

(*They glare at each other, annoyed and attracted.*)

SUSIE: . . . Forty to life, huh?

PAUL: It's better than nothing. Would you care to dance?

SUSIE: (*After a beat, looking into his eyes.*) What the hell.

(*She puts her nonhandcuffed hand onto* PAUL's *shoulder. They start up a stiff, clumsy, shin-kicking waltz.* LORRAINE *waltzes in with a* BOY-FRIEND *or two as the rest croon* "Moon River.")

END OF PLAY

THE BEST DADDY

Shel Silverstein

The Best Daddy was produced as part of *An Adult Evening of Shel Silverstein* by the Atlantic Theater Company (Neil Pepe, artistic director; Beth Emelson, producing director) in New York City on September 9, 2001. It was directed by Karen Kohlhaas; the set design was by Walt Spangler; the lighting design was by Robert Perry; the costume design was by Miguel Angel Huidor; the sound design was by Malcolm Nicholls; the general manager was Ryan Freeman; the production manager was Kurt Gardner; and the production stage manager was Christa Bean. The cast of *The Best Daddy* was as follows:

LISA	Alicia Goranson
DADDY	Jordan Lage

LISA: Okay?

DAD: A little further.

LISA: Here? Can I open my eyes?

DAD: Hold my arm.

LISA: I'm going to bump into it.

DAD: You won't bump into anything. Keep your eyes closed. Now hold my arm, a couple more steps here.

LISA: Can I look now?

DAD: All right . . . Open your eyes right . . . now.

LISA: Is that him, there?

DAD: That's right.

LISA: Why is he covered with a blanket?

DAD: Well, he . . .

LISA: He doesn't look like a pony.

DAD: Well he is, a thoroughbred gelding $350 Shetland pony.

LISA: Is he laying down?

DAD: Um, yes.

LISA: Why is he laying down? Is he sick?

DAD: Pure strain Kentucky-bred Shetland.

LISA: Why is he laying down?

DAD: Lisa . . . I didn't want to tell you this . . .

LISA: Why is he laying down? He is sick, he is.

DAD: He's dead.

LISA: He . . . he's dead?

DAD: It's a helluva thing to have to tell your daughter on her birthday.

LISA: Dead? A dead pony?

DAD: We've got to face the facts.

LISA: You . . . you got me a dead pony for my birthday?

DAD: I didn't get you a dead pony for your birth . . .

LISA: What happened to him?

DAD: Lisa, I'm going to be honest with you . . .

LISA: What happened to my pony?

DAD: You're thirteen years old now and I'm going to talk to you like an adult . . .

LISA: What happened to my pony?

DAD: I shot him.

LISA: Y—you shot him?

DAD: About an hour ago, but hear me out.

LISA: Y—you shot my pony? You . . . you shot my birthday pony?

DAD: I told you not to get excited, didn't I? Answer me, did I or did I not say, "Don't get too excited . . ."

LISA: Why did you shoot my pony?

DAD: I did not shoot your pony. He wasn't your pony when I shot him. You didn't even know he existed. He was a pony.

LISA: Why did you shoot a pony?

DAD: He bit me.

LISA: But you didn't have to shoot him. You didn't have to . . . he's only a little pony. He didn't know what he was doing.

DAD: You weren't there, you don't know the situation.

LISA: My pony is dead. I'm thirteen years old today and you gave me a dead pony for my birthday.

DAD: I told you, he bit me.

LISA: But you gave him to me anyway. You took me out here to show me a dead pony?

DAD: Well, I thought about that. I thought, Well, if I take her out here and show her a dead pony that will upset her, but if I don't give her anything she'll think I forgot her birthday.

LISA: What could be worse than getting a dead pony for your birthday?

DAD: Listen now, someday you'll have children of your own. I never shot a pony before. I want you to believe that, never in my life before today.

LISA: You hated my pony, you always hated him.

DAD: I didn't always hate him, I never even . . .

LISA: You did. You hated him because you knew I loved him.

DAD: When I saw him I liked him, he was cute.

LISA: You knew he loved me and he could show his feelings and you couldn't stand that. Oh no, 'cause you could never love anyone. You're all bottled up. You keep all your feelings all bottled up. And he could show his love. He could swish his tail and toss his head, and lick my hand when I gave him sugar. And late at night when I'd ride him bareback through the gray mountains . . .

DAD: You never rode him—I just bought him . . .

LISA: (*Music.*) You didn't know. I used to sneak out late at night when you thought I was sleeping. I'd climb out of my bed-room window and I'd run to the pasture . . .

DAD: Pasture? What pasture?

LISA: And he'd smell my scent and come galloping toward me, and I'd leap onto his back, and we'd go galloping over the moonlit moor . . .

DAD: Moonlit moor?

LISA: . . . with the wind in my hair. And now he's dead. You killed my pony. You killed Black Thunder.

DAD: Black Thunder?

LISA: You killed the only thing I ever loved.

DAD: I didn't.

LISA: You did.

DAD: I didn't.

LISA: You did. You said you did. (*Music stops.*)

DAD: (*Blows party whistle.*) APRIL FOOL! (*Laughing.*)

LISA: April Fool? But, but it's not April, it's my birthday.

DAD: BIRTHDAY FOOL! (*Blows whistle, laughs.*)

LISA: You mean Black Thunder's not dead? Then who is under that blanket?

DAD: Not "who," but "what."

LISA: Wh-what? Wh-what's under there?

DAD: Three guesses.

LISA: I . . . I don't know. You're cruel. You're the cruelest daddy in the whole world.

DAD: Three guesses.

LISA: A . . . a candy bar?

DAD: Uh-uh.

LISA: A . . . a turtle, a big gigantic turtle?

DAD: Nope, two down, one to go.

LISA: A . . . a . . . a rubber raft?

DAD: No . . .

LISA: What then, what is it?

DAD: It's your sister!

LISA: What?

DAD: It's your big fat sister!

LISA: Cathy? It's Cathy?

DAD: Big fat Cathy!

LISA: Why is she hiding under there? And you said it was a what, not a who. Cathy is a who.

DAD: Not exactly.

LISA: Not exactly? Cathy? Ca—Cathy?

DAD: It's a . . . what . . . it's Cathy's body.

LISA: Cathy's body?

DAD: She's the one that bit me.

LISA: You shot Cathy?

DAD: Teeth like a damn wild grizzly.

LISA: You gave me my dead sister's body for a birthday present? First you tell me my pony is dead, and now you tell me you shot my favorite sister? You are the cruelest meanest most vicious . . .

DAD: DOUBLE APRIL FOOL! (*Blows whistle, laughs.*)

LISA: Double April Fool?

DAD: It's not your sister. I wouldn't shoot your fat little sister. Three more guesses!

LISA: (*Crying.*) I'm not guessing anymore. You ruined my birthday. You're a mean, cruel . . .

DAD: It's the motorcycle you wanted!

LISA: The Honda?

DAD: Uh-huh.

LISA: The red one?

DAD: Uh-huh.

LISA: (*Screams.*) Really and truly?

DAD: Mmm-hmm.

LISA: No April Fool?

DAD: No.

LISA: No Birthday Fool's day?

DAD: Mmm-mmm.

LISA: Oh, Daddy. (*Kisses him.*) Daddy, you're the bestest daddy in the whole wide world! (*Kisses, kisses, kisses.*)

END OF PLAY

THE FLYING WOLIMSKIES RETURN

David Smilow

The Flying Wolimskies Return premiered at Actors & Writers, Olive-bridge, New York, on October 25, 2003. The cast was as follows:

ZIGMUND WOLIMSKI	John Seidman
HECTOR WOLIMSKI	Mikhail Horowitz
DWIGHT WOLIMSKI	David Smilow
FLORENCE WOLIMSKI	Carol Morley

A cramped, seedy circus trailer. Makeup mirrors, street clothes on hangers, tired furnishings. Offstage music and audience noises—oohs, ahs, and applause—can be heard: a circus performance in progress.

Standing before a full-length mirror adjusting the corset he wears beneath his magenta unitard (with a wrinkled yellow cape) is seventy-year-old ZIGMUND WOLIMSKI. *He sports padded shoulders too—and a wig, false teeth, and dyed eyebrows. Also in the magenta unitards and cape are* HECTOR WOLIMSKI, *sixty, who's humming a snappy tune to himself and making a series of hand gestures, and* DWIGHT WOLIMSKI, *forty-five, who sullenly watches* ZIGMUND.

ZIGMUND *admires his reflection, then peers more closely at it and rubs an eyebrow.*

ZIGMUND: (*Eastern European accent.*) Is running! Bastard.

DWIGHT: That's it, then. Substandard eyebrow dye? We can't go on.

ZIGMUND: We go on. (*Re his reflection.*) What the hell now, with this? (*He tugs at his cape, trying to smooth the wrinkles.*) Two weeks in box. You'd think it was full year.

DWIGHT: Are we talking about the cape or Mom?

(*Hector perks up, looks around.*)

HECTOR: (*Accent similar to* ZIGMUND*'s.*) Where is Audrey? Audrey!

ZIGMUND: *Bratch nih skooyah. Pepescu?*

(HECTOR *is stricken, then sobs.*)

DWIGHT: He remembers now. Dad, I'm asking you again. Call it
   off. (ZIGMUND *makes a dismissive sound.*) We're still eating the
   krevnici from the funeral and you expect us to go back up
   there. (*Lowers his voice.*) Like this. (*Indicates* HECTOR.) With
   her. (*He jerks a thumb toward a closed interior door.*)

ZIGMUND: "If contract is binding . . ."

(HECTOR *perks up again, joins in.*)

ZIGMUND/HECTOR: ". . . the Wolimskies are flying."

ZIGMUND: (*To* DWIGHT *re* HECTOR.) He ready.

(ZIGMUND *fine-tunes his shoulder pads so that they're symmetrical.
The tempo of the offstage music picks up.*)

DWIGHT: This is insane!

(ZIGMUND *extends his arm and squints at the watch on his wrist, then
calls toward the interior door.*)

ZIGMUND: We going up in eight minutes!

(HECTOR *begins to limber up with a series of arcane calisthenics.*)

DWIGHT: Do you remember the last thing out of Mom's mouth?

(HECTOR *thinks hard, brightens.*)

HECTOR: Aiiiieeee!

DWIGHT: Before that. When we were walking to the tent.

ZIGMUND: Hector. Chalk.

(HECTOR *passes an open tin of powdered chalk to* ZIGMUND, *who begins rubbing some into his hands.*)

DWIGHT: She said, "For God's sake, stop it!" Yes, on the surface, it was because you kept stepping on the back of her slippers. But there's deeper meaning to it now. She might as well have been talking about the act.

(ZIGMUND *presses the chalk tin on* DWIGHT.)

ZIGMUND: Prepare yourself.

DWIGHT: It's suicide! Or murder. Maybe both if we really click.

ZIGMUND: Such a worrier. You are like your mother.

HECTOR: Where is Audrey?

DWIGHT: Here's a hint: aieeeee!

(HECTOR's *stricken again, obsessively begins to chalk his hands, mewling.*)

ZIGMUND: (*To* DWIGHT.) Why just not take ax and cut my heart out?

DWIGHT: It's tough with an ax. A hatchet might do it, though. (*Beat.*) Dad, come on. Is the money that important?

ZIGMUND: A man work. When he work, he get paid.

(*A burst of offstage applause. The music changes.* HECTOR *perks up again.*)

HECTOR: I always liked this musics!

ZIGMUND: (*Calling toward the interior door.*) Six minutes!

(HECTOR *resumes his calisthenics.*)

DWIGHT: Screw the money for once. We're not ready. It's not safe. Tell them no. Tell them . . . we have a problem.

ZIGMUND: What problem?

(*The interior door latch moves, but the door doesn't open. There's furious scrabbling on the other side. Then the door flies open and* FLORENCE WOLIMSKI, *sixty-five, staggers out, wearing glasses and a too-loose unitard. She's unaware that the cape is tucked inside her collar—and that a long streamer of toilet paper is stuck to her slipper heel.*)

DWIGHT: (*To* ZIGMUND.) Make one up.

FLORENCE: (*Jittery but game.*) All set. I wouldn't go in there (*Indicating the room she just came from.*) for a bit. Something at lunch disagreed with me.

ZIGMUND: Is not possible. You look like the blooming young dew.

FLORENCE: Oh bull roar. (*But she smiles—at* HECTOR.) You boys. Always flirting.

DWIGHT: Aunt Florence, you don't have to do this . . .

ZIGMUND: *Chimbleh!*

DWIGHT: . . . unless you haven't fallen to your death recently.

(ZIGMUND *and* HECTOR *reflexively clap their right hands over their eyes and stick their left arms straight up in the air, faux-spitting three times as they turn their heads from left to right—an anti-hex gesture.*)

ZIGMUND: (*To* FLORENCE.) You don't listen to him.

(*But* FLORENCE *isn't listening to him, suddenly scanning the trailer.*)

HECTOR: Something you are losing?

FLORENCE: My glasses. (HECTOR *grins, points to the glasses on* FLORENCE's *face.*)

HECTOR: You are funny, funny lady, lady.

FLORENCE: (*Blushing furiously.*) I'm blind as a bat without these.

DWIGHT: (*Sotto to* ZIGMUND.) At least she won't see it coming. (*To* FLORENCE.) Better put a string or something on them or they'll fly off up there.

ZIGMUND: No! No string! Is bad luck.

HECTOR: Like net.

FLORENCE: There's no net?

HECTOR: (*Gaily.*) "Nyetski on the netski!"

FLORENCE: (*To* ZIGMUND.) You didn't tell me there's no net.

DWIGHT: (*Whisper.*) Then tell him you're out. There's still time.

(ZIGMUND *elbows* DWIGHT *out of the way, walks* FLORENCE *off a few steps.*)

ZIGMUND: Florence, Florence. What that I was to telling you after funeral?

FLORENCE: That I could be your new star—and make a few bucks.

DWIGHT: We'll mention that at your funeral.

FLORENCE: Excuse me. I did all right at the . . . the what-do-you-call-it.

DWIGHT: Rehearsal. It comes from the root word meaning "when we had a net."

(FLORENCE *is unsettled, and only now notices the toilet paper stuck to her heel. Reaching down to pull it off, she loses her balance and stumbles into a wall.*)

HECTOR: So, so funny!

(*He grins, and his nose gushes blood.*)

DWIGHT: Jesus. Hector.

(HECTOR *just blinks at him.*)

ZIGMUND: *Shlimpu coffblees.*

(HECTOR's *hands go to his nose and he tilts his head back, unfazed.*)

HECTOR: *P'dah ho.*

FLORENCE: Hector, you poor baby! (*She picks up a box of tissues and manages to push all the tissues back through the opening.* HECTOR *waves her off.*)

HECTOR: Is okay. After accident, nose happens few times. A day.

FLORENCE: What accident?

DWIGHT: I know: It's hard to keep them all straight.

HECTOR: Was after act in Tulso. Amarilli? Somewhere . . . out far. We come down from wire, like always; one by one down rope—boom, boom, boom. Big hand from crowd. We make the line, arm up in salute. Smile. Bow. And boom again.

FLORENCE: What happened? Noxso never told me this story.

ZIGMUND: This was after . . . his time.

DWIGHT: On Earth ended.

HECTOR: A pipe like this . . . (*Flings out arms to indicate length.*) . . . like this . . . (*Forms a big O with his hands.*) come loose in rigging. Way high. Then (*Makes plunging sound and gestures.*). Next stop—here. (*Taps the back of his head.*)

FLORENCE: Mercy! It's a miracle you weren't killed.

ZIGMUND: Ninety-seven hundred dollars for the plate in his head. He gots the best!

DWIGHT: They just have to replace it every couple of months.

FLORENCE: (*Horrified.*) No!

HECTOR: No.

FLORENCE: (*To* DWIGHT.) How can you joke about something like this? Your uncle must have suffered terribly.

DWIGHT: As opposed to Noxso, who went like that. (*Snaps his fingers.*) Let's hope that's how it is if anyone buys it tonight.

ZIGMUND: Nobody are falling! (*He and* HECTOR *repeat the anti-hex gesture; then Zigmund rechecks his watch.*) Three minutes.

FLORENCE: Zigmund, maybe we do need a smidge more practice. I watched for years when Noxso was alive, of course, bless his soul. But this is the first time I've . . . put on the old tights myself.

ZIGMUND: Is unitard. And we go on!

DWIGHT: A man *and* a woman works.

ZIGMUND: I proof we're ready. We going over whole act right now—quick. Make a circle! (HECTOR *describes one in the air.*) No. With us. (*He gestures to form a circle. They do.*) Music start. (*He begins to scat the snappy tune* HECTOR *was humming earlier.*) I go up to platform. (*He makes a hand-over-hand gesture to pantomime climbing a rope.*) Then . . . (*He cues* HECTOR, *who does the same, then* DWIGHT, *and finally* FLORENCE.) Okay. We all up. Ladies and gentlemen, the Flying Wolimskies!

(*He scats again, then cues the others to represent their first moves with their hands. With each measure of music, they change hand position to approximate the progress of the act. They look like four people using a bizarre semaphore.* HECTOR *gets into it and starts scatting along with* ZIGMUND, *who in turn starts to smile and bop in place. As the older men's enthusiasm peaks, they and* DWIGHT *suddenly stop dead and fall silent, staring at* FLORENCE's *latest hand position.*)

FLORENCE: Is this wrong?

(*She quickly turns her head to check her own odd arm position, and her glasses fly off.*)

DWIGHT: (*To* ZIGMUND.) How many minutes now?

ZIGMUND: Is first-night jitters.

DWIGHT: Dad, she can't do it.

FLORENCE: Now, wait just a minute.

HECTOR: (*Half to himself.*) Twenty-seven feet from wire to ring.

DWIGHT: With no pesky net to get in the way.

FLORENCE: I can too do this!

ZIGMUND: And she need the money.

FLORENCE: Noxso left me with zip, the cheap . . . (*Catches herself. Then to* ZIGMUND *and* HECTOR.) Your brother wasn't much on planning ahead.

HECTOR: *Byosta.* We go give it a try. (FLORENCE *melts.*)

DWIGHT: Give it a try? This isn't a new carrot cake recipe we're testing out. It's not an alternate route to the dry cleaner's. You don't get to try with this. You either do it or there's a memorial service. Again. What are you, idiots?

FLORENCE: Hold it right there, bub. Where do you get off, pissing and moaning, all holier than thou? I notice you're wearing your little purple onesy. If you think this is so nuts, why don't you quit and let the old farts drop from the sky!

(DWIGHT *and* ZIGMUND *exchange a look. An odd silence falls.*)

ZIGMUND: Wolimskies fly now for a hundred fifty years. My father. His father. His father. His father. All. This is only life we know how to live! (*He thumps his corseted, unitarded self.* HECTOR's *so moved he bursts into tears and hugs* ZIGMUND.) You see? One way. Same costume.

DWIGHT: (*To* FLORENCE.) He's got a note in his corset they'll find if he falls.

FLORENCE: What?

DWIGHT: It says he's dead because his son left the act and broke his heart. He didn't want to live anymore.

(FLORENCE *looks at* ZIGMUND, *who touches a spot under his armpit. We hear the crinkle of paper.*)

FLORENCE: Wow.

DWIGHT: That's how you get a hundred and fifty years of Wolimskies to fly.

(*Loud offstage applause. The music changes again.* ZIGMUND *looks at his watch one more time.*)

ZIGMUND: We go on.

HECTOR: On!

(ZIGMUND *and he straighten up and march out the door, one after the other.* DWIGHT *holds the door for* FLORENCE *and looks her in the eye. Hard.*)

DWIGHT: Break a leg.

END OF PLAY

STREAK

Tommy Smith

CHARACTERS

CESARE: *The third baseman. Number 7. Slight Spanish accent.*
JERRY: *Third base coach. American.*
ANNOUNCER

Lights.

Third base at a large stadium. Roaring crowd.

CESARE, *the third baseman. Number 7. Slight Spanish accent.*

JERRY, *third base coach. American.*

(*Beat.*)

CESARE: So. How are you, Jerry?

JERRY: Fine.

(*Beat.*)

CESARE: Kids?

JERRY: Kids are fine.

(*Beat.*)

CESARE: How's the team doing this year?

JERRY: Fine without you.

(*Beat.*)

CESARE: That so?

JERRY: Yeah, Caesar, doing fine without you.

CESARE: It's pronounced "Cesare."

JERRY: Always called you Caesar.

CESARE: Caesar's an emperor. Caesar's a salad.

(*Beat.*)

JERRY: So. New team working out?

CESARE: Sure is.

JERRY: Not what I hear.

CESARE: Oh?

JERRY: Hear you're not hitting like you did for us. Hear your game's gone to shit.

CESARE: Game's fine.

JERRY: Ain't got on base since Boston. What was that, July?

CESARE: Late August.

JERRY: It's late September.

CESARE: I know.

JERRY: I know you know. What, you waiting for something?

CESARE: My stride, man. Waiting for my stride.

JERRY: Stride better come soon. Got a shot at a series, but only if you start playing. New team gonna regret signing away half their revenue to a firecracker with no fuse.

CESARE: Come up with that one yourself?

JERRY: Like it?

CESARE: Regular fucking Shakespeare Jesus Mary Joseph.

(CESARE *signs cross.*)

ANNOUNCER: . . . and with the score tied in the bottom of the ninth, Tetsuo Tanaka steps up to the plate!

(*Crowd roars.*)

CESARE: My replacement.

JERRY: Mmm-hmm.

CESARE: Tokyo, right?

JERRY: Kyoto.

CESARE: Saw him on Sports Center. Kid plays pretty well.

JERRY: Pretty well? He's the Japanese Babe Ruth.

CESARE: Ain't that good.

JERRY: Two for three every at bats is pretty fucking genius.

CESARE: (*Signing cross.*) Watch the swearing, man.

JERRY: You swear much as me.

CESARE: But I give it one of these.

(CESARE *signs cross.*)

Gonna swear, give it to the Father, Son, and Holy, all right? Don't wanna be next to you, lightning strikes you dead.

JERRY: Don't believe that shit.

CESARE: (*Signing cross.*) I'm not kidding, man!

JERRY: Stuff, don't believe that stuff.

CESARE: You better, man. Believe me. When you least expect, religion bitch-slap you.

JERRY: You said *bitch*.

CESARE: I can say *bitch*. *Bitch* is a dog.

ANNOUNCER: Strike one.

CESARE: Look! He ain't that good.

JERRY: Just wait. Kid's on a streak. Never seen a player run like him. Time the ball's past the pitcher, he's already at first. And the power on his bat. In the cage the other day, he cut one through the chain-link fence. Straight through, jagged metal busting out the other side. Mark my words, kid's gonna get MVP.

CESARE: Said that about me last year.

JERRY: No I didn't.

CESARE: Sure did.

JERRY: Well, if I did, I don't remember.

ANNOUNCER: Ball one.

(*Beat.*)

CESARE: You still like me, Jerry?

JERRY: Sure. Sure.

CESARE: Acting like I killed your mother.

JERRY: You did what you had to do.

CESARE: Right.

JERRY: But you still abandoned us.

(*Beat.*)

CESARE: So maybe I shouldn't have left the team. All right? Maybe I shouldn't have left this city. Left the people. But I signed the contract. I signed the contract. Never have to worry about being poor. Game's gone to shit, can't play ball, so what? So what?

JERRY: Sold your soul.

CESARE: Don't get biblical, man.

JERRY: You're the Catholic.

ANNOUNCER: Ball two.

(*Beat.*)

CESARE: Can I tell you something, Jerry?

JERRY: Depends.

CESARE: I confided in you before, man. Last year, bit of a coke problem. You helped me out, Jerry. Helped me kick it. And you didn't tell nobody. I appreciate that. But this. I don't know how you're gonna take this.

JERRY: Nothing incriminating?

CESARE: No, man, nothing like that.

JERRY: Then what?

CESARE: You were right.

JERRY: Right about what?

CESARE: I sold my soul to the devil.

ANNOUNCER: Strike two.

(*Beat.*)

JERRY: Oh, look, I know how sensitive you get about this religious shit. I didn't mean to give you a complex about it, I was just kidding around.

(*Beat.*)

You're serious.

(CESARE *nods.*)

The devil.

(CESARE *nods.*)

The actual devil. Horns. Hooves. The devil, forked tongue, the devil.

CESARE: Looked like a regular guy at first. Knocked on my door, said he had a proposition for me. I said okay, let him in. Seemed like a nice enough guy. Suit. Tie. But sulfur, he smells like sulfur. Fresh, burning. Offer him a drink, he says No, I won't be staying. Pulls out a pack of papers, says Got a deal for you. New expansion team opening up on the other side of the country, am I interested? Not really, I say, but then he shows me the salary. You can buy a small island with this, he says. Next thing I know, his pen's in my hand, I'm signing my name. He takes the pen away, takes the contract, and smiles. And his teeth are fire. And his tongue is a snake. And his eyes are black. And he says good.

ANNOUNCER: Strike two.

JERRY: So what I hear you saying is you got recruited by . . . Satan.

CESARE: It's the only explanation.

JERRY: I knew it.

CESARE: You did?

JERRY: You're snorting again.

CESARE: No, man.

JERRY: You're coked up now, aren't you? It's why you can't play.

CESARE: Didn't read the fine print is why I can't play. I sold my game to the devil.

JERRY: I don't believe any of this.

CESARE: You don't believe in nothing man. That's your problem. I come to you with this, you can't even deal. I put my soul on the line, you front with this fucking atheist bullshit—Jesus Mary Joseph, Jesus Mary Joseph.

(CESARE *signs cross twice.*)

JERRY: Whoa, whoa. Soul on the line?

CESARE: He said I tell anyone about this, bad things gonna happen.

JERRY: What bad things?

CESARE: I don't know, man, bad things! Devil says bad things, better believe he can do bad things to a guy!

JERRY: Why did you tell me, then?

CESARE: Had to tell someone. Thing's been eating me up.

JERRY: All right, all right. Let's think logically. Where's the contract?

CESARE: He took both copies.

JERRY: Supposed to give you the pink.

CESARE: Devil don't play by the rules, man, get some sense.

JERRY: Does he have an office?

CESARE: No. I checked. No one knows him.

ANNOUNCER: Ball three.

(*Beat.*)

CESARE: I'm fucked.

JERRY: Jesus Mary Joseph.

CESARE: No, man, I'm fucked. All I ever wanted to do was play baseball. Now it's gone. Fuck all the money. Give a fuck about the money. Just wanted to play for the majors. But I fucked up. Got greedy.

JERRY: You did what any player would have done. You did what many players have done. Metaphorically.

CESARE: Doesn't make it right. I betrayed the team, betrayed my fans. I deserve what's coming to me.

JERRY: You're a good kid, you just got confused.

CESARE: He's gonna get me.

JERRY: Don't get all dramatic. Still have to play the rest of the game.

CESARE: He said I shouldn't tell anyone and now I told you! He's gonna wax me!

JERRY: You ain't getting waxed! Concentrate on the game!

CESARE: It doesn't matter, man, don't you see? He always gets his man! Strike three, I'm out!

JERRY: Shut up with that talk! Now, listen here! You were the best goddamned player this team has seen! Don't care what you think happened, you're gonna be fine! You're gonna get your stride! You're gonna get into a series! You're gonna win, man, you're gonna win it all! Because I believe you can! Fuck this devil shit! You're not going to die, Cesare!

(*Beat.*)

CESARE: You did it.

JERRY: Did what?

CESARE: You pronounced my name right.

(*A baseball whizzes into* CESARE. *He falls.*)

ANNOUNCER: . . . and a line drive by Tanaka knocks third base-man Caesar Cruz to the ground!

(*Crowd roars.*)

JERRY: Cesare?

ANNOUNCER: . . . and Tanaka is rounding first . . .

JERRY: Cesare!

ANNOUNCER: . . . he's making his way to second . . .

JERRY: Cesare.

ANNOUNCER: . . . Tanaka is barreling full speed toward third base! Ladies and gentlemen, what a play!

(*Roaring from crowd reaches a deafening level as* JERRY *stands over the* motionless CESARE. *Black.*)

END OF PLAY

ROSA'S EULOGY

Richard Strand

Rosa's Eulogy was commissioned by Actors Theatre of Louisville and premiered at the Humana Festival of New American Plays in March 2001 as part of *Heaven and Hell (on Earth): A Divine Comedy*. It was directed by Sullivan Canaday White and Meredith McDonough; the set design was by Paul Owen; the lighting design was by Tony Penna; the sound design was by Jason Tratta with Martin R. Desjardins; the costume design was by Kevin McLeod; the stage manager was John Armstrong; and the dramaturgs were Amy Wegener, Tanya Palmer, and Michael Bigelow Dixon. The cast of *Rosa's Eulogy* was as follows:

JEANNE   Jennifer Taher

JEANNE *stands over a cardboard box which she has surrounded with lit votive candles. Occasionally she will fondly stroke the contents of that box.*

JEANNE: Dear Lord, I am here before you to honor this cat, who I don't actually know but who I found in the street outside my apartment where some bastard hit her with his car and then just left her for carrion. I call her Rosa because, because, I don't know her real name and I like the name Rosa. What do we know about Rosa? We know that she is one of your creations and therefore precious. We know, in fact, that she was more worthy in your eyes than the bastard who probably got her as a kitten because she was cute but didn't take even a second to consider that getting a cat is a lifelong responsibility so he just tossed her out of his car onto Foothill Boulevard when he got bored with her where the chances of her surviving even two days are about nil because—Foothill Boulevard, for Christ's sake—that's a busy street and if she's not hit by a car she's going to get sick or eaten by a coyote—whatever— what we know is that Rosa is going to heaven and the bastard who called himself her owner is going . . . (JEANNE *stops herself.*) Sorry. Sorry. Not my decision. That's up to you, of course. Sorry. Didn't mean to overstep. (JEANNE *returns to her eulogy.*) Even though I never met Rosa when she was alive, I can tell—anyone could tell just looking at her lifeless

419

corpse—that she was a Maine Coon, which is one of the most beautiful breeds of cat that you ever thought to place on this earth. Well, you know, you gave breeders the gift of scientific insight so they could create the Maine Coon breed, but still, your fingerprints are all over this. We know Rosa was a Maine Coon by the striped tail and the distinctive dark patches over her eyes and the nose which, well, um, seems a little longer than would be considered show quality . . . (JEANNE *looks closer at Rosa.*)

Okay, she's probably not a purebred Maine Coon, but she is clearly . . . (JEANNE *takes another close look at Rosa.*) Holy cripe, she's a raccoon. What the hell am I doing petting a raccoon? Eoo. Eoo. (JEANNE *is wiping her hands on her pants.*) Sorry. (JEANNE *blows out a candle.*) Sorry. (JEANNE *blows out another candle.*) Didn't mean to bother you over a raccoon. (JEANNE *blows out another candle.*) Oh, man. Gotta wash my hands. Sorry, God. Sorry. Go back to whatever you were doing. I'll take care of the raccoon. (JEANNE *blows out the remaining candles.*) Toss this in the Dumpster. Sorry, Lord. Sorry.

END OF PLAY

CHOCOLATE

Frederick Stroppel

Chocolate was produced by the Theatre Artists Workshop of Westport in Norwalk, Connecticut, in July 2001, as part of their annual Word of the Week Festival. The play was directed by Carole Schweid and had the following cast:

DETECTIVE   Herb Duncan
MRS. COLBY   Dorothy Bryce

A DETECTIVE, *notebook in hand, is speaking with* MRS. COLBY, *a housewife, in her living room.*

DETECTIVE: So you have no idea where your husband is?

MRS. COLBY: (*Cheerfully.*) No idea! Not a *clue*! He could be *anywhere*!

DETECTIVE: When was the last time you saw him, Mrs. Colby?

MRS. COLBY: Well, let's see. This is Thursday, it must be . . . oh, two weeks now.

DETECTIVE: Two weeks?

MRS. COLBY: Yes, it was right after the harvest moon. Because I remember saying to him, "Look, Clive. It's the harvest moon!" And he didn't answer. And I was a little miffed at the time, but now I realize he wasn't even here. Which just goes to show, you should never jump to conclusions.

DETECTIVE: So Mr. Colby has been missing for two weeks, and you never reported this fact to the police?

423

MRS. COLBY: Heavens, no. My husband is a very private person. I wouldn't want the police intruding on his personal life. Would you like some coffee, Detective?

DETECTIVE: No, thank you. Mrs. Colby, you don't seem especially concerned about your husband's disappearance.

MRS. COLBY: Well, of course I'm concerned. But I'm a worrier by nature, so I don't give that much weight.

DETECTIVE: I see.

MRS. COLBY: Besides, this is hardly unusual for Clive. He's a whimsical fellow and possessed of strong idiosyncratic urges that often defy description. Once he walked out on us in the middle of Christmas dinner, and he called us three days later from British Columbia. He was trying to join up with the Mounties! Well, we all had a good laugh about that, you can imagine.

DETECTIVE: Mrs. Colby, we have reason to suspect that the circumstances here are a little more serious than that.

MRS. COLBY: Well, I should hope so.

DETECTIVE: We've spoken to your neighbors, and they reported that there was some kind of disturbance here at the house the night that your husband disappeared.

MRS. COLBY: Really? Here? How funny!

DETECTIVE: Yes, they said there was a lot of shouting and arguing . . . profane language. Strange animal noises.

MRS. COLBY: Animal noises? That's *so* interesting! Would you like some apple juice, Detective?

DETECTIVE: No, thank you. Now, did you and your husband have any sort of disagreement that evening?

MRS. COLBY: Lordy, no. My husband and I were always in perfect concordance. Our evenings were invariably spent in sedate, placid self-satisfaction.

DETECTIVE: There was no shouting?

MRS. COLBY: Oh, the shouting—I can explain that. Clive is getting a little hard of hearing, and I may have raised my voice a tad asking him what kind of topping he wanted on his ice cream frappé.

DETECTIVE: (*Consults notebook.*) There was an overheard statement, and I'm quoting here: "Fat cow? I'll show you who's a fat cow!"

MRS. COLBY: Well, I can explain that. You see, we were playing a little game in the privacy of our bedroom, the details of which are rather salacious and not at all relevant to this investigation.

DETECTIVE: Perhaps not, but the words in question were spoken in the living room.

MRS. COLBY: Well, we were moving around. It was spirited fun.

DETECTIVE: The neighbors reported screaming, lights going on and off, . . . some sort of violent struggle with the venetian blinds.

MRS. COLBY: Yes, that was Clive. He was pretending to be a parrot, you see.

DETECTIVE: A parrot?

MRS. COLBY: Yes. We were playing the Parrot and the Cow.

DETECTIVE: I see.

MRS. COLBY: So naturally he was jumping around on the furniture, scratching the blinds . . . knocked over one of my best lamps. It was very comical, and yet profoundly erotic.

DETECTIVE: I see.

MRS. COLBY: Would you like a muffin, Detective?

DETECTIVE: No, thank you. Now, Mrs. Colby, we checked on some of your credit purchases in the last two weeks and discovered a bill from Home Depot for a load of mixing cement, which was delivered to this address. *Forty sacks* of cement, to be precise.

MRS. COLBY: Forty sacks . . . Yes, that sounds about right.

DETECTIVE: On the face of it, that's a lot of cement, Mrs. Colby.

MRS. COLBY: Well, I can explain that. You see, I make birdbaths as a hobby.

DETECTIVE: Birdbaths?

MRS. COLBY: Yes. I design my own birdbath molds, mix the cement personally, pour it in, let it set . . . and voilà!

DETECTIVE: I didn't notice any birdbaths in your backyard.

MRS. COLBY: Oh, no, I give them all away, to friends and passersby. For me, the joy is in the creation.

DETECTIVE: What I *did* notice, out behind the garage, was a very large cement plot, about three by six feet, which appeared to be quite freshly laid.

MRS. COLBY: Yes, well, that's all the excess cement. There are so many false starts in birdbath construction, you have no idea.

DETECTIVE: Apparently not.

MRS. COLBY: I eventually intend to build a shrine to Saint Anthony out there.

DETECTIVE: I see.

MRS. COLBY: Could I get you some sardines, Detective?

DETECTIVE: No, thank you. Now, forgive me for pointing this out, but it's my job to pick up on any discrepancies, and there appears to be a large shovel tucked behind the couch there.

MRS. COLBY: Oh, yes.

DETECTIVE: Now, am I to assume that that's the customary spot for your heavy garden tools?

MRS. COLBY: No, not for the most part, but I use that particular shovel to clean away the cobwebs that tend to gather in the vestibule.

DETECTIVE: Most people would use a broom for that purpose.

MRS. COLBY: Yes, most people would. The more fools, they.

DETECTIVE: I *have* observed that on the whole you do keep a very tidy home, Mrs. Colby.

MRS. COLBY: Why, thank you, Detective.

DETECTIVE: Which makes that stain on the carpet there all the more conspicuous.

MRS. COLBY: Oh? Is there a stain?

DETECTIVE: Yes, right there? It looks for all the world like dried blood.

MRS. COLBY (*Looks.*) Yes, it does, doesn't it?

DETECTIVE: But I take it it's not?

MRS. COLBY: My stars, no. It's chocolate.

DETECTIVE: Chocolate?

MRS. COLBY: Yes, we had a box of Godiva chocolates sitting around here for the longest time, and then one day, oh, about two weeks ago, I just dipped into them and couldn't stop. I must have dropped a praline crunch on the floor. I was wondering what happened to it.

DETECTIVE: Excuse my presumption, ma'am, but that doesn't look like Godiva chocolate.

MRS. COLBY: Oh, but it is. Look.

(*She bends and scrapes a bit off the carpet and proceeds to eat it.*)

Mmmm . . . See? Still retaining its rich decadent flavor. Would you like some?

DETECTIVE: No, thank you. But when I say it doesn't look like Godiva chocolate, I'm referring to the fact that it looks more like . . . how shall I say this?

(*Dramatic pause.*)

Nestlé's.

MRS. COLBY: (*Gasps.*) I beg your pardon?

DETECTIVE: In the course of my various investigations over the years, I have had occasion to make a comparative study of the grades and qualities of foreign and domestic chocolates. This has a decidedly processed milk-chocolaty look, Mrs. Colby. How do you explain that? Or can you?

MRS. COLBY: (*Stammers.*) Well, I . . . I . . .

DETECTIVE: Yes?

MRS. COLBY: (*Sheepish.*) You've caught me out, Detective. I should have known better than to try to hoodwink a man of your acute perspicacity. Yes, it's a KitKat bar. My secret is out: I eat commercial, candy-store chocolate on the sly. Oh, if the girls at the country club knew this . . . I'm so embarrassed.

DETECTIVE: There, there, Mrs. Colby. Don't be hard on yourself. Many a decent citizen will resort to lies and prevarications when social pressures come to bear. Needless to say, this will be our little secret; it goes no farther than this room.

MRS. COLBY: I'm very grateful, Detective. You're a man of rare delicacy and perception.

DETECTIVE: Yes, I suppose I am.

(*Flips his notebook shut.*)

Well, I guess everything else checks out. Thank you for your time, ma'am.

(*He heads out and then stops.*)

Oh, one more thing.

MRS. COLBY: Yes?

DETECTIVE: This game you mentioned—the Parrot and the Cow?

MRS. COLBY: Yes?

DETECTIVE: Does it have to be a *parrot*?

MRS. COLBY: Why, noooo. The species are flexible, so long as the usual rules obtain. You could be a snake, or a duck, or—what you will.

DETECTIVE: (*Pleased.*) I see. Well, we'll be in touch.

(DETECTIVE *exits.*)

END OF PLAY

THE EARRING

Joyce Van Dyke

The Earring premiered at the Calderwood Pavilion as part of the annual Boston Theater Marathon in May 2005. It was directed by Patricia Riggin and produced by New Repertory Theatre. The cast was as follows:

YELENA	Bobbie Steinbach
ANDRUSHA	Matt O'Hare
ALEXANDRA	Anne Gottlieb
MANUEL	Juan Luis Acevedo

CHARACTERS

YELENA: A hotel maid, in her fifties.
ANDRUSHA: Her son, nineteen, a gang member.
ALEXANDRA: A theatrical agent, in her early forties.
MANUEL: An actor (mixed race), in his early twenties.

SETTING

The living room of a New York hotel suite. In the middle of the room is a hotel maid's cleaning cart.

TIME

The present, around ten in the morning.

NOTE ON DIALOGUE

YELENA and ANDRUSHA speak English with a Russian accent throughout (very heavy for YELENA, lighter for ANDRUSHA). When YELENA and ANDRUSHA speak to each other, the convention is that they are speaking Russian. When they speak to the Americans, however, they are speaking broken English.

Lights come up on ANDRUSHA *listening to music on a New York side-walk and* YELENA *vacuuming in the hotel room. The vacuum cleaner repeatedly approaches an earring lying on the floor that she is not at first in a position to see. When she catches sight of the earring, she turns off the vacuum cleaner.* ANDRUSHA *disappears.* YELENA *picks up the earring: It's gold, with a large diamond. She goes over to examine it in the light. It's obvious that she has a very practiced eye and knows what she is looking for.*

YELENA: O bozhe!*

(*She closes her hand tightly over the earring.*)

Holy mother of God.

(*She opens her hand and looks at it again.*)

Saint Boris, Saint Nikolai, Saint Vladimir—just look away, don't watch me, let me do what I need to do, don't judge me! What's one little sin in this city. No, a sin's a sin, no matter where, but you yourself, Saint Vladimir! How many terrible things you did before you became a saint! One earring in one room in one hotel in New York City!

*Aw-BOH-zhe: Oh my God!

(*She wraps the earring in a handkerchief, tucks it into her bra, goes to the phone and dials out.* ANDRUSHA *appears. He's still loitering on the sidewalk. His cell phone rings and he pulls it out of his pocket.*)

ANDRUSHA: I told you not to call me at work.

YELENA: Andrusha, Andrusha—

ANDRUSHA: I'm not a kid. I'm waiting for a call.

YELENA: I found something, Andrusha, something valuable, I want to give it to you, but you have to come right away. Can you come? I'm in room 1919. Can you—

(*The door opens and* ALEXANDRA *and* MANUEL *enter with a room key.*)

MANUEL: I want to audition for it, why not?

ALEXANDRA: You're not what they're looking for. (*Seeing* YELENA.) Oh!

(YELENA *smiles and nods at them.*)

YELENA: (*On the phone.*) It's too late. But maybe not. (*To* ALEXANDRA *and* MANUEL.) I don't think you can understand me, can you.

ALEXANDRA: What language is she speaking?

MANUEL: Russian? I think.

YELENA: (*On the phone.*) They checked out early, but it looks like they've come back, they must be looking for it.

ANDRUSHA: What did you find?

YELENA: (*On the phone.*) How am I gonna give it to you with them here?

ALEXANDRA: (*To* YELENA.) Pardon me . . .

ANDRUSHA: Look, should I come, or what?

YELENA: (*On the phone.*) I have to go. Yes, come, come. Room 1919. I'll think of something. Bye.

(YELENA *and* ANDRUSHA *both hang up.* ANDRUSHA *exits.*)

ALEXANDRA: Hi. Um. Do you speak English?

YELENA: Excuse.

ALEXANDRA: I lost my earring. (*Showing.*) My earring. I lost my other earring. Did you find it in here by any chance?

YELENA: (*Admiring the earring* ALEXANDRA *shows her.*) Ah!

ALEXANDRA: No, I *lost* it. It must've fallen off somewhere—

MANUEL: She's not following you.

ALEXANDRA: Have you vacuumed? Vacuum?

YELENA: Vacuum, da. Okay.

(*She turns on the vacuum cleaner.*)

ALEXANDRA: No, no! Don't!

(YELENA *turns off the vacuum cleaner.*)

(*To* YELENA.) You didn't find an earring like this, did you? (*To* MANUEL.) She understands exactly what I'm saying. I'm sure she does.

MANUEL: (*To* YELENA.) You know, I just have to say this—you are such an attractive woman. Ever since we walked in, it's driving me crazy. I'd really like to sleep with you.

(ALEXANDRA *stares at him.*)

YELENA: (*To* MANUEL.) Excuse?

MANUEL: (*Complacently.*) Nope. Doesn't speak English.

ALEXANDRA: She understands body language. She has to know what I'm talking about. What if she found it and isn't telling us? I'm calling hotel security.

(*The phone rings.* MANUEL *picks up.*)

MANUEL: Hello?

(MANUEL *is puzzled by what he is hearing. Tentatively he extends the phone to* YELENA, *and she takes it.*)

YELENA: (*To* MANUEL *and* ALEXANDRA.) Excuse.

ALEXANDRA: She takes her calls in our room? It's still our room.

YELENA: (*On the phone.*) Hello?

(ANDRUSHA *appears in a spot.*)

ANDRUSHA: I'm in the lobby.

YELENA: (*On the phone.*) They're still here. This woman won't give up.

MANUEL: It was a guy. (*Speculatively.*) Young guy.

YELENA: (*On the phone.*) Wait in the lobby, I'll call you.

ALEXANDRA: She's not going anywhere. What if she has it on her? And I left her a tip. That's gone, she took it already.

ANDRUSHA: I can't wait around. I got an appointment.

YELENA: (*On the phone.*) Andrusha, I'm doing this for you. I know you need the money. I take the sin on myself—

ANDRUSHA: Don't preach to me.

(ANDRUSHA *hangs up and disappears.*)

YELENA: (*On the phone.*) Andrusha, please.

ALEXANDRA: I couldn't have lost it! I don't lose things.

YELENA: (*On the phone.*) Andrusha . . .

MANUEL: That's kind of an arrogant thing to say.

(YELENA *hangs up.*)

ALEXANDRA: I mean, I'm careful. I don't lose things. Like my cell phone.

MANUEL: I told you, I didn't even want that part.

ALEXANDRA: But that's one you could've gotten! You take what you can get.

MANUEL: Any suck-ass script.

ALEXANDRA: At your stage, yes.

MANUEL: I want a gift! I want the hand of God to—like the part Eric got!

ALEXANDRA: Eric? Eric is blond and blue-eyed. Who looks more American—Eric, or you? Wake up, Manuel! How often do you think you can get cast in this country?

MANUEL: I thought I was gonna be the "jewel in your crown." Or was that just to seduce me?

ALEXANDRA: I can't believe you're attacking me now. When I'm heartsick about this loss. (*To* YELENA.) Excuse me, I don't know how to say this. (*Turning away.*) I can't do this. This is so embarrassing. (*To* YELENA, *beckoning.*) Excuse me, do you mind?

(ALEXANDRA *indicates turning her pockets inside out.* YELENA *complies. A cigarette lighter falls out of one of her pockets.*)

Okay, now she knows I suspect her. Jesus Christ.

YELENA: Jesus Christ. Da.

(*She pulls a crucifix on a chain out of her uniform and points at a small gold crucifix around* ALEXANDRA*'s neck.*)

ALEXANDRA: Oh, yeah. Da. That's right.

(ALEXANDRA *touches her cross.*)

Christian, yes, we're both Christians. What the hell am I saying?

(MANUEL *picks up the lighter and offers* YELENA *a cigarette. She accepts. He lights it for her.* ALEXANDRA *watches them.*)

She likes you.

YELENA: (*To* MANUEL.) What beautiful eyes you have.

ALEXANDRA: What's she saying?

MANUEL: How charming I am.

(*He smiles at* YELENA.)

YELENA: The way you light my cigarette—a real gentleman! My son, he only smokes marijuana. He tears a page out of my Bible to roll a joint! I've lost him. He's in this gang, on the streets all day. Like in Moscow, the gang that stole Papa's store—he had a jewelry store. Small. We lost everything. Then we came to America. Now my son is gone, too.

MANUEL: I love the sound of Russian, it's so dark and stewy.

(*A knock on the door.* ALEXANDRA *opens it. It's* ANDRUSHA. YELENA's *face lights up.*)

ANDRUSHA: You still have it?

YELENA: Yes. You're looking well.

MANUEL: (*To* ALEXANDRA.) She's his mother.

ALEXANDRA: (*Amazed.*) How do you know?

ANDRUSHA: (*To* MANUEL *and* ALEXANDRA.) I go to college. In neighborhood. So I come by.

YELENA: (*To* MANUEL *and* ALEXANDRA.) This is my son, my Andrusha.

ANDRUSHA: (*Embarrassed.*) She's telling I'm her son.

(ALEXANDRA *squeezes* MANUEL's *arm.*)

ALEXANDRA: (*To* MANUEL.) You're good.

ANDRUSHA: (*To* MANUEL *and* ALEXANDRA.) Also I work full-time. College. Work. Not much time for visit.

ALEXANDRA: Yeah. I see. Could you ask her if she's found an earring? Like this? I think I might have lost it in here.

ANDRUSHA: (*To* YELENA.) It's an earring?

(YELENA *nods.*)

Don't nod! Tell me in words.

YELENA: A diamond earring. How can I give it to you?

ALEXANDRA: What did she say, did she find it?

ANDRUSHA: No.

ALEXANDRA: Why did she nod?

ANDRUSHA: She nods because she understands you look for it.

ALEXANDRA: But she hasn't seen it anywhere.

ANDRUSHA: No. This makes you so unhappy?

ALEXANDRA: It has a lot of sentimental value. As well as financial.

ANDRUSHA: But you are rich woman. You are rich.

MANUEL: Hey, man, she just wants her earring back.

ANDRUSHA: (*To* YELENA.) She stays in hotels, she has a boyfriend, she has a nice figure, and she isn't happy! It takes all kinds.

YELENA: I'm happy to see you, Andrusha. (*Smoothing his hair.*)
My dear. Now you hug me, kiss me—and I'll give it to you.

(*He kisses her and embraces her. During the embrace she pulls out the
handkerchief to wipe away her tears and passes the earring to him.*)

I love you, Andrusha darling. I love you.

ANDRUSHA: Mama.

YELENA: (*Moved.*) Go now. Go. Call me.

(ANDRUSHA, *blushing and embarrassed, straightens himself. He nods to*
ALEXANDRA *and* MANUEL *and goes out.*)

ALEXANDRA: Gee, what a nice son.

MANUEL: A lucky son. To have a mother like that? The way she
looks at him . . .

ALEXANDRA: I love you. It's still our room. For a little while. Why
don't you ask her to go?

MANUEL: (*In a heavy, perfect Russian accent.*) I don't speak Russian,
only Russian accent.

(YELENA *gives him a look. She is putting the vacuum on the cart.*)

ALEXANDRA: Anyway, I think she gets it.

(YELENA *motions the two of them together. She pushes her cart out.*)

END OF PLAY

THE BLUEBERRY HILL ACCORD

Daryl Watson

The Blueberry Hill Accord was first staged by students during the final week of the Summer Teenage Conservatory Rehearsal and Performance Program at Stella Adler Studio, New York, on August 12, 2005. The program was directed by Melissa Ross, and the cast was as follows.

HANNAH   Emma Fernberger
LINDSAY   AJ Luca

Lights up on the Blueberry Hill diner. High school students HANNAH *and* LINDSAY *are sitting across from each other in a booth.* HANNAH *is reading a magazine while* LINDSAY *eats from a plate of fries and does homework.*

HANNAH: . . . and I'm like, "Just because I let you do it a year ago doesn't mean I have to let you do it now!" And then Stephanie—and I can't believe she says this—she goes, "Okay, *Ebenezer*." And I'm, like, "What?" And she goes, "Why don't you lighten up a little?" And I'm, like, "Why don't you get herpes and *die*, you crack ho from *Long Beach*!" Unbelievable, right? Can I have a fry?

LINDSAY: A small one.

(*Beat.*)

HANNAH: Excuse me?

LINDSAY: If it's a small one, yeah.

(*Beat.*)

HANNAH: Eeew!

LINDSAY: I have clarinet rehearsal tonight until ten! There's no dinner break; this has *got* to hold me over.

HANNAH: *Forget it.* So anyways, Stephanie, she comes off like this total saint—

LINDSAY: Why do you do that?

(*Beat.*)

HANNAH: Do what?

LINDSAY: That!

HANNAH: What?

LINDSAY: That! That whole passive-aggressive thing you're . . .

HANNAH: Passive-aggress . . . *what?*

LINDSAY: . . . doing, that you always do, so that I end up feeling like a *bitch*.

HANNAH: I seriously have no idea what you—

LINDSAY: If you want a fry, take a fry.

(*Beat.*)

HANNAH: I don't want one.

LINDSAY: Do you not want one because you don't want one, or do you not want one because you want me to feel bad for not wanting you to have one?

HANNAH: I don't want one. Can I finish the story now, please?

LINDSAY: Just take a fry.

(*Beat.*)

HANNAH: No.

LINDSAY: Take a fry.

HANNAH: You obviously don't want me to.

LINDSAY: It's fine if you take a small one.

HANNAH: Lindsay, I don't care—

LINDSAY: TAKE A FRY!

HANNAH: ALL RIGHT! GOD!

(*She grabs a fry and eats it.*)

There! Are we done now?

(*Beat.*)

LINDSAY: I can't do this.

HANNAH: Share food? I agree.

LINDSAY: No, I mean . . . I don't think I can do this anymore.

HANNAH: Do what?

LINDSAY: This. Us. This whole *us* thing. I don't think it's working out. The friendship.

HANNAH: (*Laughing.*) What is this? A breakup?

(*A very long beat.*)

Are you breaking up with me?

(*Beat.*)

LINDSAY: I just think that we're in different places in our lives. We want different things—

HANNAH: This is the breakup speech! I know that speech when I hear it. You're giving me the speech!

LINDSAY: Hannah . . .

HANNAH: You're breaking up with me?

LINDSAY: Would you stop saying that? It's not—

HANNAH: You're breaking up with me over french fries?

LINDSAY: It's not about the french fries.

HANNAH: Then what is it?

LINDSAY: I don't know! A lot of things! God, we've been friends since the third grade. Aren't you ready to . . .

HANNAH: To what?

LINDSAY: To move on. Meet other people!

HANNAH: Meet other pe . . . *What are you talking about?* If you want to meet people, go! Meet! That's the great thing about friends. You can have more than one.

LINDSAY: That doesn't work for me.

HANNAH: That's how it works for EVERYBODY!

LINDSAY: I'm very particular about who I hang out with! I can only deal with about five acquaintance friends and one really good friend. I don't have the energy for anything else. You know I'm like this. I don't know why you're surprised.

HANNAH: I thought I was your really good friend.

LINDSAY: You were, but . . . honestly, lately, when we're together, I feel like . . .

HANNAH: What?

LINDSAY: Like we're two ships sailing past each other in the night.

(*Beat.*)

HANNAH: I don't know what that means.

LINDSAY: It means you and I are two ships. And it's night.

HANNAH: Yes, I got that part.

LINDSAY: And we keep sailing right past each other!

HANNAH: Isn't that better than crashing into each other?

LINDSAY: It's a metaphor.

HANNAH: I don't get it.

LINDSAY: That's my point! You don't get me. I don't get you. You talk about things that I don't really care about, and I definitely talk about things that you don't care about.

HANNAH: I care about the things you talk about.

LINDSAY: No, you don't.

HANNAH: Yes, I do.

(*Beat.*)

You think I'm boring?

LINDSAY: No.

(*Beat.*)

HANNAH: You think I'm boring!

LINDSAY: No, you're not listening.

HANNAH: Yes, I am. I'm listening to you call me boring.

LINDSAY: No, Hannah. There's a difference between you being boring and you just saying things that I don't find interesting.

HANNAH: Well, if I'm being uninteresting, you can say something.

LINDSAY: I can't.

HANNAH: Yes, you can.

LINDSAY: I can't.

HANNAH: Why?

LINDSAY: Because . . . I'd be saying something all the time.

(*Beat.*)

HANNAH: That's really mean.

LINDSAY: I'm sorry.

HANNAH: That was really, really mean.

LINDSAY: I'm being honest.

HANNAH: Yeah? You're also being a bitch! How's that for honesty?

(HANNAH *rises and heads toward the exit.*)

Enjoy your freedom.

LINDSAY: Hannah, wait! Hannah!

(HANNAH *pauses.*)

Please. Sit down. Hannah, sit down. Please.

(HANNAH *slowly walks back over to the table and sits down. Beat.*)

Before we leave here today . . . there's a few things I'd like to get in writing.

(LINDSAY *leans over, pulls her book bag up from the floor, and opens it. She removes several pieces of paper from the bag and sets them on the table.* HANNAH *stares at her in disbelief.*)

I've compiled some notes here . . . they're more bullet points, actually . . . I was thinking we could go over them and both sign at the bottom.

HANNAH: Is this a joke?

LINDSAY: Well . . . no . . .

HANNAH: I'm not signing anything.

LINDSAY: But—

HANNAH: NO! This is stupid.

LINDSAY: I feel this is the best.

HANNAH: I don't give a shit what you feel.

(HANNAH *rises again.*)

LINDSAY: LOOK, I KNOW THINGS ABOUT YOU!

HANNAH: Are you threatening me?

LINDSAY: No! You know things about me too. Okay? So it's in both of our best interests to settle this on paper.

(*Beat.*)

HANNAH: You're serious.

LINDSAY: Yes.

HANNAH: You really wanna do this.

LINDSAY: Yes.

HANNAH: You wanna add yet another layer of insanity to this whole thing.

LINDSAY: Well, I wouldn't—

HANNAH: No, no, no! You wanna do it, let's do it!

(HANNAH *sits down and grabs the papers, flipping through them.*)

First of all, I want all my stuff back from you.

LINDSAY: Right.

HANNAH: My Norah Jones CD . . .

LINDSAY: My copy of *Pride and Prejudice*.

HANNAH: My green top. My Magic 8-ball.

LINDSAY: You gave me the Magic 8-ball.

HANNAH: I lent you the 8-ball. You just never gave it back.

LINDSAY: You never asked for it. I've had it for three years.

HANNAH: Better late than never.

LINDSAY: Fine. And just so we're clear, I don't want you to say anything about me to other people.

HANNAH: Fine. And you better not say anything about me either.

LINDSAY: Fine.

HANNAH: And you know what? I don't want you telling the Joey Feinberg story anymore.

LINDSAY: WHAT? Why?

HANNAH: Because it's my story.

LINDSAY: But I always tell that story! It's a good story!

HANNAH: It's a great story! And you butcher it every time you tell it.

LINDSAY: I do not.

HANNAH: Lindsay, you could find a lottery ticket on the street, win a million dollars, get kidnapped by Colombian drug lords and held for ransom, go on *Oprah* to tell the whole world about it . . . and you'd still make it the most boring, yawn-inducing story ever. You have a knack for it.

LINDSAY: That's so mean!

HANNAH: It's the truth. I only let you tell the Joey Feinberg story because you're my friend. But if we're not friends anymore, you can't tell the story.

LINDSAY: Well, then, you can't tell the Lake Mead story.

HANNAH: What sense does that make?

LINDSAY: If I can't tell the Joey Feinberg story, you can't tell the Lake Mead story.

HANNAH: Excuse me! The Joey Feinberg story happened to me and Joey Feinberg. It's my story.

LINDSAY: And the Lake Mead story happened to both you *and* me. It's fifty percent mine, by rights, and I'm saying I don't want you telling it.

HANNAH: Fifty percent of it is mine too!

LINDSAY: Well, you can tell your fifty percent of it.

HANNAH: This is ridiculous.

LINDSAY: I'm serious. You can only talk about the stuff that happened to you. Leave me out of it.

HANNAH: Fine.

LINDSAY: And you can't tell anybody what I told you about my parents.

HANNAH: Okay.

LINDSAY: Promise me.

HANNAH: I promise. I'm writing it down. See? And you can't tell anybody about the time I got my period during that softball game.

LINDSAY: I thought everybody knew that.

HANNAH: Everyone thinks it was Jackie.

LINDSAY: Nuh-uh!

HANNAH: Why do you think they call her Jackie Swab-inson?

LINDSAY: Gross! That's awful!

HANNAH: Whatever. It's payback from when she told everybody I had mono, when I so didn't.

LINDSAY: I guess.

HANNAH: You guess right. She's a bitch.

LINDSAY: Did you know she went after Tommy Marth, even after she knew I liked him?

HANNAH: 'Cause she's *like* that. I told you not to tell her you wanted him. But for the record, I can date Tommy now.

LINDSAY: WHAT?

HANNAH: Once we sign this, all's fair.

LINDSAY: So does that mean I can date Adam?

HANNAH: Yeah. Sure. Whatever. I don't care.

LINDSAY: All right.

HANNAH: You can't tell anybody I'm seeing a therapist.

LINDSAY: You can't tell anybody *I'm* seeing a therapist. And you can't tell anybody I kissed Rachel Bumgardner at that party.

HANNAH: YOU KISSED RACHEL BUMGARDNER?

LINDSAY: Wait, you didn't know?

HANNAH: NO!

LINDSAY: Oh my God. I cannot believe I just told you that.

HANNAH: So what happened? You *have* to tell me.

LINDSAY: It was so crazy . . .

(LINDSAY *stops herself. Long beat.*)

LINDSAY: I can't think of anything else to put down.

HANNAH: Actually . . . I have one more thing.

LINDSAY: What?

HANNAH: Neither of us can eat here. Ever.

LINDSAY: No way.

HANNAH: We can't or I won't sign.

LINDSAY: Why?

HANNAH: Because Blueberry Hill is our spot! This is our place. This is where I told you about losing my virginity—

LINDSAY: Shhh!

HANNAH: . . . and you told me about you losing yours!

LINDSAY: SHHH!

HANNAH: We've stayed up late studying here, we've had all the big talks here: guys, religion, college, everything. It's holy ground. I don't care who you pick for your "really good friend," but you better not bring her here.

LINDSAY: I don't know . . .

HANNAH: Am I wrong? Doesn't that history mean anything to you?

LINDSAY: No, it does. I just . . .

HANNAH: What?

LINDSAY: I don't know! This is hard!

HANNAH: Well . . . I don't know what to tell you. I would have been perfectly happy if you'd just given me the silent treatment for eight months and talked shit behind my back while I went crazy trying to figure out what happened. That's how normal people end friendships. You're the one that wanted to turn it into the Geneva Convention.

LINDSAY: Okay.

HANNAH: So we're agreed? Blueberry Hill's off limits?

LINDSAY: Yeah.

HANNAH: Okay.

(*Beat.*)

So where should I sign?

LINDSAY: Well, we can't sign it like this.

HANNAH: Why not?

LINDSAY: It's all scribbles. It should be typed up in legalese so that it at least looks legible.

(*Beat.*)

HANNAH: So who's going to do that?

LINDSAY: I guess I will.

(*Beat.*)

HANNAH: So in the meantime . . . verbal agreement?

LINDSAY: I don't trust those. No one ever agrees on what was actually agreed upon. That's why you get things in writing. I mean . . . I'm willing to wait if you are.

HANNAH: I guess.

LINDSAY: At least until I get this typed up.

HANNAH: Right.

LINDSAY: You know?

HANNAH: Okay.

(*Beat.*)

Wait . . . I'm confused! So are we still friends?

LINDSAY: Well . . . I mean, until we sign this, technically, yeah. We are.

(*Beat.*)

HANNAH: Does that mean you're still coming over this weekend?

LINDSAY: Oh . . .

HANNAH: Because I'm just going to be hanging out, so . . . if you don't think you'll be done by then . . .

LINDSAY: We'll see. I got a lot of homework and rehearsal, so maybe I won't get to it. I don't know.

HANNAH: Or if you do finish it, you can bring it over, we can hang out, and then we'll sign it before you leave.

LINDSAY: Okay.

HANNAH: Whatever. We'll see what happens.

LINDSAY: Yeah.

(*Long beat.*)

HANNAH: *Rachel Bumgardner?*

LINDSAY: Okay, first of all, I was trashed beyond reason . . .

(As LINDSAY *ad-libs the story, the lights fade to black.)*

END OF PLAY

WEDDING DUET

Lauren Wilson

Wedding Duet was first performed at the Downstage Theatre, Sarah Lawrence College, in December 2005. It was directed by Lori Leigh. The cast was as follows:

BRIDE   Lindsay Doleshal
GROOM   Randall Whittinghill

A closed door. Laughter behind it. A key is put into the lock—more laughter. The knob turns and the door opens. The GROOM *stands on the threshold, carrying the* BRIDE.

BRIDE: Oh my God. This is so perfect!

GROOM: Can you lift up your dress any?

BRIDE: It's so adorable! Look at the little fireplace!

GROOM: Very cute. Here, can I put you down while I get a better grip?

BRIDE: You can't put me down here!

GROOM: Okay, let me just give you a boost then.

(*He does.*)

BRIDE: Watch the train!

GROOM: I will.

(*Boosts her again.*)

That's better.

BRIDE: Hang on, my veil's pulling.

GROOM: Why don't you just take it off?

BRIDE: I can't take it off yet! I think your foot's on it.

GROOM: It is?

(*He steps aside.*)

BRIDE: No, other way.

(*He moves again.*)

GROOM: Look, let's just go in. My arms—

BRIDE: Okay, but wait. The photographer's not here.

GROOM: We don't need a picture of this. Let's just remember it.

BRIDE: You're right. Let's take it all in so we'll never forget this moment.

(*They do.*)

GROOM: Honey?

BRIDE: Wait a minute. Just one more second.

GROOM: My arms—

(*He drops her on the threshold.*)

BRIDE: Oh my God!

GROOM: Are you all right? Did you hit your head?

BRIDE: No, I'm all right. Are you all right?

GROOM: Sure, I'm fine. I just couldn't hold on anymore.

BRIDE: I'm sorry. It was my fault. I shouldn't have made you—

GROOM: No, it was my fault. I should have braced my—

(*They look at each other and laugh.*)

BRIDE: Can you believe this? Who else but us?

(*More laughter.*)

GROOM: Dropping you right on the threshold!

(*They laugh again. Her laughter turns to crying.*)

Honey?

(*She is sobbing hard now. She turns away and faces the door frame.*)

GROOM: Sweetheart?

BRIDE: It's just so—

(*Sobs more.*)

GROOM: Is it the dress? I'm sure your mother can—

BRIDE: It's not the dress! It's the whole thing! The whole disgusting, hideous thing!

GROOM: Which disgusting, hideous thing?

BRIDE: Everything!

(*He contemplates this. She sobs.*)

I mean, of course I fall down in the threshold! Of course! I can never do anything right!

GROOM: Well, but like I just said, it wasn't your fault.

BRIDE: Yes, it was! And now it's all ruined!

GROOM: Now, look. Let's not turn this into a . . . you know, okay? So you fell down in the threshold. Big deal!

BRIDE: It is a big deal. It's a symbol!

GROOM: No, it's not. It's just something that happened. And the longer we talk about it . . .

BRIDE: But we have to talk about it. If we don't talk about it I'll just keep feeling bad about it.

GROOM: Okay, let's talk about it. Why don't we go in and make a fire in the little fireplace?

BRIDE: No! We can't just go in there!

(*He considers this. He sits down beside her, squeezed into the door frame.*)

I just feel this huge sense of, I don't know . . . doom.

GROOM: Doom.

BRIDE: Like when I woke up this morning. I just had this feeling that I was totally alone. It's not that I didn't want to get married, that's not what I'm saying at all. I wanted to get married. It's just . . . Oh, God, I don't know!

GROOM: So are you saying—

BRIDE: And then all those roses. My God! My God!

GROOM: (*Waits for more.*) You mean—

BRIDE: All I could think about was how much money it cost, and how one day my parents are going to die, and how tomorrow—tomorrow!—the roses are all going to be thrown in the trash somewhere. Or tonight! They're going to be rotting in some Dumpster and filling up a landfill and I'm going to have to put my parents in the ground one day and throw dirt on them.

GROOM: I think this is getting kind of . . . I don't know.

BRIDE: What?

GROOM: Blown out of proportion. I mean, if I hadn't dropped you, would we be having to sit here and talk about all this stuff? No, we'd be in there having fun.

BRIDE: You mean you're not having fun?

GROOM: No! Well, I mean, not right this second.

BRIDE: Are you unhappy?

GROOM: What do you mean? I just said—

BRIDE: I mean, being married. Are you unhappy being married?

GROOM: No! How do I know? We've been married for three and a half hours!

(*She looks at him, he looks at her. They burst out laughing. The laughter grows, becomes hysterical, then subsides.*)

Okay? Are we okay now?

BRIDE: I think so. I just had to—

GROOM: I know. You don't have to explain.

BRIDE: Will you carry me across now?

GROOM: Absolutely. Let's do this thing.

(*They stand and prepare.*)

BRIDE: Ready?

GROOM: Ready.

(*She jumps into his arms.*)

BRIDE: Here we go!

(*He hesitates.*)

Honey?

GROOM: Hang on.

BRIDE: What is it? What's wrong?

(*He puts her down.*)

GROOM: It's . . . I don't know.

BRIDE: What?

GROOM: It's the thing about the symbol. I wish you hadn't said that.

BRIDE: I just meant—

GROOM: I know what you meant. But I hadn't been thinking that way until then, and now that you said it, it's all I can think about. Suddenly I'm just this groom person and you're just this puffy bride—

BRIDE: Puffy?

GROOM: I don't mean puffy.

BRIDE: But you said puffy.

GROOM: I was just trying to make a point, which is that as long as we're talking about the symbol, what does it mean that I'm carrying you, anyway?

BRIDE: I think it means you're going to support me and hold me for the rest of my life.

(*He looks at her. He considers this. He sits down.*)

Honey?

GROOM: Just give me a minute.

BRIDE: Isn't that what it means?

GROOM: I don't know what it means. I thought we were just walking through a door.

BRIDE: Maybe it's not a symbol at all.

GROOM: Oh, it's a symbol, all right. It's definitely a symbol.

BRIDE: Well, if you don't want to carry me, why don't you just say so?

GROOM: Why don't I? Well, because . . . Do you really want to know?

BRIDE: Yes.

GROOM: Because you'll flip out.

BRIDE: No, I won't.

GROOM: You won't?

BRIDE: No.

GROOM: All right. I don't want to carry you.

(*She considers this.*)

BRIDE: Would you rather shove me?

GROOM: See, I knew you'd flip out.

BRIDE: I'm not flipping out. I'm joking.

GROOM: No, you aren't.

BRIDE: Yes, I am!

GROOM: And now that you're flipping out it means we're going to spend the next three hours—

BRIDE: But I'm not flipping out! I'm trying to tell you that I'm not flipping out!

(*A pause.*)

GROOM: Look—

BRIDE: Oh, great. Here we go.

GROOM: What?

BRIDE: Nothing. Go on, I'm listening.

GROOM: I was going to say, the vein in my temple is starting to throb, and maybe if I just lay down on the bed for a minute—

BRIDE: On the bed!

GROOM: Yes . . .

BRIDE: In there?

GROOM: Did you want room service to put a cot in the hallway?

BRIDE: But you can't lay down on the bed! You can't just ignore it! We have to resolve this!

GROOM: But we're not going to resolve this by standing here and talking!

BRIDE: I can't believe this. You'd actually do that to me?

GROOM: Do what?

BRIDE: Leave me standing here alone on the threshold?

GROOM: No! No! Just for, like, ten minutes. I'll come get you as soon as my head stops pounding.

BRIDE: (*Crying.*) And what am I supposed to do in the meantime? Just stand out here in the hall?

GROOM: I don't know. Maybe some of the guests are still down at the party.

BRIDE: Down at the party! Down at the . . . The bride can't go back to the party!

GROOM: Okay, fine. I give up. You don't want to come in, you don't want to go downstairs, you just want to stand here and be miserable for the rest of our lives.

BRIDE: No! No! Not be miserable. Talk it over! Talk it over!

GROOM: Talk what over? We've already talked so long I can't even remember what we're fighting about!

BRIDE: You can't remember?

GROOM: No! I have no idea what we're fighting about! We're not fighting about anything except about how we're fighting!

BRIDE: I can't believe you just said that.

GROOM: Oh, fine, sure. I'm a jerk because I can't remember. All right then, you tell me—what are we fighting about? I bet you can't remember either.

BRIDE: We're fighting because you're not willing to work through conflict.

GROOM: Not willing to! Are you kidding? I've never worked so hard in my life! It's like pulling a train uphill with my goddamned teeth! And no, that was not a reference to your weight!

(*They glare at each other.*)

BRIDE: Now you listen to me, buster. We're married now!

GROOM: Oh, yeah, you got that right. You got that perfectly right!

BRIDE: Either you stay here and talk about this with me or . . .

GROOM: Or what?

BRIDE: Or I'm leaving!

GROOM: You're leaving.

BRIDE: Yes.

GROOM: You're leaving.

BRIDE: Yes.

GROOM: You're leaving.

BRIDE: That's what I said.

GROOM: Leaving as in leaving to walk around the block, or leaving as in leaving sayonara?

BRIDE: What?

GROOM: As in leaving for good!

BRIDE: Well, I don't know. All I know is, I can't be with someone who doesn't know how to work through conflict.

GROOM: Okay. Okay, I get it now. It's all making perfect sense. What you're saying to me, what you're actually saying to me on our wedding night is that if I don't stand here in the goddamned threshold of this cheesy-ass shithole friggin' backwoods country inn—

BRIDE: Shithole?

GROOM: —until I drop dead from exhaustion in the attempt to find whatever combination of words is going to "resolve the conflict"—

BRIDE: Shithole? Shithole?

GROOM: —and make you feel like the world isn't ending, which is not my responsibility, you know, and which I refuse to—

BRIDE: I wanted to get married in Cancun, remember? You were the one who—

GROOM: Don't—

BRIDE: You were the one who said let's save the money—

GROOM: Don't change the subject—

BRIDE: I brought all the brochures home and had the whole thing—

GROOM: I'm not talking about that! I'm talking about the fact that you—

BRIDE: No, I'm talking about—

GROOM: Would you please stop interrupting me?

BRIDE: But you told me to find an inn!

GROOM: I didn't mean—

BRIDE: And now all of a sudden—

GROOM: That's not the point! That's not the point! I didn't even want to get married!

(*A silence. She screams. He tries to stop her, but she won't stop. He slaps her hard across the face. She slaps him back. They wrestle each other in the doorway, trying to kill each other, until they wear themselves out. She lies panting on the ground; he leans exhausted against the frame. He reaches into his mouth and removes a tooth, spits blood onto the floor. He cleans his mouth with his tie.*)

Are you all right?

(*She doesn't answer.*)

I said, are you all right?

BRIDE: No.

GROOM: Maybe we should—

BRIDE: Don't talk to me.

(*She pulls herself up the door frame to her feet. One of her ankles hurts.*)

GROOM: Here, let me—

BRIDE: Don't touch me. Don't ever touch me again!

GROOM: Fine.

(*They stand next to each other.*)

BRIDE: I think my ankle's broken.

GROOM: Do you want me to look at it?

BRIDE: No. All right.

(*He kneels and does this. She winces.*)

GROOM: Maybe you should get it X-rayed.

BRIDE: I just want to lie down.

GROOM: Here—

(*He puts an arm around her. They stand awkwardly like this.*)

Do you want to lay on the bed?

BRIDE: All right. No. Wait.

GROOM: What?

BRIDE: You really didn't want to get married?

GROOM: Of course I did.

(*He smiles at her. She smiles at him. They kiss passionately. She pushes him away.*)

BRIDE: Your mouth's bleeding.

GROOM: I know. Let's go in.

BRIDE: Okay.

(*They kiss again. She pushes him off.*)

Why did you say it, then?

GROOM: Say what?

BRIDE: That you didn't want to get married.

GROOM: I don't know. Did I say that?

(*He tries to kiss her; she holds him off.*)

BRIDE: Yes.

GROOM: I meant at first. When you brought the brochures home. That's all I meant.

BRIDE: Oh, good.

(*They kiss again.*)

When did you change your mind?

GROOM: Jesus Christ! Can we not do this?

BRIDE: Do what?

GROOM: Start fighting again?

BRIDE: Okay.

(*He puts his arm around her.*)

GROOM: Can you walk?

BRIDE: I think it's broken.

GROOM: Here.

(*He picks her up in his arms.*)

BRIDE: Honey?

GROOM: Yeah?

(*He waits for a response.*)

What is it?

BRIDE: Nothing. Never mind.

(*They look at the room through the doorway. He gives her a boost. Lights down.*)

END OF PLAY

PLEASE HAVE A SEAT
AND SOMEONE WILL
BE WITH YOU SHORTLY

Garth Wingfield

Please Have a Seat and Someone Will Be with You Shortly was originally produced by the Vital Theatre (Stephen Sunderlin, producing artistic director; Linda Ames Key, producing director) at the McGinn/Cazale Theatre in New York City on December 15, 2005. It was directed by Laura Josepher, and the cast was as follows:

DAVID   Michael Anderson
SUE   Karin Sibrava

A waiting room. SUE *and* DAVID *sit in chairs next to each other reading magazines. At rise: A long beat;* DAVID *considers* SUE, *who's lost in her magazine. Then finally.*

DAVID: Sue?

SUE: Excuse me?

DAVID: Your name is Sue, right?

SUE: (*Uneasy.*) It is . . .

DAVID: (*A little overcome.*) Wow . . .

SUE: What?

DAVID: So we're finally talking . . .

SUE: (*Even more uneasy.*) We are . . .

DAVID: I mean, after all this *time* . . .

SUE: It's been . . . a while now, I guess . . .

DAVID: And it was just as easy as saying that one word: Sue. Who knew it would be that easy?

481

SUE: You know what? And please don't take this the wrong way.
But I'm not sure I like it that we're talking.

DAVID: You don't?

SUE: I think . . . no, I'm pretty sure I *preferred* it when we never
spoke at all.

DAVID: Oh, shit. Oh, God. I crossed a line. I crossed a line and
you hate it.

SUE: I think you might have crossed a line.

DAVID: I am so sorry.

SUE: That's okay.

DAVID: So I should shut up now.

SUE: I think that would be for the best.

DAVID: Gotcha. Right. I'll stop talking to you. I can do that. The
end.

(*A long beat.*)

SUE: (*Then.*) You know my name. Okay, that's a little weird.

DAVID: No, it's not.

SUE: Yes, it is. I'm sorry, but it is.

DAVID: Of course I know your name, Sue. Do you mind if I call
you Sue?

SUE: Look, okay, I'll have you know I have *Mace* in my purse.

DAVID: Calm down! Hey, easy there! I know your *name* because your *therapist* has come through that door, stood there, smiled at you, and said "Sue?" every Monday night for the last eighteen months. Hello?

SUE: (*A little flattered at this.*) I didn't realize . . . that you'd paid attention to that.

DAVID: Of *course* I'd paid attention to that!

SUE: Huh.

DAVID: (*Gently playful; not pissed.*) But I wouldn't want to upset you anymore. And I wouldn't want you to Mace me.

So like I said . . . the end.

(*Another long beat.*)

SUE: (*Almost embarrassed to admit this.*) I . . . I'm afraid I don't know *your* name.

DAVID: Excuse me?

SUE: You remembered my name. I don't know yours; I feel bad.

DAVID: Well, that . . . that's because *my* therapist comes through the door, stands there, glowers, and says, "It's time."

(*Then.*)

He's this super-strict, super-scary Freudian.

SUE: Oh my God, he *does* seem scary. Is he German?

DAVID: Oh my God, he is! We do the whole routine. I lay on the couch. He sits behind me. All very formal.

(*Then.*)

Actually, I'm not entirely sure if *he* knows my name.

SUE: I bet it's Albert.

DAVID: What?

SUE: Your name.

DAVID: Albert?

SUE: Yeah. You just . . . look like an Albert. If I had to guess.

DAVID: Ouch. Okay, that hurts.

SUE: You don't want to look like an Albert?

DAVID: Uh, no. No self-respecting man wants to look like an Albert.

SUE: Fine, I bet it's Herman then.

DAVID: Double ouch.

SUE: Or Thaddeus.

DAVID: Okay, you're not making any friends here, Sue.

SUE: Or Simian.

DAVID: *Simian?*

SUE: I went to college with a guy named Simian. I'm kidding. I always thought that was, like, the meanest name ever.

DAVID: Please, Simian's *parents* should be in therapy!

SUE: For child abuse. Thank you!

(*A beat.*)

DAVID: My name is David. Nothing exciting. But that's my name.

SUE: That's a nice name.

Please, my name is Sue. So I'm not one to judge in the naming department.

DAVID: It's nice to meet you, Sue.

SUE: Likewise, David.

(*A beat. They finally smile at each other.*)

DAVID: So . . . so hold on. You've never really noticed me during all these months we've been waiting out here?

SUE: I never said I didn't notice you . . .

DAVID: Because I sure noticed *you.*

SUE: You did?

DAVID: Absolutely. Lots.

SUE: Okay.

DAVID: In fact, I spent the first couple of months trying to catch your eye over the magazines we were reading. I made a huge effort trying to do this.

SUE: *That's* what you were doing?

DAVID: I was.

SUE: Because I honestly . . . I swear I thought you either had an astigmatism or a tic.

DAVID: Are you serious?

SUE: You'd do this thing where you'd read your magazine, then lower it . . . read it, then lower it . . . read it, then lower it.

It was almost hypnotic to witness out of the corner of my eye.

DAVID: Okay, I'll be up-front here: I have obsessive-compulsive issues that I am dealing with during my sessions here.

SUE: Well, that explains so much.

DAVID: I'm doing much better with that stuff now, I'm happy to say.

SUE: I'm glad to hear that.

DAVID: Dr. Reifenschneider has me on a very mild antidepressant, a wonderful side effect of which is that it's wiped out that OCD stuff altogether.

SUE: Not entirely. You still do this thing where you run your forefinger back and forth across your upper lip while you read.

DAVID: (*Pleasantly surprised to hear this.*) So you really *have* noticed me . . .

SUE: I don't know.

(*Pulling back a little.*)

Maybe. Sometimes. Now and then.

(*A beat.*)

DAVID: Okay, I don't mean to cross *another* line here, but now that we're talking, and since we only have who knows how many more minutes before one of our doctors walks through the door . . . I've also thought about you. Outside of this room, I'm talking now. I feel I should come clean about this.

SUE: You've thought about me?

DAVID: I have.

SUE: (*Turning away a bit.*) But why . . . why would you do that?

DAVID: Am I scaring you?

SUE: A little.

DAVID: I'm sorry, it's just I've thought about what kind of apartment you'd have. I've thought about what your life is like.

(*Then.*)

I've imagined you're a first-grade teacher.

SUE: (*Taken aback by that.*) You have?

DAVID: Yeah. I don't know . . . there was just something about you. Your demeanor. Your scarf. The impeccably patient way you turned the pages of *Us*. I could just see you reading *Where the Wild Things Are* to a class of screaming six-year-olds and keeping your calm while children all around you pulled one another's hair and vomited.

SUE: That's . . . wow.

(*Then.*)

Okay, I'll be up-front with *you*: In my sessions here, I've been dealing with the ways I put up walls and push people away. And while part of me wants to run screaming into the night now that you've told me all this—or promptly change my sessions to *Tuesdays*, I won't . . . and I'll just . . .

Say thank you.

DAVID: (*Smiles.*) You're welcome.

And just so you know, there's no need to worry about changing your therapy night. Because this is my final session with Dr. Reifenschneider. He's closing up his practice and moving to Vermont to spend his twilight years running this little candle shop. And I only wish I was making that up because that is JUST SO FREUDIAN. I mean, CANDLES?

SUE: (*Laughing.*) Oh my God.

DAVID: So starting next Monday, I'll be seeing Dr. McBee down in the Village. Dr. Reifenschneider says he's around my age and wears shorts in the summer. I'm looking forward to a change of pace.

SUE: I'm sure.

DAVID: But I saw you sitting here tonight, and I don't know, I just decided I had to say hello to you before I could say goodbye.

(*A little beat.*)

SUE: I imagined you were a carpenter.

DAVID: Oh my God, you *did*?

SUE: On several occasions.

DAVID: A carpenter. Holy shit.

SUE: This is very hard for me to say out loud. I'm also dealing with issues of trust and abandonment in my sessions. So you're really pushing all my buttons here tonight.

DAVID: A carpenter, I'm sorry. That's the kind of thing guys *dream* about being mistaken for.

SUE: You have very strong forearms. And I could just tell you knew a clean line when you saw one. I imagined you designed and made your own furniture. These very rough-hewn chairs and benches that you'd rub with linseed oil while NPR played in the background.

DAVID: I love NPR!

SUE: Oh my God, so do I! I'm sorry, *Car Talk*?

DAVID: Please. I don't even have a car, and I live and breathe by *Car Talk*!

SUE: Absolutely!

DAVID: (*Boldly plowing ahead.*) I imagined you lived in Chelsea.

SUE: I imagined you lived up by Columbia.

DAVID: And that you have a cat.

SUE: And that you have this enormous moosehead thing left over from your college years.

DAVID: And that I'd ask out for coffee first, but things would move quite fast from there. We'd have dinner at Gramercy Tavern.

SUE: See, now, I pictured Balthazar.

DAVID: And we'd take buggy rides in Central Park.

SUE: And Rollerblade there on the weekends—and I've never Rollerbladed in my *life*!

DAVID: And we'd move in together after about a year.

SUE: This very shabby loft out in Williamsburg . . .

DAVID: . . . with a very wheezy radiator, but we'd love everything about it. And we'd adopt a dog!

SUE: And join the local food commune!

DAVID: And make casseroles!

SUE: And bake banana bread!

DAVID: And have a kid or maybe two. Or three! You and me . . . and the dog and the kids . . . out in Williamsburg . . . forever.

(*A long beat. The mood shifts.*)

I'm an accountant.

I really . . . God, I wish I were a carpenter. But I'm sorry, I'm so not.

SUE: I'm a marketing person at Publishers Clearing House. It's basically the devil's work.

DAVID: And I live in this shitty walk-up in Spanish Harlem.

SUE: I live on Roosevelt Island. No one lives on Roosevelt Island. *I* do. What's that about?

DAVID: (*Then.*) And my name is Albert.

I'm not kidding. I never tell anyone that my name is Albert when I meet them because it makes the worst first impression *ever*.

SUE: (*Apologetic.*) And I have a boyfriend. A fiancé, actually.

We have issues of intimacy and respect . . . which is essentially why I'm here in couples therapy by myself. I'm terrified at the thought of marrying him.

But *this* . . . this was so great, David. Albert.

DAVID: Yeah, it was, Sue. It was.

(*Just then there's a faint light from offstage to indicate a door opening.*)

THERAPIST'S VOICE: Sue?

(*She stands and moves toward the door.*)

DAVID: So wait, before you go . . . I just wanted to say . . .

(*She stops and turns to him.*)

Good-bye.

SUE: (*Then, with a small smile.*) Hello.

(*She stands there for a beat, not moving toward the door . . . just standing there . . . as the lights fade.*)

END OF PLAY

CONTRIBUTORS

DAVID AUBURN's play *Proof* premiered at Manhattan Theatre Club, then transferred to Broadway, earning him a Tony Award and the Pulitzer Prize for Drama. He is the recipient of the Guggenheim Foundation Grant and the Joseph Kesselring Prize for Drama. Other plays include *Skyscraper, Fifth Planet,* and *The Next Life.* Screenplay credits include *St. George and the Dragon, The Lake House,* and *Proof.* Mr. Auburn was a member of the Juilliard playwriting program.

ALAN BALL won the Academy Award for Best Original Screenplay for *American Beauty,* which starred Kevin Spacey and Annette Bening. He went on to create and produce the Emmy-winning HBO series *Six Feet Under,* which ran for six seasons. Additional TV credits include ABC's *Grace Under Fire* and supervising producer for the CBS series *Cybill.* Mr. Ball's plays include *Five Women Wearing the Same Dress* and *All That I Will Ever Be.*

GINA BARNETT is an actress, singer, teacher, playwright, and screenwriter. Her plays include *After All* (Hudson Stage Company), *Donna Morelli* (New York Stage & Film), *T for 2* (Detroit Rep), *Four Play* (Ensemble Studio Theatre), and *Alone at Last!* (Manhattan Punch Line). Honors include the JR Humphries Award; winner in TheatreFest Regional Playwriting Contest; finalist in Kaufman and Hart New American Comedies

Contest; and two-time finalist in Louisville's 10-Minute Play Contest.

GLEN BERGER's plays include *Underneath the Lintel* (L.A. Ovation Award), *Great Men of Science, Nos. 21 & 22* (Ovation Award; *L.A. Weekly* Award), and *A Night in the Old Marketplace* (Loewe Award). Mr. Berger received a Manhattan Theatre Club Sloan Foundation fellowship and a Children's Theatre of Minneapolis commission. TV work includes the PBS children's series *Arthur* (two Emmy nominations), *Postcards from Buster*, and *The Time Warp Trio*. He is a member of New Dramatists.

DAVID CALE is the author and performer of the solo shows *A Likely Story, Lillian, Deep in a Dream of You, Smooch Music, The Redthroats*, and the duet show, *Betwixt*. His monologues have been featured on NPR's *This American Life* and *The Next Big Thing*. He is the author, lyricist, and cocomposer of the musical *Floyd and Clea Under the Western Sky*.

ERIC COBLE was born in Edinburgh, Scotland, and bred on the Navajo and Ute reservations in New Mexico and Colorado. His plays, including *Bright Ideas, The Dead Guy, Natural Selection*, and *For Better*, have been produced Off-Broadway and on four continents. Awards include the AT&T Onstage Award and the National Theatre Conference Playwriting Award.

SHARON E. COOPER, a playwright, educator, and yoga instructor, is an artistic associate of the Milk Can Theatre Company and a member of the Dramatists Guild. Productions include *For Camille* (Theatre Virginia's New Voices), *Door of Hope* (Makor/92nd Street Y), *Lifeline* (the American Theatre of Actors), *In the Midst* (Best Short Play, Spotlight On), and *The Match* (the Milk Can Theatre Company). She attended the Kennedy Center's Playwrighting Intensive Program.

LAURA SHAINE CUNNINGHAM is a playwright, journalist, and author of seven books. Ms. Cunningham's fiction and non-fiction have appeared in the *New Yorker* and the *New York Times*. She has seven full-length plays including *Sleeping Arrangements*, *Beautiful Bodies*, and *Bang*. She is widely produced, and has several other short plays in the Vintage anthologies *Take Ten*, *Take Ten II*, and *Leading Women*.

ADRIENNE DAWES is a graduate of Sarah Lawrence College. Her plays have been produced by Sarah Lawrence, Off My Back Theatre Productions, Revolving Stages, the American Repertory Theatre of London, and Live Girls Theatre!, among others. She received the Lipkin Prize for Playwriting for *Love and Happiness* and *You Are Pretty*. *Jesus Loves Good Christians* was named semifinalist for the Panowski Playwriting Award. Ms. Dawes is a core member of St. Idiot Collective in Austin, Texas.

STEVEN DIETZ's twenty-plus plays have been produced at over a hundred regional theatres in the United States, as well as Off-Broadway. International productions of his work have been seen in England, Japan, Germany, France, Australia, Sweden, Russia, Slovenia, Argentina, Peru, Singapore, and South Africa. Recent plays include *Fiction*, *Inventing van Gogh*, and *Last of the Boys*.

PAUL DOOLEY is primarily an actor, as well as a writer. In the seventies he was the cocreator/head writer of the award-winning show *The Electric Company*. He is best known as the father in the classic film *Breaking Away* and as Molly Ringwald's dad in *Sixteen Candles*, but most of all as Winnie Holzman's husband (in Burbank).

CHRISTOPHER DURANG's plays include *A History of the American Film* (Tony nomination), *Sister Mary Ignatius Explains It All for You* (Obie Award), *Beyond Therapy*, *Baby with the Bathwater*, *The Marriage of Bette and Boo* (Obie Award, Hull Warriner Award), *Laughing Wild*, *Durang/Durang*, *Betty's Summer Vacation* (Obie award), *Mrs. Bob Cratchit's Wild Christmas Binge*,

Miss Witherspoon (Pulitzer Prize finalist), and *Adrift in Macao* with Peter Melnick.

PETER HEDGES's plays include *Baby Anger* (Playwrights Horizons), *Good as New* (Manhattan Class Company), and *Imagining Brad* (Circle Repertory Theater). He is the author of two novels, *An Ocean in Iowa* and *What's Eating Gilbert Grape*, and the screenplays for *What's Eating Gilbert Grape*, *About a Boy*, and *Pieces of April*, which he also directed.

WINNIE HOLZMAN is a graduate of Princeton University and the NYU Musical Theatre Program. She began her writing career on the popular television series *Thirtysomething*. She was also the creator and co-executive producer of the acclaimed drama *My So-Called Life*, and writer/co-executive producer on TV's *Once and Again*. Ms. Holzman is best known as coauthor with Stephen Schwartz of the hit Broadway musical *Wicked*.

MIKHAIL HOROWITZ is the author of *Big League Poets* (City Lights, 1978) and *The Opus of Everything in Nothing Flat* (Red Hill, 1993). His poetry is widely anthologized. Stageworks/Hudson produced his short play *Mere Vessels* as part of its Play-by-Play Festival in 2005. He has been performing poetry, music, comedy, political satire, and pataphysical acrobatics professionally since 1973.

SETH KRAMER is a playwright originally from Chicago whose work has been produced in fifteen states across the United States. His one-acts have been selected by the Nantucket Play Festival, the Strawberry One-Act Competition, the Turnip One-Act Competition, and the Annual Offbeat New York Festival. Honors include the George R. Kernodle Award, the New York Thespian Award, and three-time finalist in Actors Theatre of Louisville's 10-Minute Play Contest.

ERIC LANE's plays include *Heart of the City*, *Times of War*, *Ride*, and *Dancing on Checkers' Grave*. Honors include the Berrilla Kerr

Playwriting Award, the La MaMa Playwright Award, and a Writers Guild Award. Mr. Lane has written and produced two award-winning short films, *First Breath* and *Cater-Waiter*, which he also directed. He has received fellowships at Yaddo and the St. James Cavalier Centre for Creativity in Malta.

WARREN LEIGHT's *Side Man* won the Tony Award for Best Play. His other theatre work includes *Glimmer, Glimmer & Shine*; *Fame Takes a Holiday*; and *No Foreigners Beyond This Point*. His new play *James and Annie* is scheduled for production by the Drama Department. *Dark No Sugar*, a new collection of his one-act plays, is published by DPS. Mr. Leight is currently co-executive producer on *Law & Order: Criminal Intent*.

MARK HARVEY LEVINE's short plays have been produced hundreds of times around the world. *Surprise* was also part of *Cabfare for the Common Man*, an evening of his short plays, which premiered at the Phoenix Theatre in Indianapolis. It was included in another collection of his plays, *Aperitivos*, translated into Portuguese and produced by Pausa Companhia in São Paulo, Brazil.

DAVID LINDSAY-ABAIRE's plays produced by Manhattan Theatre Club include *Fuddy Meers*, *Kimberly Akimbo*, *Wonder of the World* (starring Sarah Jessica Parker), and *Rabbit Hole* (starring Cynthia Nixon), which received a Tony Award nomination for Best Play. Honors include the L.A. Drama Critics Circle Award and a Helen Hayes Award nomination. He is a graduate of Sarah Lawrence College and the Juilliard Playwriting Program, and a proud member of New Dramatists, Dramatists Guild, and the WGA.

STEVE MARTIN has enjoyed a prolific career as an actor, comedian, and writer spanning four decades in film, television, and theatre. Film roles include *The Jerk*, *Pennies from Heaven*, *Dead Men Don't Wear Plaid*, *Little Shop of Horrors*, *All of Me*, *Dirty Rotten Scoundrels*, *Roxanne*, *Father of the Bride*, *Parenthood*, and

Shopgirl. He has hosted TV's *Saturday Night Live* and the Academy Awards. His plays include *Picasso at the Lapin Agile* and *WASP.*

ELAINE MAY is half of the celebrated comedy team Nichols and May. She later reunited with Mike Nichols to write the screenplay for *The Birdcage* and *Primary Colors* (British Academy Award). Ms. May has carved out successful careers as an actress, writer, and director. Films include *A New Leaf, The Heartbreak Kid,* and *Heaven Can Wait* (Oscar nomination for Best Screenplay). Plays include *Adaptation, Death Defying Acts, Power Plays, Adult Entertainment,* and *After the Night and the Music.*

MARK O'DONNELL won a Tony as a coauthor of the musical *Hairspray.* His plays include *Fables for Friends, The Nice and the Nasty, Strangers on Earth, That's It, Folks!,* and the musical *Tots in Tinseltown.* His humor has appeared in the *New Yorker,* the *Atlantic,* and *McSweeney's.* Among his books are the novels *Getting Over Homer* and *Let Nothing You Dismay.*

JONATHAN RAND is author of three of the top five most produced short plays in North American high schools in 2004–2005, according to the Educational Theatre Association: *The Least Offensive Play in the Whole Darn World* was number five, *Hard Candy* was number three, and *Check, Please* topped the list as the most produced short play of the season. Mr. Rand is a graduate of the University of Pennsylvania and currently lives in New York City.

WAYNE RAWLEY is the creator of the hit action–adventure series for the stage *Money & Run,* which first debuted in Seattle in 1999. Other plays include *God Damn Tom, Live! From the Last Night of My Life,* a present-day adaptation of Anton Chekhov's *The Seagull,* and a multimedia adaptation of George Orwell's *1984. Controlling Interest* has been produced by the Actors

Theatre of Louisville, City Theatre in Miami, and Impact Theatre in Berkeley.

JACQUELYN REINGOLD's plays include *String Fever, Girl Gone, Dear Kenneth Blake, Tunnel of Love, Freeze Tag, Acapulco, A.M.L.,* and *Joe and Stew.* They have been produced in New York at EST, MCC Theatre, Naked Angels, HB Playwrights, and across the country. Awards include EST/Sloan Foundation, Kennedy Center Roger Stevens, and New Dramatists' Whitfield Cook. Published works include *Women Playwrights: Best Plays, Best American Short Plays,* and *Things Between Us,* a collection of her one-acts from DPS. www.jacquelynreingold.com

EDWIN SÁNCHEZ's newest play, *La Bella Familia,* was work-shopped at ACT in San Francisco and at Primary Stages in New York. Other recent productions include *Diosa, Trafficking in Broken Hearts, Unmerciful Good Fortune,* and *Barefoot Boy with Shoes On.* His plays have been produced throughout the United States as well as in Brazil, Russia, and Switzerland.

NINA SHENGOLD's plays include *Homesteaders* (Samuel French), *Finger Foods* (seven shorts; Playscripts), *War at Home* (written with Nicole Quinn; Playscripts), and the adaptation *Romeo/Juliet* (Broadway Play Publishing). She won the Writers Guild Award for *Labor of Love,* starring Marcia Gay Harden. Her short play *No Shoulder* was filmed by Suzi Yoonessi. Her novel *Clearcut* is published by Anchor Books.

SHEL SILVERSTEIN was a renowned poet, playwright, illustrator, screenwriter, and songwriter. He was best known for his popular children's books including *The Giving Tree, A Light in the Attic,* and *Where the Sidewalk Ends.* He wrote the play *The Devil and Billy Markham,* and cowrote with David Mamet the screenplay *Things Change.* His song "I'm Checking Out," from the film *Postcards from the Edge,* was nominated for an Academy Award.

DAVID SMILOW is a playwright, actor, and Emmy Award–winning television writer. He has received a Writers Guild Award for his work on both *One Life to Live* and *Guiding Light*. Two of his short plays—*Brights* and *Brief Intel-ude*—have been made into equally short films. He lives in upstate New York.

TOMMY SMITH is a New York–based playwright whose works include *Air Conditioning*, *Sunrise*, and *April's Subject*. With composer Michael McQuilken, he cocreated *Extropia*, *A Day in Dig Nation*, and *The Tale*. Mr. Smith is a two-time finalist for the Heideman Award, and a two-time winner of the Lecomte du Nouy Prize for emerging writers. He recently completed a fellowship at the Juilliard School under Marsha Norman and Chris Durang.

RICHARD STRAND has had premieres at Actors Theatre of Louisville, Victory Gardens Theater, GeVa Theatre, Steppenwolf Theatre, The Z Collective, Mixed Blood Theatre, and a number of other venues. *The Bug* has been translated into German, Italian, Greek, and Spanish and continues to be performed in the United States and in Europe. He is a professor at Mount San Antonio College.

FREDERICK STROPPEL's comic plays and one-acts have been produced throughout the country and as far afield as Budapest and Australia. New York productions include *Fortune's Fools* at the Cherry Lane Theater, his musical *Tales from the Manhattan Woods* at the Wings Theatre, and his one-act evenings *Kidney Stones*, *One Man's Vision*, and *Spider Holes*, all at the Nuyorican Poets Café. Mr. Stroppel has written several screenplays, and has worked in television for HBO, Nickelodeon, Disney, and PBS.

JOYCE VAN DYKE's *A Girl's War* premiered at New Repertory Theatre and was an American Theatre Critics Association New Play Award nominee. The play was published in *Con-*

temporary Armenian American Drama. Ms. Van Dyke received the 2006 EST/Sloan Commission for *Oil Play*. A MacDowell Colony fellow and alum of Boston University's playwriting program, she lives in the Boston area with her husband and two sons.

DARYL WATSON's plays include *Prime Time*, *Snap*, and *Idle Gods*. He currently serves as cocreator/writer for the Disney TV series *Johnny and the Sprites*. He is also the cofounder and president of Real TheatreWorks (www.realtheatreworks.org). Mr. Watson holds a BFA in drama with a second major in English and American literature from New York University.

LAUREN WILSON was born in Baltimore, Maryland. Her plays include *The Golden State*, *Chemical Imbalance*, *Heads Will Roll*, *A Little Snippet*, *Bluff*, and several plays for children. Her work has been produced by many physical theatre ensembles, including the Dell 'Arte Company, Workhorse, Bloomsburg Theatre Ensemble, and Touchstone Theater. She currently lives in New York with her husband, Daniel.

GARTH WINGFIELD's plays include *Flight*, *Are We There Yet?*, *Sunday Styles*, *Bump*, and *Adonis*, as well as many one-acts. His work has been performed in New York, Los Angeles, Miami, and London. For television, Mr. Wingfield wrote several episodes for the first season of *Queer As Folk* and was a staff writer on the ABC sitcom *Clueless*. He lives in New York City.

ABOUT THE EDITORS

ERIC LANE and NINA SHENGOLD are editors of a dozen contemporary play collections. Their other titles for Vintage Books include *Under 30: Plays for a New Generation*, *Talk to Me: Monologue Plays*, *Plays for Actresses*, *Leading Women: Plays for Actresses II*, *Take Ten: New 10-Minute Plays*, and *Take Ten II: More 10-Minute Plays*. For Viking Penguin, they edited *The Actor's Book of Contemporary Stage Monologues*, *The Actor's Book of Scenes from New Plays*, *Moving Parts: Monologues from Contemporary Plays*, *The Actor's Book of Gay and Lesbian Plays* (Lambda Literary Award nominee), and *Telling Tales: New One-Act Plays*.

NINA SHENGOLD's first novel *Clearcut* (Anchor Books) was selected as one of 2005's Best Books by the *Seattle Post-Intelligencer*, *San Francisco Bay Times*, Out.com, and InsightOut Book Club. She received the ABC Playwright Award and the L.A. Weekly Award for *Homesteaders*, and a Writers Guild Award and GLAAD Award nomination for her teleplay *Labor of Love*, starring Marcia Gay Harden. Other screenwriting credits include *Blind Spot*, with Joanne Woodward and Laura Linney, *Unwed Father*, *Double Platinum*, and the short film *No Shoulder*, starring Melissa Leo and Samantha Sloyan. Shengold's ten-minute plays have been widely performed; seven of them are collected in Playscripts' anthology *Finger Foods*. *War at Home: Students Respond to 9/11* (written with Nicole Quinn and the Rondout Valley High School Drama Club) has been produced in England, Australia, Singapore, Canada, and throughout the United States. She is artistic director of the upstate New York theatre company Actors & Writers, now in its fifteenth year. For more information, see www.ninashengold.com.

ERIC LANE is an award-winning playwright and filmmaker. Plays include *Heart of the City*, *Times of War*, *Ride*, *Cater-Waiter*, and *Dancing on Checkers' Grave*, which starred Jennifer Aniston. He has written and produced two short films: *First Breath* stars Victor Williams, Kelly Karbacz, and Melissa Leo. *Cater-Waiter*, which Mr. Lane also directed, stars David Drake, Tim Deak, Lisa Kron, and John Kelly. For his work on *Ryan's Hope*, he received a Writers Guild Award. Honors include the Berrilla Kerr Playwriting Award, the La MaMa Playwright Award, and a five-time finalist for the Heideman Award. Mr. Lane has received fellowships at Yaddo, VCCA, the Millay Colony, and St. James Cavalier Centre for Creativity in Malta. He is an honors graduate of Brown University, and is artistic director of Orange Thoughts Productions, a not-for-profit theater and film company in New York City.

INDEX BY CAST SIZE

PERMISSIONS
ACKNOWLEDGMENTS

David Auburn: *Miss You* by David Auburn, copyright © 2002 by David Auburn (first published in *Fifth Planet and Other Plays*, Dramatists Play Service, Inc.). Reprinted by permission of the author and Paradigm.

Inquiries: Stage performance rights to *Miss You* are controlled exclusively by Paradigm, 500 Fifth Avenue, New York, NY 10110, Attn: William Craver. No professional or nonprofessional performance of the play may be given without obtaining in advance the written permission of Paradigm and paying the requisite fee.

Alan Ball: *Your Mother's Butt* by Alan Ball, copyright © 1994 by Alan Ball (first published in *Five One-Act Plays*, Dramatists Play Service, Inc.). Reprinted by permission of the author and The Gersh Agency.

Caution: The English language stock and amateur stage performance rights in this play are controlled exclusively by Dramatists Play Service, Inc., 440 Park Avenue South, New York, NY 10016. No professional or nonprofessional performance of the play may be given without obtaining in advance the written permission of Dramatists Play Service, Inc., and paying the requisite fee. Inquiries concerning all other rights should be addressed to The Gersh Agency, 41 Madison Avenue, 33rd Floor, New York, NY 10010, Attn: Peter Hagan.

Gina Barnett: *Alone at Last!* by Gina Barnett, copyright © 2007 by Gina Barnett. Reprinted by permission of the author.

Inquiries contact: Sonia Pabley, Rosenstone/Wender, 38 E. 29th Street, New York, NY 10016.

Steven Dietz: *The Spot* by Steven Dietz, copyright © 2003 by Steven John Dietz. Reprinted by permission of the author.

Inquiries contact: Sarah Jane Leigh, Sterling Standard LLC, 445 W. 23rd Street, # 1E, New York, NY 10011, telephone: 212-242-1740, fax: 212-242-1735.

Paul Dooley and Winnie Holzman: *Post-its (Notes on a Marriage)* by Paul Dooley and Winnie Holzman, copyright © 2007 by Paul Dooley & Winnie Holzman. Reprinted by permission of the authors.

Inquires: For Winnie Holzman, contact George Lane or Michael Cardonick, Creative Artists Agency, 162 Fifth Avenue, 6th Floor, New York, NY 10010, telephone: 212-277-9000.

Christopher Durang: *Wanda's Visit* by Christopher Durang, copyright © 1995 by Christopher Durang. Reprinted by permission of the author.

Inquiries contact: Patrick Herold, International Creative Management, Inc., 40 W. 57th Street, New York, NY 10019.

Peter Hedges: *The Valerie of Now* by Peter Hedges, copyright © 1991 by Peter Hedges. Reprinted by permission of the author.

Inquiries contact: George Lane, Creative Artists Agency, 162 Fifth Avenue, 6th Floor, New York, NY 10010.

Mikhail Horowitz: *We Cannot Know the Mind of God* by Mikhail Horowitz, copyright © 2007 by Mikhail Horowitz. Reprinted by permission of the author.

Inquiries contact: Mikhail Horowitz, 302 High Falls Road, Saugerties, NY 12477, email: horowitz@bard.edu.

Anthologies edited by Eric Lane and Nina Shengold

TAKE TEN
New Ten-Minute Plays

In this splendid collection, thirty-two of our finest playwrights hone their skills on a form that has been called the haiku of the American stage. The plays range from monologues to an eight-character farce and contain parts that span the entire spectrum of age, race, and gender. Eminently producible, ideally suited for the classroom and audition, *Take Ten* is a marvelous resource for teachers and students of drama, as well as a stimulating read for lovers of the theater.

Drama/978-0-679-77282-8

TAKE TEN II
More Ten-Minute Plays

In this splendid follow-up to *Take Ten*, Eric Lane and Nina Shengold have put together a veritable bonfire of talent. *Take Ten II* provides a fast-track tour of the current theatrical landscape, from the slapstick ingenuity of David Ives's *Arabian Nights* to the searing tension of Diana Son's 9/11 drama *The Moon Please*. This diverse anthology includes thirty-five short plays by major American playwrights, alongside a host of exciting new voices.

Drama/978-1-4000-3217-4

PLAYS FOR ACTRESSES

Gather any group of actresses, from students to stars, and someone will inevitably ask, "Where are all the great roles for women?" They are right here, in this magnificently diverse collection of plays with female casts. Their characters include uprooted Japanese war brides, outrageously liberated Shakespearean heroines, and nuns who double as Catholic schoolgirls. Whether you're looking for a script to produce, a scene for acting class, or a new audition speech, this book will provide you with a wealth of juicy, challenging female roles.

Drama/978-0-679-77281-1

LEADING WOMEN
Plays for Actresses II

Eric Lane and Nina Shengold have again gathered an abundance of strong female roles in an anthology of works by award-winning authors and cutting-edge newer voices. The characters who populate these full-length plays, ten-minute plays, and monologues include a vivid cross section of female experience: girl gang members, Southern debutantes, pilots, teachers, and rebel teenagers. Each play in *Leading Women* is a boon for talented actresses everywhere.

Drama/978-0-375-72666-8

TALK TO ME
Monologue Plays

This unique collection of monologue plays includes a breathtaking array of human voices and stories by master playwrights and emerging new writers. Each of the plays, ranging from one-act to ten-minute plays to full-length works, creates a rich and specific world. Because each monologue is complete, rather than an excerpt, *Talk to Me* is an unprecedented source for actors in search of material for auditions, classes, and performances, as well as a literary gold mine for anyone who loves drama.

Drama/978-1-4000-7615-4

UNDER THIRTY
Plays for a New Generation

The plays presented here include insights into the caste system of American high schools as well as heartbreaking, edgy portrayals of twentysomethings adrift in the city. There are romantic duets, large-cast ensembles, and everything in between, populated by mold-breaking characters: misfit cheerleaders, nurturing drifters, rich petty thieves—even a rogue SAT tutor. For the generation of actors in their teens and twenties, *Under Thirty* is an unparalleled source of diverse and challenging roles, created by some of today's finest writers.

Drama/978-1-4000-7616-1

VINTAGE BOOKS
Available at your local bookstore, or call toll-free to order:
1-800-793-2665 (credit cards only).